W9-AQN-100

TORONTO, ONTARIO, CANADA
M4Y 2R5

WITHD

Exodus

INTERPRETATION
A Bible Commentary for Teaching and Preaching

INTERPRETATION
A BIBLE COMMENTARY FOR TEACHING AND PREACHING

James Luther Mays, *Editor*
Patrick D. Miller, *Old Testament Editor*
Paul J. Achtemeier, *New Testament Editor*

TERENCE E. FRETHEIM

Exodus

INTERPRETATION

A Bible Commentary
for Teaching and Preaching

BS
1245
.3
F.72

Regis College Library
15 ST. MARY STREET
TORONTO, ONTARIO, CANADA
M4Y 2R5

John Knox Press
LOUISVILLE

99119

Scripture quotations from the *Revised Standard Version of the Bible* are copyrighted 1946, 1952, © 1971, 1973 by the Division of Christian Education of the National Council of the Churches of Christ in the U.S.A. and are used by permission.

Scripture quotations marked NRSV are from the *New Revised Standard Version of the Bible,* copyrighted © 1990 by the Division of Christian Education of the National Council of the Churches of Christ in the U.S.A., and are used by permission.

Library of Congress Cataloging-in-Publication Data

Fretheim, Terence E.
    Exodus / Terence E. Fretheim.
        p.   cm. — (Interpretation, a Bible commentary for teaching and preaching)
    Includes bibliographical references.
    ISBN 0-8042-3102-8

    1. Bible. O.T. Exodus—Commentaries.   2. Bible. O.T. Exodus—Homiletical use.   I. Title.   II. Series.
BS1245.3.F72 1991
222'.1207—dc20   90-40392
                                                          CIP

© copyright John Knox Press 1991
10 9 8 7 6 5 4 3 2 1
Printed in the United States of America
John Knox Press
Louisville, Kentucky 40202-1396

SERIES PREFACE

This series of commentaries offers an interpretation of the books of the Bible. It is designed to meet the need of students, teachers, ministers, and priests for a contemporary expository commentary. These volumes will not replace the historical critical commentary or homiletical aids to preaching. The purpose of this series is rather to provide a third kind of resource, a commentary which presents the integrated result of historical and theological work with the biblical text.

An interpretation in the full sense of the term involves a text, an interpreter, and someone for whom the interpretation is made. Here, the text is what stands written in the Bible in its full identity as literature from the time of "the prophets and apostles," the literature which is read to inform, inspire, and guide the life of faith. The interpreters are scholars who seek to create an interpretation which is both faithful to the text and useful to the church. The series is written for those who teach, preach, and study the Bible in the community of faith.

The comment generally takes the form of expository essays. It is planned and written in the light of the needs and questions which arise in the use of the Bible as Holy Scripture. The insights and results of contemporary scholarly research are used for the sake of the exposition. The commentators write as exegetes and theologians. The task which they undertake is both to deal with what the texts say and to discern their meaning for faith and life. The exposition is the unified work of one interpreter.

The text on which the comment is based is the Revised Standard Version of the Bible and, since its appearance, the New Revised Standard Version. The general availability of these translations makes the printing of a text in the commentary unnecessary. The commentators have also had other current versions in view as they worked and refer to their readings where it is helpful. The text is divided into sections appropriate to the particular book; comment deals with passages as a whole, rather than proceeding word by word, or verse by verse.

Writers have planned their volumes in light of the requirements set by the exposition of the book assigned to them. Biblical books differ in character, content, and arrangement. They also differ in the way they have been and are used in the liturgy, thought, and devotion of the church. The distinctiveness and use of particular books have been taken into account in decisions about the approach, emphasis, and use of space in the commentaries. The goal has been to allow writers to develop the format which provides for the best presentation of their interpretation.

The result, writers and editors hope, is a commentary which both explains and applies, an interpretation which deals with both the meaning and the significance of biblical texts. Each commentary reflects, of course, the writer's own approach and perception of the church and world. It could and should not be otherwise. Every interpretation of any kind is individual in that sense; it is one reading of the text. But all who work at the interpretation of Scripture in the church need the help and stimulation of a colleague's reading and understanding of the text. If these volumes serve and encourage interpretation in that way, their preparation and publication will realize their purpose.

The Editors

PREFACE

The book of Exodus has long been a special resource for those who wish to study the beginnings of Israel as the people of God. It not only has generated a considerable volume of scholarly literature but has also been given extraordinary "confessional" attention by those who see the exodus and its God as having decisively shaped who they are as individuals and communities. As I have attempted to gain some control over this material, I have been humbled by its richness and depth. At the end of the journey, I have a profound sense that the book of Exodus is holy ground indeed.

This work would not have been possible without the help of many persons. I wish to express my appreciation to students at Luther Northwestern Seminary and the Divinity School at the University of Chicago who have responded to this material in earlier forms. Special thanks are due to the series editors, Patrick D. Miller, Jr., and James L. Mays, whose encouragement and assistance have been invaluable. I am also grateful to the Luther Northwestern Administration and Board of Directors for granting a sabbatical leave and to Lutheran Brotherhood of Minneapolis for financial assistance along the way. Finally, my gratitude goes to my wife, Faith, for her unfailing support, and to my daughters, Tanya and Andrea, to whom this book is dedicated.

Christmas Day, 1989

CONTENTS

CONTENTS

CONTENTS

Introduction

The book of Exodus moves from slavery to worship, from Israel's bondage to Pharaoh to its bonding to Yahweh. More particularly, the book moves from the enforced construction of buildings for Pharaoh to the glad and obedient offering of the people for a building for the worship of God. Exodus advances from an oppressive situation in which God's presence is hardly noted in the text to God's filling the scene at the completion of the tabernacle.

In between these bookends of Exodus is an amazing range of activity, from plagues to sea walls to wilderness wanderings to fiery mountains and golden calves. The nonhuman order gets caught up in these occasions as much as do people. God becomes engaged in events in a way not often paralleled in the Old Testament. The people of Israel are the focus of all of this activity, but God's purposes are creation-wide: "that my name may be declared throughout all the earth" (9:16).

Exodus as a Pre-Christian and a Christian Book

The Old Testament is the word of God for the Christian church. That is, it is a means by which God speaks words of judgment and grace to the community of faith. It may be said to have other functions: it helps to define what the Christian was and still properly is, and it assists in delineating a shape for Christian life in the world. But, at the heart of things, the Old Testament serves to bring people face-to-face with the Father of Jesus Christ, and in that encounter God speaks. Whether it be the law or the prophets or the writings, the Old Testament has for centuries served more than a preparatory function; it has actually spoken an effective word of God to Christians: calling, warning, exhorting, judging, redeeming, comforting, and forgiving. Because the church through the years has *experienced* the Old Testament as word of God in these ways, its

1

liturgies, its preaching, and its catechetics have been filled with Old Testament stories, psalms, wisdom, and prophecies.

The book of Exodus has participated in this Christian experience. Young Christians have been reared on the stories of Exodus, from the story of baby Moses set adrift on the Nile to Israelites walking through the sea on dry land to the gifts of water and manna in the wilderness. Catechisms that include the ten commandments have been impressed upon their memories and have given shape to their speech and action. Liturgies have had built into their very center the themes of passover and unleavened bread, and Exodus 15 has been appointed as a text for Easter Day, so cosmic is the victory of God seen to be. Theologies of various sorts have drawn on Exodus texts with abandon, from theories of atonement to issues of divine agency to more recent theologies of liberation from contemporary communities that truly know what oppression is all about. Christians know deeply in their own being the meaning of the cry, "Let my people go," and make their confession of faith in terms of the exodus-shaped language of redemption. The exodus is a constitutive event for Christians; without it they would not be who they are: a redeemed people of the God of Israel.

The understanding of the Christian gospel has been decisively shaped by this salvific experience. Jesus, like Israel, is "called out of Egypt" (Matt. 2:15) and tempted in the wilderness (Matt. 4:1-11). He not only celebrates the passover (Mark 14:12-25; Matt. 26:28) but, in a radical theological extension, is himself identified as the "passover lamb" (I Cor. 5:7; 11:25) and the "supernatural Rock" who followed Israel in the wilderness (I Cor. 10:4). He assumes the role of a new Moses—or is it the instructing God of Exodus 20?—as he teaches his disciples from the mountain (Matt. 5—7). And, in the most remarkable move of all, Israel's God "tabernacles" in his very person (John 1:14). Drawing upon virtually every existing interpretive means available to them, the New Testament writers used Exodus texts as a vehicle for interpreting *and* proclaiming God's act in Jesus. At the same time, Exodus texts are not only applied to Jesus; a continuity is seen between Israel and church as people of God. These texts are "written down" for the "instruction" (I Cor. 10:11) of the Christian community. They can be used as warning (I Cor. 10:6-11), apologia (Acts 7:17-44), instruction (I Cor. 9:8-12; II Cor. 8:14-15), specifications of what love requires

2

(Rom. 13:8–10; Matt. 19:16–22), examples of human faithfulness (Heb. 11:23–29), reminders of the missional purpose of the community (I Peter 2:9–10; Rev. 1:5–6; 5:10), or resources for an eschatology (Rev. 8:6—9:21; 15:1–5; 21:3; 22:4).

One can see that many parts of Exodus, along with much else in the Old Testament, are often (literally) contained within the New Testament; in being so blended into the New, it becomes as new as the New. Together they constitute a new coherent totality, yet without the Old losing its character as word of God—no word of God can lose all value—or the New losing its sense of genuine newness. One could say that the Old Testament constitutes *both* a pre-Christian word of God and, by virtue of the new totality, a Christian word. The God of the exodus is *our* God, whose salvific activity we too have experienced. We are one with those Israelites who stood on the far shore of the Red Sea and proclaimed the victory of their God. Their songs have become our songs.

But how in our study of Exodus do we do justice to both of these realities: our *knowledge* of its pre-Christian roots and our *experience* of hearing it as a genuinely Christian word?

There is no one way in which this must be done, but a two-step approach may not be the best available: first, one is to be historical, descriptive, objective; then, with that material in hand, one moves through the New Testament to a contemporary application. This often belies what actually happens in the course of interpretation, where no specific "application" step is undertaken at all; the text itself applies immediately by virtue of the text being experienced as word of God. For Christians who hear, say, Psalm 23 or the first commandment, there will be an immediacy of meaning because of the intersection with a certain life experience. Because of the high degree of commonality of experience across the centuries, one does justice to both pre-Christian and Christian dimensions of the text simultaneously.

Other texts are less immediate to contemporary experience for a variety of reasons (e.g., transcultural differences). In such cases, more "explaining" is necessary before the horizons of text and reader meet. This can take many forms, but one way is to *talk about the text itself,* but in language that both honors the realities of the pre-Christian world (e.g., avoiding obviously anachronistic terminology) and at the same time enables it to ring

3

true to common Christian experience (hence doing justice to both worlds). This is what we will seek to do in this commentary. There will usually be no specific point of "application," but an attempt will be made to *merge* into a single story the experience of the people in the text and the contemporary experience of the people of God. An elision of worlds may thereby occur.

This approach will be consonant with the *testimonial character* of the text itself. That is to say, for each successive Israelite generation this material was told and retold, *and* each retelling often was integrated into the text itself. The text thus consists of a series of retellings all interwoven with one another. This integration is so complete that it is often difficult or impossible to discern where the inherited traditions and the new retellings begin and end. Each successively larger shape of the tradition thus functioned for Israel as an ongoing witness to what God had said and done without a specific move to "application." It was a matter of retelling the story in such a way that the worlds of past generations and ever-contemporary communities of faith merged with one another. This is also a contemporary task.

This approach assumes that one does not *make* the text relevant to today but that the text *is* relevant and that the task is to enable that relevance to be seen; the task is to facilitate the urgency of the text as it intersects with ever new lives and situations. The reader's perception of what has happened will be different from a two-step approach. The reader will be left, not with an interpretation of the text in some secondary or applied fashion and abstracted from the text, but with *the text itself* whose meaning has become immediate to the reader's own life experience. Thus the text is not an object, something that is tinkered with and talked about as something back then, but rather it *becomes direct address* and hence congruent with its original function for the community of faith.

Our task, then, will be to relate to the text as if in a conversation, an asking and a listening that are open to the faith claims of the text, and with contemporary experience in view. And we will seek to do this, not as some capstone to a more objective analysis of the text, but at every step along the way. The hoped-for result will be that the text, the interpreter, and the latter's situation vis-à-vis the people of God will illumine one another. A dialogue may emerge wherein the text, tradition, criticism, and contemporary experience are constantly intersecting, and out of that mix important insights in the text may become available.

Exodus and the Critical Task

Commentaries on the book of Exodus have been few and far between in recent years. The magisterial commentary of Brevard Childs (1974) has no doubt had something to do with that; it has satisfied the demand for an exegesis that is both rigorous in its use of the critical tools and committed to a discernment of the theological dimension of the texts. Besides, it is a tough act to follow. Yet, more recent Old Testament work has moved into new vistas that were only dimly in view two decades ago. More specifically, new forms of redaction criticism and literary criticism have brought renewed attention to Exodus texts and opened up the interpretive possibilities.

For more than two hundred years, *source criticism* has been the predominant literary approach to the study of the Pentateuch. Exodus has commonly been studied as an integral part of this larger literary whole. This has usually meant that the book of Exodus is seen as a composite work, consisting primarily of three combined sources (J, E, P), with probably some deuteronomic influence. There are also texts that have often not been attributed to any major source, for example, certain legal traditions. The book thus grew by a process of accretion, with these sources gradually brought together over the course of a half millennium or more.

This long-prevailing scholarly consensus has come under sharp challenge in the last generation, particularly regarding the nature, scope, and dating of the sources. While few scholars doubt that the material in Exodus comes from widely different historical periods, the way in which it has been brought together into its present unity is much discussed, and there is at present no consensus regarding these matters. For an up-to-date survey of opinion on classical and more recent theories, see especially Whybray.

My own point of view is that Exodus is a patchwork quilt of traditions from various periods in Israel's life. Yet it is also a finished product. In its earliest form, it was probably a relatively brief narrative with the basic thread of the story, dating from the period before the monarchy. This narrative was reworked

5

from time to time over the centuries, major reworkings of which might be identified with J and E (southern and northern versions), who drew on other, as yet unintegrated, aspects of the story. Existing versions of the story were reworked and supplemented in a major way during the exile by a redactor, probably to be identified with P (rather than viewing P as a separate source). This Priestly redactor drew on materials from a wide variety of sources, older and more recent, particularly legal and cultic, and placed his stamp on the entire book, which would be identified with much of what we now call the Tetrateuch. This commentary will focus on this last major redactional stage.

One of the major continuing considerations for *form criticism* in Exodus is the relationship between the two primary genres of the book, narrative and law. The interweaving of these two types of literature is certainly one of the chief characteristics of Exodus. Of what import is it that law and narrative are so intermingled with each other? This issue, which has theological implications of some consequence, will be explored in depth at Exodus 12 and 19. One very difficult question is the degree to which one can refine the formal language regarding the narrative portions of the book. Efforts to speak of saga or legend or folktale have not been particularly helpful or fruitful, and scholars have been able to come to little consensus. To use the language of story is certainly appropriate, but it carries the disadvantages of imprecision and ambiguity. The designation of theological narrative may help capture that this literature is an admixture of Israel's story and God's story, with the intent to move the reader's heart and will as much as the mind. There are also some poetic pieces in the book, notably Exodus 15.

The *new literary approach* differs from prior studies primarily in its interest in literary criticism rather than literary history, in texts as literary objects in themselves rather than the history of the text prior to its present shape. As a literary entity, the text now has a life of its own and we have to come to terms with it as such. The concern is fundamentally a hearing of the text as we now have it. A central task is the examination of the amazing variety of the text's literary features to see how they work together to form an organic and coherent whole (e.g., repetition, point of view). While other approaches should be considered complementary to this one, it will be evident in the commentary that the literary approach is more fruitful than

6

more narrow historical ones for getting inside a text and seeing what makes it tick. Among the more prominent features in Exodus, irony will be given special attention.

It is to be noted that the movement of the book of Exodus is marked by a number of structural characteristics. One might cite the rhythm of lament, deliverance, and praise and the interconnections between liturgy and narrative as well as law and narrative. Another common structure is the way in which, through verbal and thematic links, certain narrative aspects are made to prefigure later ones (see Fishbane). For example, the actions of Pharaoh's daughter on behalf of Moses prefigure later divine activities on behalf of Israel (see at 2:1). The various activities of Moses in 2:11–22 foreshadow later actions by both God and Israel. The deadly encounter of Moses with God in 4:24–26 anticipates the passover. Each of the plagues prefigures disastrous aspects of passover and sea crossing. Each of the events in the wilderness has aspects that foreshadow Sinai realities. These internal linkages give to the overall narrative a certain mirroring effect; each story reflects aspects of another, which binds them together more closely and provides an internal hermeneutic. Key transitional sections also serve to interlock the major portions of the book (1:1–7; 2:23–25; 6:28—7:7; 11:1–10; 15:19–26; 19:1–8; 24:12–18). Each section looks both backward and forward, catching the reader up on what has preceded, while anticipating future developments. These sections tend to "interrupt" the flow of the story, providing interludes or summaries or advance announcements.

There are relatively few problems in the Hebrew text of Exodus. This commentary will be based on that text as used by the New Revised Standard Version. References are based on the divisions of the NRSV.

History and Faith in the Book of Exodus

The book of Exodus is not historical narrative, at least in any modern sense of that phrase. Its primary concern is with issues that are theological and kerygmatic. That is to say, those responsible for the material at various compositional stages were persons of faith who were concerned to speak a word of God to other persons of faith, who in turn would have heard it as word of God. We hear in this book the living voice of the community of faith which was Israel. In that sense the material is profoundly historical in purpose. Exodus is not socially or historically disinterested; it was written with the problems and possibilities of a particular audience in view and shaped to address that setting. The author(s) did not write for everybody in general or for nobody in particular. This is less obvious in the case of narratives than it is with, say, the prophets, and the audience is particularly difficult to discern in books such as Exodus. This question is complicated by the fact that at various stages of redaction different audiences were in view.

It seems likely that the basic shape of the present book of Exodus had an exilic provenance. Israel in exile finds itself in straits similar to its forebears in two major respects: (1) captive to outside forces and (2) suffering under just judgment because of its disloyalty to God. It faces a situation not unlike that portrayed in both chapters 1—6 and chapters 32—34. The community of faith stands in need of *both* deliverance and forgiveness. Exodus issues related to law and obedience, to divine presence and absence, and appropriate worship places and practices would also have been important for Israel in an exilic setting. From time to time over the course of the commentary, texts will be related to this setting. Yet the texts are presented in a form that is general enough to fit many comparable situations in the life of the people of God. Hence, wherever there is a correspondence of life situations, a word of God addressed back then can once again function as such a word.

The vehicle in and through which this word of God is addressed is a story about Israel's past. Yet no historiographical purposes or methods are evident, and the text makes no such claims for itself. The concern is not to reconstruct a history of this earlier period but to tell the story of a people in which God has been actively engaged. Nevertheless, the concern for "what really happened" has often occupied the attention of modern scholars. This task has been made difficult not only by the nature of the material but also by the fact that no extrabiblical sources document what the book narrates. It is a matter of reconstructing the history from clues of various sorts, both within and without the text.

8   Much remains uncertain in this reconstructive effort. There is some consensus that some of later Israel's ancestors lived in Egypt for a time, as did other Semitic foreigners during the

second millennium. Some linguistic influence is evident, seen, for example, in Moses' Egyptian name. Construction activity by certain pharaohs in which slave labor was employed, particularly in the fourteenth and thirteenth centuries B.C., lends a certain plausibility to the Egyptian oppression of Israel (see 1:11). This suggests an early thirteenth century B.C. date for the exodus. Yet the times and places associated with the exodus or the wilderness wanderings or the Sinai event are all quite uncertain, occasioning much ongoing scholarly debate, but on the basis of little evidence (see at 14:1–18; 17:1–7; 19:1–8). It is probable that stories of a number of movements by various tribal groups have been integrated to form a single narrative (for a helpful survey of the issues, see Ramsey).

The end result, without going into detail, is that Exodus contains a very mixed set of materials from a historiographical perspective. While a nucleus is probably rooted in events of the period represented, the narratives also reflect what thoughtful Israelites over the course of nearly a millennium considered their meaning(s) to be. In such an ongoing reflective process, the writers no doubt used their imaginations freely (e.g., when they put forward the actual words of a conversation); in so doing, they believed they were doing justice to what they had inherited. It is also likely that the celebration of these events in Israel's worship generated materials for these stories; liturgy has shaped literature (see at 12:1–28). Such a community valuing of these materials means that they have a continuing value quite apart from the question of "happenedness." Even where the historiographer's judgment may be quite negative, the material does not lose its potential value to speak a word of God across the centuries, in Israel's time or ours.

A question often raised in this regard is, How important *for faith* is the happenedness of the reported events? To paraphrase the apostle Paul: If the exodus did not occur, was Israel's faith in vain? A few interpreters would make no distinctions among biblical events; the happenedness of every event is crucial for faith. But most would say that certain biblical texts give us an innerbiblical warrant to make distinctions among events. So-called historical recitals are found throughout the Old Testament (e.g., Deut. 26:5–9; Josh. 24:2–13). Certain key events—for example, the exodus itself (in a general way, not in detail)—are isolated in these confessions. It would appear that such events

9

are so specified because they are considered constitutive of the community and hence important for faith, while other events are not given such significance. As a constitutive event, the exodus is recognized as an event of such import that the community would not be what it is without its having occurred. Generally, the pervasiveness of the references to the exodus in the Old Testament would seem to constitute a warrant for such an understanding. The event so captured the imagination of Israel that it not only served to illuminate Israel's most basic identity but also functioned as a prism for interpreting all of Israel's subsequent history (e.g., Isa. 43:14–21; 51:9–11).

Exodus and the Theological Task

The relationship between theology and narrative is a problem of some consequence. That the book of Exodus is filled with matters of theological interest is clear; one need only note the extent to which God is the subject of the speaking and the acting that occur. At the same time, Exodus is not a systematic treatise, presenting an ordered reflection on theological issues. Five observations are in order on this point.

1. The fundamental purpose of Exodus is "kerygmatic"; that is, it seeks to confront the reader with the word of God, not a constructive theological statement. Hence its theology is in the service of its message. Particular theological statements have been formulated in relationship to concrete situations faced by the audience. We therefore have to do with an "applied theology," the occasional character of which must not be forgotten in any move to modern reformulation. The word spoken is a timely word. Yet, because its "timeliness" may cut across generations, it has the potential of becoming comparably timely in another time and place. Some theological work in this commentary will be of this sort.

2. The word spoken may also be a "timeless" word (e.g., convey a universal truth or an aspect of the divine nature), but the particular formulation of it is context related and hence is potentially inadequate or even unsuitable for any or every subsequent generation. For example, the claim that "Yahweh is a man of war [warrior]" (15:3; RSV/NRSV) may convey an important truth, but its specific formulation may no longer be adequate for other times and places. Both those who seek simply

10

to describe the text's theology (the content/formulation distinction is implicit in the text) and those who raise the issue of continuing relevance (see above) must struggle with the implications of this. This distinction will be evident from time to time in this commentary (cf. 21:1—23:19).

3. The narrator does not stake out theological positions that iron out all tensions. It is not always clear what this might mean (e.g., the move from 23:21 to 34:7 or from 24:9–11 to 33:11 to 33:20). Differing views in the inherited traditions may have been allowed to stand alongside one another. Or, the narrator is seeking to mediate among competing points of view in subtle ways. Or, there is some theological development in the narrative itself. Or, the tension may be inherent in the theological position of the narrator. In this commentary, all of these will be recognized, while assuming that a basic theological coherence is available in the present text.

4. The theology in Exodus is carried by certain types of literature: story, law, and liturgy. One best hears its theological views by reconveying them in literary forms closely related to those of the text itself: retelling the story, reformulating the laws, and recelebrating the liturgies. At the least, all theological work with the text must take into account the genres in and through which theological statements are made. At points in the commentary a simple redescription in the form of the text will be undertaken as the best way to make its theological views clear.

5. Nevertheless, the text itself invites, indeed provides, a warrant for more general theological reflections. *(a)* The liturgical material directly invites the question, What does this mean? (12:26; 13:14; cf. 13:8; 10:2). *(b)* The legal material is explicitly grounded in generalized statements about God: "I am compassionate" (22:27). *(c)* Theological generalizations are introduced into the narratives, giving some internal direction as to who the God of the story is. Truth claims are made concerning this God and the divine relationship to the world that both convey certain convictions and delimit the possibilities of meaning. Story and generalization do not stand opposed to each other; in fact, they are integrated with each other. For example, 34:6–7 makes explicit statements about the nature of the God who is engaged in Israel's history: gracious, merciful, slow to anger, and abounding in steadfast love. While not many statements move within

11

this more abstract sphere, that they exist at all indicates that the God who is the subject of sentences in the narrative is to be understood in some way relative to those abstractions. *(d)* The hymnic material in Exodus 15 supports this move. It makes explicit claims about the nature of the God who has been active in the story.

These considerations both limit and open up possible theological approaches to the text. The primary approach of this commentary is to draw out the theology inherent within each text that is being considered, and in such a way as to honor the type of literature and the concern of the text to address a word of God to its audience. In this undertaking, I make two distinctions: *(a)* Between the theology *in* the present form of the text and the theology of the sources that the redactor may have used. My concern is with the former. A determination of the latter is a precarious enterprise, not least because we do not know how well these sources have been preserved in the present redaction. Generally speaking, this means that the theology I seek to explicate is relatively late in its present form—from the exilic period. *(b)* Between the theology in the text and the history of Israel's religion. The latter would seek to discern the degree to which these texts reflect aspects of Israel's early religious traditions, institutions, and practices. Some issues to consider would be the origins and early history of festivals, priesthood, sanctuaries, law, monotheism, and covenant. I will only incidentally be concerned with these questions in the commentary, as they may help us discern some of the historical depth in the text (on these matters, Sarna is a brief and reliable guide).

Leading Theological Issues

A recognition of the special theological interests of the narrator will provide some keys to the interpretation of the book (see Fretheim, "Suffering God and Sovereign God in Exodus").

A Theology of Creation

Until recently, the interpretation of Exodus has been almost exclusively concerned with the theme of redemption, so much so that standard introductions to the Old Testament often start at this point. The theme of creation is often ignored or noticed

12

only occasionally (e.g., in the tabernacle texts). It is my conviction that the book of Exodus is shaped in a decisive way by a creation theology. This will be recognized in the book's verbal, thematic, and structural concerns.

Generally, God's work in *creation provides the basic categories and interpretive clues* for what happens in redemption and related divine activity. It is the Creator God who redeems Israel from Egypt. God's work in creation has been shown to be life-giving, life-preserving, and life-blessing (e.g., 1:7, 12, 20). What God does in redemption is in the service of these endangered divine goals in and for the creation. For example, the hymnic celebration of that redemptive act in Exodus 15 is permeated with creation talk, in terms of vocabulary, structure, and theme. Not only is an *experience* of God's work as creator necessary for participation in the exodus—otherwise there would be no people to redeem, an *understanding* of God's work as creator is indispensable for the proper interpretation of what happens— there would be no exodus *as we know it* without its having been informed by that understanding.

1. A creation theology provides the *cosmic purpose* behind God's redemptive activity on Israel's behalf. While the liberation of Israel is the focus of God's activity, it is not the ultimate purpose. The deliverance of Israel is ultimately for the sake of all creation (see 9:16). The issue for God is finally not that God's name be made known in Israel but that it be declared to the entire earth. God's purpose in these events is creation-wide. What is at stake is God's mission for the world, for as 9:29 and 19:5 put it, "All the earth is God's" (cf. 8:22; 9:14). Hence the *public character* of these events is an important theme throughout.

2. God's redemptive activity is set in terms of a *creational need.* The fulfillment of God's creational purposes in the growth of Israel is endangered by Pharaoh's attempted subversion thereof. If Pharaoh succeeds in his antilife purposes at that point at which God has begun to actualize the promise of creation (1:7–14), then God's purposes in creation are subverted and God's creational mission will not be able to be realized. God's work in redemption, climaxing in Israel's crossing of the sea on "dry land," constitutes God's efforts at re-creation, returning creation to a point where God's mission can once again be taken up.

13

3. God's redemptive activity is *cosmic in its effects.* Generally, the Lord of heaven and earth is active throughout Exodus, from acts of blessing to the use of the nonhuman creation in the plagues, the sea crossing, the wilderness wanderings, and the Sinai theophany. More specifically, Exodus 15 confesses that God's victory at the sea is not simply a local or historical phenomenon but a cosmic one. God's defeat of the powers of chaos results not simply in Israel's liberation but in the reign of God over the entire cosmos (15:18).

4. God's calling of Israel is given *creation-wide scope.* The theme of "All the earth is God's" is picked up again in 19:4–6, a divine invitation to Israel to be a kingdom of priests and a holy nation. Israel is called out from among other nations and commissioned to a task on behalf of God's earth. Israel is to function among the nations as a priest functions in a religious community. Israel's witness to God's redemptive activity (see 18:8–12) and its obedience of the law are finally for the sake of a universal mission.

The redemptive deeds of God are not an end in themselves. The experience of those events propels the people out into various creational spheres of life. Redemption is for the purpose of creation, a new life within the larger creation, a return to the world as God intended it to be.

A creation theology is also built into the structure of the book, seen not least in the parallels between Exodus and Genesis 1—9: *(a)* a creational setting (cf. 1:7 with Gen. 1:28); *(b)* anticreational activity (cf. chaps. 1—2, 5 with Gen. 3—6); *(c)* Noah and Moses (see at 2:1; 25:1; 33:12); *(d)* the flood and the plagues as ecological disasters (see at 7:8); *(e)* death and deliverance in and through water, with cosmic implications (see at 15:1); *(f)* covenant with Noah/Abraham and at Sinai with commitment and signs (see at 24:1; cf. 31:17); and *(g)* the restatement of the covenant (see at 34:9). Chapters 25—40 may be viewed in terms of a creation, fall, re-creation structure. The commentary will explore these elements in greater detail.

The Knowledge of God

The book of Exodus is concerned in a major way with the knowledge of Yahweh. Ironically, Pharaoh sets this question: Who is Yahweh? (5:2). The pursuit of this question is primarily undertaken by God: "that you may know that I am Yahweh." The object of this divine quest includes Pharaoh and the Egyp-

14

tians (7:17; 8:10, 22; 9:14, 29; 11:7; 14:4, 18) as well as Israel (10:2; 29:46). God's concern for self-disclosure is thus not confined to Israel; it includes the world (see 18:8–12). The exodus events are not, however, the only medium for this knowledge. In God's first words in Exodus, the divine self-identification is as the God of Abraham, Isaac, and Jacob (3:6; cf. 3:13–16; 4:5; 6:3–8), and the covenant with them is a primary motivating factor in what God is about to do (2:24). Whatever its historical foundations, the narrator claims that this electing and promising activity of God constitutes an important element in the identity of Yahweh.

Moreover, the text testifies that God's personal disclosure to Moses (chaps. 3—6), in what might be termed an internal event, decisively shapes the interpretation of the events. The significance of the exodus is made available to Moses prior to its occurrence; it is thus not understood as an inference drawn from an experience of the event. Even more, while the initiative with respect to the divine identity lies with God, Moses' persistent inquiries into the divine name and other matters draw God out and consequently more knowledge becomes available. The experience of the event itself, of course, enhances the understanding of what occurs. Yahweh also defines himself in other speeches to Israel and Moses (e.g., 20:2). In fact, the profound self-identification in 34:6–7 is revealed in a personal way in the wake of Israel's apostasy!

This suggests the following typology for the understanding of revelation in Exodus: (1) the faith heritage of the community; (2) God's specific disclosure to and interaction with Moses; (3) the experience of the event itself; and (4) Moses' interpretation of the event to Israel and to others (see 18:8).

This is not simply a matter of "progressive revelation" on God's part or "progressive understanding" on Israel's part, as if the identity of Yahweh is set from the beginning and only needs to be unfolded. God does not remain unchanged by all that happens. God does some things that God has never done before; the interaction with other characters also shapes the divine identity. God is not only one who is; God is also one who in some sense becomes. Hence the identity of Yahweh, not very clear at the beginning of the narrative, achieves a depth and clarity as the narrative progresses through divine speech and action as well as human alertness and boldness.

It is apparent from this "divine economy" that human

agents are of central importance. Their character and abilities make a difference, not only to Israel but to God. Exodus is concerned throughout with the proper role and reputation of such persons, not least the nature of their relationship with both God and people. Moses is obviously the primary individual in view, but the texts seem to reflect a concern for a more general theology of leadership (or, we might say, ministry).

Images for God

Exodus presents God as one highly engaged in the events of which it speaks, though a more unobtrusive, behind-the-scenes activity is evident in chapters 1—2; 5; and 18. Images of sovereignty are certainly prominent. God as lord is evident in the proclamation of the law and the call to obedience; God as judge is experienced by both Egyptians and Israelites; God's kingship is explicitly affirmed in 15:18; God as warrior is professed at the Red Sea (15:3); and God as ruler of heaven and earth is manifest in all of God's activity in the nonhuman order.

Nevertheless, the nature of the divine sovereignty seems to be differently conceived depending on whether the nonhuman or the human order is in view. God seems to work in the nonhuman order at will; God meets no resistance there. At the same time, God does not act in nature independent of the created order of being. That is, God's work in nature is not arbitrary; it is congruent with nature's way of being and in coordination with human activity (see at 7:8).

Human beings, however, have sufficient freedom and power to be resistant to the word and will of God. God must contend with intransigence, cruelty, and disloyalty in the human order. Positively, a stress on divine suffering and divine dependence on the human means that God is portrayed in terms other than absolute rule or control. These factors will mean that common understandings of sovereignty are subverted and redefined.

The book of Exodus is enclosed by speeches of divine self-portrayal (3:7–10; 34:6–7; cf. 2:23–25). The first is programmatic; the God who acts in the narrative is understood to be the kind of God portrayed here. God's sovereignty is evident in the divine initiative, the setting of the agenda, the will to deliver Israel, and the announced ability to accomplish this. Alongside this, however, are images not commonly associated with sovereignty. It is a divine sovereignty qualified by divine

16

suffering, by a divine move of compassion, that enters deeply into the sufferings of the people (see at 3:7). This is congruent with one of the last speeches of God in Exodus (34:6–7). Here the divine self-portrayal is sharply oriented toward images of grace, love, and mercy. Because this or a similar statement recurs in all corners of the canon, it has a creedal status; it may be said to be a statement about God toward which the entire Exodus narrative is driving.

In addition, any definition of divine sovereignty must take into account the fact that God does not act alone in these events. The opening chapters set this divine mode in place (see at 1:15; 2:1): God works in and through five lowly women to carry out the divine purpose. Ironically, they prove to be highly effective against ruthless forms of power, but choosing such human vehicles means that God works in unobtrusive, unlikely, and vulnerable ways.

Moses is also an instance of such a divine way. Both God and Moses are the subject of the exodus (see at 3:8, 10; cf. 6:13, 26–27; 32:7). God depends on Moses in carrying out the tasks involved and hence must work in and through Moses' frailties as well as strengths. This means that God gives up total control of the ensuing events; this is for God a risky venture, fraught with negative possibilities. For example, in the face of Moses' resistance, God adapts the original plan and chooses Aaron to be a co-leader rather than overpowering Moses. God is angry at this development (see at 4:14) but goes with what is possible, even though it is less than the best (witness Aaron's later failure as a leader in chap. 32). Another dialogue between Moses and God in chapters 32—34 shows again how God is responsive to what Moses has to say. In view of Moses' prayer, God reverses himself with respect to the announced judgment on an apostate people (see at 32:14). More generally, one might cite how God takes the context into account in making decisions and charting directions (see at 13:17–21; 2:23–25). (On God and Pharaoh, see the excursus at 7:3.)

Certainly these images focus on one major concern of Exodus: Who will finally be recognized as the sovereign one, Yahweh or Pharaoh? Whom will Israel serve? But an oft-forgotten parallel issue is: What kind of sovereignty is being exercised? Pharaoh's and Yahweh's ways of being sovereign are contrasted in the narrative (cf. 3:7–10 with 5:5–18). The force of these texts is that Yahweh's sovereignty is qualified by suffering images, while Pharaoh's is not. It is Pharaoh who is the unmoved mover; he chooses to intensify Israel's oppression rather than identify with those who suffer. The God of Israel is a suffering sovereign.

The Meaning of Liberation and Exodus as Paradigm

For centuries the exodus has functioned as a paradigm, especially for those who have been victimized by oppressive systems of one kind or another (see Walzer; van Iersel). God is the champion of the poor and those pushed to the margins of life; God is one who liberates them from the pharaohs of this world. As God acted then, so God can be expected to act again. In the United States, Negro spirituals have carried on these Exodus themes, and Black Theology is permeated with them. In the last generation, South American and other liberation theologians have also considered the exodus to be paradigmatic for their reflections on the experience of oppression (see Croatto). The exodus is not believed to stand alone as a biblical foundation for such a theological perspective, but it is the generative event. Numerous texts from both Testaments are understood to stand in this tradition, from the prophets to the Psalms to the Gospels (cf. I Sam. 2:1-10; Luke 1:46-55).

In such formulations, this liberating activity of God is often believed to be explicitly political. God's salvific activity is directed not just toward internal change but toward societal change, the external conditions of life. Salvation is thus conceived in holistic terms as the work of God affecting change in all aspects of life: religious and political, social and individual. Perhaps above all, the exodus is seen to be a sign of hope that poverty and oppression are not the last word, for God is at work on behalf of a different future. Those who interpret the book of Exodus must take time to listen to these interpretations from the "underside" of life, whatever they might think about liberation theology; these people have a clearer sense than most of what oppression is like. The commentary will draw on such reflections particularly concerning chapters 1 and 5.

This way in which Israel's liberation has been interpreted has not gone uncontested, however. There are at least three difficulties with many such interpretations.

18   1. It has been objected that the people of Israel do not engage in military or other violent revolutionary activity to initiate or ensure their escape, even though they are armed and

could have done so (13:18). It is highly precarious to suggest that an earlier stage of the tradition had them doing battle. Even if they did do so, the final stage of the redaction sets it aside. In fact, Israel is expressly forbidden to engage in such activity; Israel is to watch and "see the salvation of the Lord, which he will work for you today." It is only God who does the fighting, as recognized by both Israelites and Egyptians (14:13–14, 25; 15:3–12). All the violence comes from God working in and through various aspects of the nonhuman order. The end result is not a takeover of Egypt but a withdrawal to another land; Exodus is not a journey that begins and ends at home.

It may be said, and this is no small matter, that Moses engages in deception (3:18; 5:1–3) and is bluntly confrontational in his approach to the authorities. The civil disobedience of the midwives and Moses' mother may also be cited (see at 1:15; 2:1); so may Moses' killing of the Egyptian, though that functions to prefigure *divine* activity (see at 2:11). Such Israelite actions may certainly be said to be subversive, and they do prepare the way for what God does.

Above all, it is God's activity that can serve as a paradigm. The exodus is a powerful symbol that the present situation does not define what is possible for God. With God, change and newness are lively possibilities. Moreover, there can be no doubt that Israel's God is deeply engaged on behalf of Israel's counterparts in every age and that their liberation from bondage to oppressive systems is a high divine priority from which they can take hope. Israel's own typological use of God's actions in the exodus can help show the way (e.g., Isa. 41:17–20; 43:14–21; 52:11–12). At the same time, the interpreter must use care so as not to lose sight of the fact that God's actions in the exodus are on behalf of a very particular elect people, the people of Israel.

2. From another perspective, while there can be little doubt that salvation is understood in a holistic way in Exodus (as in the entire Bible), political interpretations have often ignored other dimensions of the event. The identity of the anti-God forces in the narrative is a matter of no little import in this regard. Pharaoh is not simply another tyrant, and the event is more than historical. The text makes clear that God's activity is also directed against Egypt's gods (12:12; 15:11; 18:11). Pharaoh is seen to be both a human being and an embodiment of cosmic

forces working against God's creational designs. Redemption is thus both mythically and historically conceived and hence is universal in scope. The historical redemption is real and constitutive in character because it participates in *a cosmic victory.* To interpret salvation in sociopolitical terms only or primarily scales down the import and effect of what happens at the Red Sea (see at 15:1–21).

The exodus redemption finds its closest parallels in the victory announced by Second Isaiah and in the cross and resurrection of Jesus in the New Testament. It would then need to be asked whether the image of God as warrior has not in these instances been transmuted to such an extent that sociopolitical violence is now problematic in talk about the redemption that *God* works (see the article by Zenger in van Iersel).

3. Finally, it must be remembered that the book of Exodus insists that one cannot speak of liberation as a freeing from all restraints; it is not a declaration of independence. As we have noted, Exodus moves from one kind of slavery to another, from bondage to Pharaoh to the service of Yahweh. One cannot bypass Sinai on the way to the promised land. Hence, any who would use Exodus as a paradigm for liberation should then move to the question, Whom will we now serve? Exodus would claim that true freedom is found only in the service of Yahweh.

These factors suggest that the exodus ought not function as a paradigm in any direct or simple way.

Israel's Worship and Yahweh's Presence

Worship is a central theme of Exodus. The overall movement of the book is from slavery to worship. The concern for the proper worship of Yahweh is also evident throughout the book, seen both in specific content and in the fact that liturgical usage of this material has shaped the literature.

Worship themes are made especially prominent by the redactional placement of the passover ritual and the songs of chapter 15. Their enclosure of the exodus story gives it a liturgical character, contributing to a sacramental understanding of the events and their commanded reactualizations. Liturgy and narrative are interconnected (see at 12:1). The centrality of praise in chapter 15 has also been closely tied to the lament character of earlier chapters. This rhythm of lament, deliverance, and praise is shown by the psalms to be a common liturgi-

20

cal rhythm in Israel's worship. This suggests a liturgical character for the entirety of chapters 1—15. Their interpretation cannot be separated from the meaning given to these events in the life of worship.

Worship themes continue in the eating and drinking of the wilderness, and especially at Sinai. The Sinai events of theophany, law-giving and covenant-making, perhaps shaped by subsequent liturgical reactualizations, are permeated with worship themes and concerns. Chapters 25—40 are obvious in their explicit worship focus. Most of this material centers on the plan and construction of the tabernacle, the worship center of the community. Between the planning and the building, however, come chapters 32—34. At issue in the apostasy of the golden calf and its aftermath is the proper worship of Yahweh.

The question of Exodus thus becomes not only, Whom will Israel serve? but, Of what does the proper worship of Yahweh consist? Certain negative possibilities are rejected, while positive directions are encouraged and commanded. Proper worship is understood to have both sacrificial and sacramental dimensions. On the one hand, it is a means by which Israel can bring public honor to its God through praise, thanksgiving, and other expressions of faithfulness (see at 15:1). On the other hand, it is a means in and through which God can act in faithfulness on behalf of those who worship (see at 12:1).

Closely related to this is the movement in Exodus from seeming divine absence to the fullness of presence in the tabernacle. Especially following the golden calf incident, the divine presence with the people becomes the central problematic. Will God go with Israel on its journeyings or not (33:1–3)? Finally, after the planning and building of the tabernacle, God in all the divine glory does dwell among the people (40:35). It is apparent that what Israel does and says in worship has an effect on the nature of the divine presence in its midst. God will be faithful, but Israel can drive Yahweh away by its disloyalty. Israel's faithfulness in worship is seen to be absolutely central to its life as the people of God.

Law, Covenant, and Israel's Identity

The identity of the Israelites is of considerable interest to the narrator. Over the course of the narrative they are more and more revealed for who they are, both positively and nega-

21

tively. Unlike Genesis, Exodus has to do, not with the family of Jacob, but with *a people,* the people of Israel. This change in identity is established in the opening verses, and in God's first speech ("my people," 3:7). Israel's status as God's elect people is in place from the beginning. They are the people of the covenant made with Abraham; the promises to Abraham are also their promises (2:24). Peoplehood is the presupposition of these events, not the result. The narrative is concerned with how these people more and more take on their identity, becoming in life what they already are in the eyes of God.

The order of the central events in the book of Exodus is theologically important. First comes the redemptive work of God on behalf of the people. This serves to ground their precarious existence in the deliverance from both historical and cosmic enemies that God accomplishes on their behalf. The elect people is now a redeemed people. Only then is the law given at Sinai. The law is a gift to an already redeemed community. The law is not the means by which the relationship with God is established; God redeems quite apart from human obedience. But then the concern for the law suddenly fills the scene, not only in Exodus, but in the remainder of the Pentateuch. Central to the law is the issue of faithfulness to God alone, particularly as manifested in proper worship (see above). Such faithfulness and other forms of obedience are certainly in Israel's own interests for the best life possible (see Deut. 4:40). But Israel is called beyond itself to a vocational covenant within the Abrahamic covenant (see at 19:1; 24:1). Israel's obedience is ultimately for the sake of being a kingdom of priests among the other peoples of the world (19:4–6). The golden calf debacle, however, demonstrates that Israel does not remain faithful. Israel's future with God stands at the edge of the abyss. Only God's gracious act of forgiveness enables a new future for Israel (see at 34:9–10). But the importance of obedience is not thereby set aside. Obedience remains central for the sake of witness and mission to the world. And God's tabernacling presence undergirds Israel on that journey.

PART ONE

Growth and Bondage in Egypt

Exodus 1—2

This section contains a series of vignettes that set the stage for the remainder of the book. It is certainly a composite, drawing on various traditions. Yet the pervasive use of irony and the almost complete absence of God language help tie the section together literarily and theologically. (See especially the studies of Ackerman, Isbell, and Exum.)

God's *creational and historical promises are fulfilled* among the people of God *in Egypt.* But this resolution is *threatened by chaotic forces embodied in an oppressive Pharaonic regime.* Initially, God works behind the scenes against this creation-threatening situation in and through *the wisdom and courage of five lowly women.* Their *creative disobedience* preserves a future for Israel and enables the emergence of a leader in the person of Moses. His early life experiences both *embody Israel and anticipate the divine action.* A *new intensification of divine activity* (2:23–25) gives promise for a changed future.

The *wide-ranging scope* of these chapters is breathtaking. They move back and forth from the familial to the national, from the personal to the cosmic, from courageous women to arrogant kings, from endangered babies to a concerned God.

Exodus 1:1–7
The Land Was Filled with Them

The opening passage of a book is important. Exodus 1:1–7 is no exception. Very quickly the narrator moves the story away from Genesis into a new world, from twelve sons to seventy persons to a full land. The focus is on issues of *continuity with both creation and promise themes in the Genesis narrative,* while setting the stage for what follows. It also serves to note the passage of a considerable period of time.

A key to this section is the repetition of the phrase "the sons of Israel [Israelites]" at the beginning and at the end. In verse 1 the phrase stresses continuity with Gen. 46:8–27, which names those who went down to Egypt (the LXX has seventy-five persons; cf. Acts 7:14; Luke 10:1). The opening of Exodus is thus a verbal link back to Genesis, interlocking the two narratives. The phrase in verse 7 stresses discontinuity, moving from a particular family to an entire people, from Jacob/Israel to Israel. The latter use of the phrase occurs only twice in Genesis (32:32; 36:31); in Exodus it will occur 125 times. This is a major shift in vocabulary usage. The reader is thus asked to shift attention to this new reality—Israel, the people of God. This shift is accentuated in verse 6; not only has Joseph died (so Gen. 50:26), but the entire Genesis generation. The perspective of the narrator is evident: the beginnings of Israel as the people of God are to be traced to this pre-exodus (!) time. However much modern historians wish to argue about the time when we can first speak of an Israel—most would say only after the settlement in Canaan—the narrator claims otherwise. What follows is the story of Israel, the people of God.

Verse 7 multiplies language regarding the growth of this people. Five verbs are used to stress *an extraordinary increase in numbers* (one verb is used for the plague of frogs, 8:3!). This language connects with the promise of fruitfulness to Israel's ancestors (cf. Gen. 17:2–6; 48:4), the fulfillment of which is anticipated in Gen. 47:27. Still further language of growth is used as the chapter progresses (1:9, 10, 12, 20), highlighting the *ful-*

24

fillment of promises made to this family. Yet there is no specific language of fulfillment and no reference to God until 1:17. Readers familiar with the story would make the connections (cf. Deut. 10:22; 26:5; Ps. 105:24). They would observe that God language had been rare in the story of Joseph; God was at work in the history of this family in unobtrusive ways (Gen. 50:20). Yet the paucity of explicit God language invites further reflection.

Verse 7 connects not only with historical promises but also with the creation/re-creation accounts of Gen. 1:28 and 9:1, 7. Israel has been fruitful, has multiplied, and fills the earth/land (Hebrew *'ereṣ* can be translated either way; it refers both to the "earth" in Gen. 1:28 and 9:1 and to Egypt—to have mentioned Egypt would have obscured this verbal link). The point here is that *God's intentions in creation are being realized in this family;* what is happening is in tune with God's creational purposes. This is *a microcosmic fulfillment of God's macrocosmic design* for the world (cf. 40:34–38). Israel is God's starting point for realizing the divine intentions for all. The reader should be prepared to see other such realizations of creative design in Exodus.

These growth passages are *testimony to God's ongoing work of creation and blessing,* that flowing, rhythmic, non-dramatic divine activity. In the reticence to speak of God, this is recognized as a behind-the-scenes kind of activity in which God works in and through gifts given in creation. This creational activity is an indispensable foundation for the later work of redemption. Without this, there would be no people to redeem. The God who redeems has been at work in life-giving ways all along the journey (cf. Gen. 45:5–7; 50:20). God's redemptive work should thus not be seen in interventionist terms but as an intensification of the ongoing activity of the Creator God. In both instances it is activity which brings forth and fosters life and blessing. Because God is a God of life and blessing, God will do redemptive work, should those gifts ever be endangered or diminished. The next section testifies that such a danger is real; divine redemptive activity will be needed.

The long period of time covered in these verses is thus recognized, not as a time when God has been absent, but when God's work of blessing has been substantial (Gen. 45:17–20). It is ironic that this marvelous creative activity occurs *in Egypt,*

25

in the world outside the promised land, in a hospitable setting provided by people who have experienced (if not yet known) God's work as creator. It will also be experienced by Moses in Pharaoh's court and in Midian. This *creative activity* is drawn into Israel's most basic confession of faith (Deut. 26:5; Ps. 105: 24; cf. Josh. 24:3). How significant a work is here carried out by the "non-chosen" to provide life and blessing for the "chosen." How often this has been the case over the centuries since. How seldom it has been acknowledged!

Moreover, this time has been very important for both God and people as a time of preparation for a day of redemption when it would be needed. Exodus insists that God's redemptive work does not occur in a vacuum. *God's work in creation provides the basis for God's work in redemption; God's work in redemption fulfills God's work in creation.*

This narrative pushes the reader forward to what follows. If all this has happened to the people, what must be in store for the future? If God has begun to fulfill promises, and in such an extraordinary way, is there not hope that other promises will be fulfilled, not least the gift of a land? As the people have grown and filled the land, the need for a land of their own has become more pressing. But such fulfillments often bring problems in their train as well as creative possibilities. Not everyone is in tune with God's creative designs.

Exodus 1:8–14
Whom Will Israel Serve?

This section is not only filled with irony, it reveals *the symbolic character of the narrative*, whatever its historical grounding may be. Pharaoh, Joseph, the Egyptians, Pithom, and Rameses stand for much more than historical realities. This is reinforced by 12:12 and 15:11, which include the Egyptian gods among those to be judged. The issues at stake are thereby thrown onto a cosmic screen, encompassing both heavenly and earthly spheres. The struggle in which Israel and its God are engaged is both historical and creational (see at 15:1).

Into the midst of God's extraordinary creative activity enters a major effort to subvert what God has done. Seeming resolution dissolves into dissonance. A sign of blessing for Israel is a sign of disaster for Pharaoh. *The new king of Egypt counters God's life-giving work with death-dealing efforts.* A life-supporting situation becomes life-threatening. This is no minor subversion, having only local effects; it is a threat to undo God's creation. To bring death to God's microcosmic work will have negative macrocosmic ramifications. It is the Fall and its aftermath revisited at that spot in the world where God has begun the task of fulfilling the divine creative designs. *God's response will have to be comparably cosmic.* The cosmic scope of events will often be evident in what follows; indeed, all nature will become involved.

The culprit this time is not a serpent or a brother-killing Cain or the sons of God but "a new king over Egypt." The narrator introduces him in terse fashion. He is not even given a name (nor is his successor). The focus is thus placed on him, not simply as a historical figure, but as *a symbol for the anticreation forces of death* which take on the God of life. The narrator's concern is with this king's response to God's extraordinary creative activity. This is a life-and-death struggle in which *the future of the creation is at stake.*

The sole description of Pharaoh is that he does not know Joseph. "Joseph" is more than a reference to the individual; he is the one in and through whom God has preserved the people alive (Gen. 45:5–7; 50:20). This description contrasts with that given to God, who "knows" this people and their situation (2:25; 3:7; cf. 33:17). "Knowing" means more than acquaintance or being informed; it bespeaks a relationship of depth in which there is commitment to those who are known and genuine concern regarding their welfare. The king of Egypt does not know; God knows. *This difference in knowing has a profound effect on doing* (see Jer. 22:16). Not-knowing leads to oppression; knowing leads to salvation. Who knows and who does not (yet) know will be a recurrent theme in Exodus (cf. 5:2; 6:7; 7:5).

Verses 9–10 describe Israel's situation from the new king's point of view, which contrasts with that of the narrator in verse 7. What the narrator views as a blessing, the new king (cf. Gen. 47:6) considers a problem. The direct speech and the use of the narrator's vocabulary reinforces this. This is a public act, announced in "us/them" terms to the entire country in an effort to show that their future is at stake. So much is this national policy that everyone is said to be engaged in its implementation (vv. 11, 13–14; cf. Deut. 26:6). To speak of *all* Egyptians demonstrates the *symbolic character of "Egyptian."* This act is the new king's first consideration, demonstrating his singlemindedness. He is preoccupied with Israel and their extraordinary growth, that it may be beyond Egypt's capacity to control, a threat to the status quo. Unless their growth is curtailed, they may become a fifth column in time of war and escape. The Israelites become an issue of national security.

This speech is unknowingly *filled with irony.* (1) The king is the first to recognize the children of Israel as a "people," giving them a status like his own people just mentioned. (2) In echoing the narrator's words of verse 7 (cf. Gen. 18:18), and exaggerating the numbers, an "outsider" highlights the fulfillment of God's promises. His acts of oppression confirm that God's word to Abraham in Gen. 15:13 was on target. (3) His concern to act shrewdly will be shown to be folly; even with his wisest counselors (cf. 7:11) his policies will again and again be turned to Israel's advantage. Pharaoh's efforts will lead to an end precisely the opposite of his intentions. (4) Storage cities built out of a concern for life (Gen. 41:34–36) are here used as a vehicle for death. (5) Strikingly, he speaks of the exodus, echoing Joseph himself (Gen. 50:24). The phrase "escape *('alah)* from the land" is exactly the wording used in 13:18, which also uses battle language. This verb is also used for God's saving action in 3:8, 17 ("bring up"; cf. Gen. 46:4). Pharaoh says more than he knows!

Pharaoh wastes no time in implementing his new policy. His fears become structured into an oppressive system. Slavegang masters are charged to afflict Israel with heavy burdens (not an unusual practice in ancient Egypt; see Sarna, pp. 17–24). History has shown that such cruelties result not only in tighter controls over the community but in many deaths. Pithom and Rameses were cities in the delta region, part of a building project of Egypt's nineteenth Dynasty. Because these cities were much more to the Egyptians than "store-cities," however, they are used by the narrator primarily as *symbols of oppression* rather than as an effort to ground the story in historical reality.

Pharaoh's wisdom turns out not to be so wise after all. The more Israel is oppressed, the more it grows. As often for Israel,

28

it must pass in and through adversity on the way to the fulfillment of promises. Ironically, the Pharaoh's tactics once again
have the effect of furthering the fulfillment of God's promises
("spread abroad" recalls Gen. 28:14; cf. Isa. 54:3)! Egypt's fears
now turn to dread.

Oppression is the prevailing theme in this unit. Those who
live in affluence and freedom will have difficulty understanding
the true nature of this experience. Those who have had personal experience of oppression will have at least an initial advantage in hearing and interpreting this text. Readers can learn
more by consulting the literature that has emerged from those
with such experience (for further detail, see at 5:1). The reference to Egypt's fears indicates that oppression has as negative
an effect upon the oppressor as on the oppressed. Both become
less human. "As the oppressors dehumanize others and violate
their rights, they themselves also become dehumanized. . . .
Once a situation of violence and oppression has been established, it engenders an entire way of life and behavior for those
caught up in it—oppressor and oppressed alike. Both are sub-
merged in the situation, and both bear the marks of oppression"
(Freire, pp. 43–44). It is to be remembered that the *oppression
is sociopolitical in character* (see Croatto, p. 17). It is also important to recognize, however, that it is not simply so; the issues,
as we have seen, are cosmic as well as historical. When liberation does come, the *entire creation* will be affected.

Under a regime of slavery, subjects become objects. The
Hebrews, who have just been identified as a people, are in the
process of losing their identity. They are slaves of another, not
a people in their own right. The absence of overt signs of this
identity in the narrative, including religious heritage, may
dramatize this fact. From Pharaoh's perspective there will be
only one people and one heritage in the land of Egypt. Before
there can be an escape from such a situation, Israel has to regain
some sense of its own identity; that will be one concern in the
following narrative.

The language of affliction and burden is a recurrent motif
in the Exodus tradition in the Old Testament. It is incorporated
into Israel's confession of faith (Deut. 26:5; I Sam. 12:8); it will
also appear in the laws (22:21–24), where the memory of God's
deliverance is to inform Israel's relationship with the less fortunate among them. Israel's memory of oppression is thereby

29

given specific focus. Israel is not to parade its past suffering in order to occasion pity or guilt from others. *The recalling of oppression is to lead to an identification with those who suffer.* Moreover, while the oppression of Israel will continue to be noted (2:11; 5:4–5), the focus will be on God's attention and deliverance (3:7, 17; 4:31; 6:6–7). Hence the memory of the past is to be used to center the people on (1) what God has done for them and (2) how they are to respond to the unfortunate in every generation.

Verses 13–14 use repetitive language to vivify the intensification of this increasingly problematic situation ("a new pharaoh cannot afford to be wrong," Durham, p. 9). The *language is excessive in order to match the experience of oppression.* The word *perek* ("rigor") occurs twice, stressing the harshness and cruelty of the Egyptian treatment (forbidden among Israelites in Lev. 25:43, 46, 53). Words related to the Hebrew root *'abad* ("serve") are used five times (cf. the five verbs in v. 7). A chiastic structure overloads the sentence, stressing this theme:

> So they made the people *serve* with rigor,
> and made their lives bitter with backbreaking *service*
> in mortar and brick,
> and with every kind of *service* in the field;
> with every kind of *service*
> they made them *serve* with rigor.

This root provides one of the leading motifs in the book of Exodus (it is used 97 times!). It will also be used for the service and worship of God (cf. 3:20).

One key question in the book of Exodus therefore is this: *Whom will Israel serve?* Verses 13–14 would appear to make the answer to that question very clear indeed! Israel is serving Pharaoh. To be in his service, however, means harshness and bondage, the lack of freedom to be what one is called to be. That is not God's purpose for the creation. God will see this slavery (2:25; 3:7) and move to deliver Israel, so that the Israelites become God's servants. Only in service to God can service without bondage be found. With God, service is freedom. Yet Israel is not freed to do what it pleases; Israel moves from one kind of servitude to another. *The exodus does not constitute a declaration of independence, but a declaration of dependence upon God* (cf. 14:31). This is ratified in a covenant at Sinai (24:7). This servitude does not force a belonging, however, but will draw the community into a new relationship. Only God can be Lord, can lay claim to life in such a way that true freedom is the result. Within such a relationship, as in every genuine commitment, there is real freedom. When this happens, creation becomes what God intended it to be.

This text sets the stage for the kind of God it is who will shortly become involved in Israel's situation. God is a God who takes sides. God is God of the oppressed; God enters into their difficult, suffering situations to set things right. God is a God who is concerned to move people from slavery to freedom. The tradition will include the spiritual (cf. 6:9) and the cosmic dimensions of this movement, but the vivid *physical details* of the bondage and the explicit *sociopolitical realities* in the text should keep our understanding of the divine salvation very much related to all aspects of people's lives.

Exodus 1:15–22
Daughters Save Sons

Once again the narrative is *replete with ironies* as two Hebrew midwives outwit the king of all Egypt.

The narrator shifts from the king of Egypt's speech to his people, and their response, to his speech to the Hebrew midwives, and their response. This repetition invites us to note that the entire Egyptian community is parallel to two Hebrew midwives. It proves to be an uneven match! Once this irony is seen, speculation as to how two midwives could service the entire Israelite community is beside the point. It is also ironic that the king of all Egypt stoops to converse with two lowly Hebrew women in order to move his intentions forward; this is highlighted by the use of direct address and by the fact that the women are named while Pharaoh remains nameless. The irony is compounded when Pharaoh can get the entire Egyptian community to bend to his will but fails to get two daughters of Israel to so respond. Moreover, while the entire Egyptian community is finally unsuccessful, the two women are successful (in their

31

own way!). The Egyptians' fear of the Israelites leads to their failure; the women's fear of (=trust in) God leads to their success. Ironically, the efforts of both Egyptians and Hebrews have the same result: the people of Israel abound the more. (Note that these and other ironies would not be present if, as some suggest, the midwives were Egyptians.)

This narrative still moves within the sphere of creation thought. It is *a struggle over blessing and life* (these themes occur explicitly in every verse). Pharaoh is an angel of death, as he now determines to cut off life at its beginning point. He would limit creation, close it down to multiplication and fruitfulness. God, however, is on the side of life. God works in and through an aspect of the birthing process, and the children's lives are preserved. Even more, in the very face of death, the community as a whole continues to thrive; the recurrent theme of growth is once again front and center (v. 20). God's creative work enables life to abound.

The midwives' *ethic of defenseless resistance* is rooted in such an understanding of God's creative work. *God's creativity is paralleled by the midwives' creative disobedience.* Without belaboring the point or making their efforts public, they do not do what Pharaoh asks. They take this action because of their trust in the Creator God, the God of life. The "fear of God" is a prominent theme in wisdom materials (cf. Prov. 2:5–15), where the connection with creation is explicit. Rita Burns *(Exodus,* p. 30) speaks to this point: "Persons who feared God were those who acted according to a moral imperative. . . . This standard was learned through examination both of human experience . . . and of the processes of nature. . . . There, by means of keen perception and wise reflection, one could observe common patterns which in turn were thought to reflect a fundamental order in the universe. The wise, i.e., ones who feared God, were those who not only discerned this order but who also brought their actions and lives into harmony with it."

The midwives' fear of God entails the understanding that *human life is sacred.* The preservation of the lives of these babies takes priority over the murderous edict of a very important and powerful person, even at the risk of their own lives. Such noncompliance with the law on humanitarian grounds is rooted in a creation theology. While a case for civil disobedience might be rather easily developed out of this passage, the reader is invited to reflect on the wider application of a creation theology for the consideration of ethical issues.

In a response that smacks of some desperation, Pharaoh takes the low road in his preoccupation with Israelite growth. (1) He seeks to turn the Hebrews against themselves (cf. 5:10–21). It is uncertain why he should pick the midwives, except that the moment of birth is one of the key points of vulnerability in any community. It is another point of irony that midwives should be asked to be dealers in death. (2) The object of his Herod-like policy is now children, totally helpless newborns, rather than adults. (3) Life is now to be cut off directly rather than over time through oppression, and that surreptitiously. The midwives could pursue this activity only if they made it look as though the deaths were accidental. Put simply, murder now has become national, if not yet public, policy.

Irony continues. Pharaoh does not perceive that by killing off the males he would in time deplete his slave-labor force. Also, he does not recognize that this policy will rebound upon his own head; Egyptian sons, including his own, will be killed as an eventual outcome of his policies (cf. 11:5). Moreover, his decision to kill sons and save daughters is undermined by those who are saved. The daughters subvert his policy. The women, in saving the sons from the angel of death, anticipate the passover. Their activity, and civil disobedience at that, parallels the saving action of God (cf. 12:23–27).

This parallel in particular highlights *the importance of the activity of women in the divine economy.* "In the refusal of women to cooperate with oppression, the liberation of Israel from Egyptian bondage has its beginnings" (Exum, p. 63). Women will also play a significant role in chapter 2. It can rightfully be said that women are here given such a crucial role that Israel's future is made dependent upon their wisdom, courage, and vision. They make a difference, not only to Israel, but to God. God is able to work in and through these women and that creates possibilities for God's way into the future with this people that might not have been there otherwise.

Another dimension of this story is the *effective service exercised on the part of lesser-known* members of the society (cf. 2:1–10). These women are not leaders of the community, persons in a position of influence who could have an impact on governmental policy. Yet such persons are not powerless. In the

33

process of carrying out their rather mundane responsibilities they are shown to have had a profound effect on the future of their people. God is able to use persons of faith from even lowly stations in life to carry out the divine purpose. Moreover, there is no indication in the story that this courageous activity ever becomes public; it could easily have been forever lost amid all the movements of kings and nations. But the deeds of these women are made known somehow, and their names remembered, while the king of Egypt in all of his pomp and splendor remains forever nameless.

These women risk their own lives. The first-time reader would no doubt be held in some suspense upon reading verse 18. What will the king do? His direct address demands an accounting from them; his repetition of the narrator's report indicates that he has an accurate perception of events. One could now expect the worst. But, ironically, the two women completely defuse the situation with a bold and clever response: the Hebrew women are in such good physical condition that they do not need midwives. Their task has not been fulfilled, because it is not fulfillable. Their statement is doubtlessly hyperbolic and constitutes a put-down of half the king's subjects. However, it is also a testimony to the women's "life" (*hayot,* "vigorous"), which serves life rather than death. Given the issue at stake, less than a full disclosure (including their fear of God) is believed to be justifiable. Surprisingly, the women's retort puts an abrupt end to the conversation. Two lowly Hebrew women silence the king of Egypt, that paragon of wisdom, with a single remark! This is ironic, of course, for no king worth his scepter would have considered the response satisfactory, let alone from midwives. The women's retort sends the king back to the drawing boards to formulate a new policy.

The narrator turns to God's response to what has happened. God is mentioned for the first time in verse 17, as the subject of a sentence only in verse 20. Yet God language appears only from the point of view of the narrator, not of the characters. The order of these sentences is important. God's dealing well with (same root as "good" in Gen. 1) the midwives is explicitly connected with the growth of the people in numbers and strength. God's creational work is accomplished in and through these women. Only then, when the important effect of their work has been made clear, is there a statement about God's

34

creative work in the growth of their own families (and the perpetuation of their names). The fear of God does bring blessing in its train. This effect is not inevitable, of course, as if God's work in the universe were mechanically conceived. But, as Deuteronomy in particular never tires of saying (e.g., 6:24), positive human response to the will of God generally means that life and goodness will abound.

In verse 22, Pharaoh, having been foiled by the two women, returns full circle to his original addressee, the Egyptian people as a whole (v. 9), restates the policy of verse 16 (vv. 16–22 are a chiasmus), but promotes an even more murderous plan to achieve his goal. Only this time he "commands" them, indeed "all" of them, and the call for brutality, violence, and death becomes highly explicit: the public slaughter of sons newly born. This is a policy no longer designed to keep the Israelite population in control but to eliminate it altogether in time; every male child comes into the world with a death sentence on his head. If successful, it will be genocide within a few generations. The fact that this decree stands in contradiction to Pharaoh's previously stated concern about keeping the Israelites from escaping (v. 10) is testimony to his own desperate internal development about the matter.

Pharaoh's speech is again filled with irony, particularly in its reference to the Nile. Positively, it connects with the following story, where the river provides the very setting for the rescue of the baby Moses. Again, Pharaoh provides for the defeat of his own policy in its very formulation. He ends up becoming an instrument for God's saving purposes. As elsewhere in the Old Testament (e.g., Cyrus, Isa. 45:1), God is able to work through even those who do not know God. Negatively, the policy is ironic in that it portends the way in which Pharaoh's successor and his armies will meet their end, namely, by drowning (14: 26–28). Pharaoh's own decree sets a chain of events in motion that, in effect, have him signing his family's own death warrant. As if to confirm this, 1:22 is Pharaoh's last speech.

The chapter ends on an ominous note. One is left wondering what might happen with the future potentially shaped by such a murderous decree. Given the failure of Pharaoh's policies to this point, the human courage and wisdom that have positively shaped events, and the creative, purposeful God that is involved, there is reason for some optimism. But there is no

35

word in the text that even suggests that that future will be shaped only by what God will do. God too awaits a future where human activity, both negative and positive, will have an effect on God's own possibilities.

Exodus 2:1–10
Daughters Save Moses

The story of the birth and childhood of Moses is one of the most familiar in the Old Testament. Its telling and retelling have delighted young and old alike. It has just the right amount of intrigue, suspense, serendipity, irony, and human compassion, plus a happy ending. But the brutality and cruelty of the context is at times neglected: a royal appeal to violence against Hebrew infants by the general populace (1:22). It is this potential for violence, and particularly the suspense engendered thereby, that makes the story work so well. Once again, it is women who shut the violence down.

The narrative narrows from all the "sons" of Israel (1:7–14) to all male "sons" (1:15–22) to one special "son" (2:1–10) who shall save the "firstborn son" (4:22–23). Exodus 1:22 serves as a center for this theme. It brings the story of chapter 1 full circle and serves as part of an inclusio with 2:10; casting "sons" into the Nile parallels the one "son" Moses being drawn from the Nile. As Israel is under threat of extinction, so is Moses. For the first-time reader, the question is, What will happen to this baby?

Certainly Moses' family takes precautions for his safety, but the risks are apparent. There is no appeal here to leaving it "in the hands of the deity" (contra Exum, p. 77). Verse 5 suddenly heightens the anxiety: a woman from Pharaoh's household may discover the child, though she is not without compassion. The narrator uses direct speeches (four by the princess) to carry the flow of the tension. The first builds up the tension again, indicating the child's Hebrew identity. What will she do? The sister's intervention opens up a positive future, agreed to by the princess. The next speech resolves the tension, with the child back in his mother's arms; all is now well. The final speech concludes the adoption of Moses by Pharaoh's daughter. It provides the

36

assurance that Moses is in good hands for the foreseeable future. *Three daughters bring the son through death to life.*

At the same time, the story serves to defuse the threat for all other Hebrew sons. The princess's calm compassion toward the child and her commitment to long-term noncompliance with her father's brutal decree constitute a *public* demonstration of the bankruptcy of his policy. Inasmuch as the tradition never hints that this policy was carried forward, the princess's response may have had some effect (see 3:21; 9:20; 11:3, 8).

Ironies continue to abound. (1) Pharaoh's chosen instrument of destruction (the Nile) is the means for saving Moses. (2) As in 1:15–22, the daughters are allowed to live, and it is they who now proceed to thwart Pharaoh's plans. (3) The mother saves Moses by following Pharaoh's orders (with her own twist). (4) A member of Pharaoh's own family undermines his policies, saving the very person who would lead Israel out of Egypt and destroy the Dynasty. (5) Egyptian royalty heeds a Hebrew girl's advice! The princess may have been gently conned into accepting the child's own mother as a nurse, but her pity is clearly stated. (6) The mother gets paid to do what she most wants to do, and from Pharaoh's own budget (anticipating 3:22)! (7) Moses is educated to be an Israelite leader, strategically placed within the very court of Pharaoh. (8) The princess gives the boy a name that betrays much more than she knows (including a Hebrew etymology for an Egyptian name): what she has done for Moses, Moses will do for all the people of Israel.

Of what import is this ironic mode? Most fundamentally, it is revealing of a *divine irony:* God uses the weak, what is low and despised in the world, to shame the strong (cf. Jer. 9:23; I Cor. 1:26–29). Rather than using power as it is usually exercised in the world, *God works through persons who have no obvious power;* indeed, they are unlikely candidates for the exercise of power. The choice of the five women in chapters 1—2 entails much risk and vulnerability for God; that risk is real, for these persons could fail and God would have to begin again. But they prove highly effective against the ruthless forms of systemic power, and God is not the subject of a single verb in their various undertakings. Even more, God's plan for the future of the children of Israel rests squarely on the shoulders of one of its helpless sons, a baby in a fragile basket. Who would have believed that the arm of the Lord could be revealed in such a

37

one (cf. Isa. 53:1)? God moves throughout this section in unobtrusive, unlikely, and vulnerable ways.

Hence it may be said that the ironic mode fosters a sense of hope amid any situation in which God seems to be absent. What appears to be a hopeless time is actually filled with positive possibilities. But it takes faith, "the conviction of things not seen" (Heb. 11:1), to perceive that God is at work.

As in chapter 1, *parallels with Genesis* show that the story is to be interpreted in terms of *God's creative activity.* The Hebrew word for "basket" is the same as that for Noah's ark. The child's mother "saw that he was good" (God's word for the creation in Genesis). Moses is parallel to Noah (cf. 32:12–17 with Gen. 6:8). The decree of Pharaoh, with water as the instrument of death, is painted in cosmic terms, which, if successful, would plunge the world into chaos once again. God's creation (extraordinary growth for Israel) would be inundated in the Nile's waters. Both Noah and Moses are adrift in a watery chaos, but they are divinely chosen ones in and through whom the good creation will be preserved. *The saving of Moses is thus seen to have cosmic significance.* The narrator may have drawn on other infancy stories in the ancient Near East, the better to highlight this worldwide point (e.g., Sargon of Akkad; cf. Childs, pp. 8–12). Later passages in Exodus will also bring out the cosmic significance of these events.

Generally, it is due to the work of God as creator that leaders are surfaced for any community. But, once again, this divine activity is unobtrusive; God is never mentioned in the narrative. God works in and through human beings to preserve Moses alive (cf. Gen. 45:5–7). And that human activity is genuine; it is not some façade to hide an all-controlling divine activity (contra Sarna, p. 27; Plastaras, p. 41). These human beings could have failed, and God would have had to find a different way into the future with the possibilities then available. The nonmention of God must be given its full weight.

Consistent with this creation theme is *the role given to the daughter of Pharaoh.* A non-Israelite (add Moses' teachers in Pharaoh's court, Acts 7:22!) contributes in significant ways to God's activity of life and blessing. In fact, her activity is directly parallel to that of God with Israel (2:23–25; 3:7–8)! She "comes down," "sees" the child, "hears" its cry, takes pity on him, draws him out of the water, and provides for his daily needs.

38

Basic human values such as compassion, justice, and courage (cf. 1:12*b!*) as well as the active subversion of cruel and inhumane policies are seen to be present among God's creatures quite apart from their relationship to Israel; such are the product of God's activity in creation.

Even more, God's use of the gifts of non-Israelites for creative purposes sets the stage for God's redemptive purposes. In the final analysis, there is no difference in the effect of the humanitarian efforts of those who fear God and those who do not. Both Hebrew midwives and Egyptian princess are agents of life and blessing in the created order. God is able to make use of the gifts of both, and the community of faith is equally accepting of their efforts. Moreover, by telling both stories, Israel acknowledges both contributions with thanksgiving. While the redeemed will be *expected* to engage in acts of justice in view of what God has done for them (cf. 22:21–27), many who are not of this community will engage in such activity with more or less comparable results on the basis of other motivations, prompted by God's creative work within them.

The theme of *civil disobedience* (or defenseless resistance) based on a creation theology continues as these women follow the course set by the midwives. The child's mother not only hides him for three months in the face of Pharaoh's edict but seeks an alternative to death by drowning. The princess (and her servants), in relative proximity to the palace source of the edict, also knowingly responds to the Hebrew infant in noncompliant ways. The child's sister (probably Miriam, 15:20), demonstrating her cleverness and quick-wittedness in enabling her mother to be chosen as nurse for the child, assists both of these women in successfully carrying out their acts of nonviolent resistance to authority.

The narrator again shows how *women play an important leadership role* in these matters (Moses' father disappears from the story, while a great variety of language for women is used). All five women so far noted are actively engaged on the side of life against a ruler who has shown himself to be capable of considerable brutality. Bucking a male-dominated system, they risk their lives for the sake of life. As a result, they not only contribute to the prospering of the children of Israel but enable this particular child, destined to become Israel's leader, to emerge with the best possible preparation for his task. "The

39

courage of women is the beginning of liberation" (Exum, p. 82). "What the women do for Moses, God will do for all Israel" (Burns, *Exodus,* p. 25). Daughters are the saviors of sons.

This story of Moses, informed so broadly by creation theology, constitutes *a paradigm for Israel's experience of redemption.* As the activity of the princess parallels that of God, so Moses' experience parallels that of Israel. The etymology given for Moses' name (based on assonance, not historical understanding) serves this purpose. Just as Moses was safely borne through water and reeds, rescued from the brutality of the Egyptians, and provided with daily sustenance, so also was Israel. God's preservation of life in creation is paradigmatic for God's redemptive activity. The former not only prepares for the latter, it also provides the foundations for its proper interpretation. *What God does in redemption serves God's goals in and for the creation.*

This concern for creation will continue to be prominent in our discussion. It may be helpful to remind ourselves how extensively *God's work as creator in Israel's pre-exodus life* has been portrayed and how important that is understood to be for later developments. The text would claim (1) that an experience of God's work as creator is necessary for participation in the exodus—there would be no exodus without God's prior work in the community as creator; and (2) that an understanding of God's work as creator is indispensable for the proper understanding of the exodus—there would be no exodus *as we know it* without its interpretation having been informed by God's work as creator. (Note that the narrator's theological perspective may or may not be consonant with actual historical developments.)

Interests of a credentialing sort for Moses also begin to surface in this story. It is not insignificant that Moses is of the priestly family of Levi on both parents' side (2:1; cf. 6:20). They may be unnamed here to make more prominent his connection with Levi, especially in view of his being raised in an Egyptian household and his Egyptian name. This note anticipates the priestly role that Moses will later play.

Finally, we note the extensive use to which this story is put
40   in the New Testament (in contrast to the rest of the Old Testament). Christians have long observed the close relationship with the infancy narratives in Matthew 2 (see also Acts 7:20;

Heb. 11:23; cf. Childs, pp. 20–24). The story of Moses functions as a paradigm (or typology) for Matthew's story of Jesus. A fundamental continuity is seen in the way in which God works in the lives of both Moses and Jesus. Also seen is a continuity in human activity, from the senseless murder of children to the faithfulness of human beings. The Old Testament story is seen to be indispensable in *providing the proper interpretation of what God is doing in Jesus.* Both stories are working within the sphere of creation—the preservation of life and the preparation of leaders. Understanding what God is about in creation provides the necessary theological grounding for the story of redemption. And that work is, as always, quite unobtrusive, not apparent (except to eyes of faith), but a means in and through which God is at work in the world to bring fullness of life to as many as possible.

Exodus 2:11–22
Moses as Embodiment of the Future

These stories report three incidents in Moses' early adult life, bringing him into contact with three different groups: the Egyptians, his own people, and the Midianites. Each incident functions to provide a transition to what follows, to identify the adult Moses as an Israelite, to anticipate key events in the subsequent narratives, and to characterize Moses, especially as one who responds to injustice. Moses' own point of view is little in evidence (2:13, 14, 22). We hear more from others than we do from him. He is not yet the character he will be in narratives to come.

The reader is immediately informed that much time has passed (cf. Acts 7:23). One of the first questions would thus be, What has happened to Moses' relationship with his own people? Has Moses been so fully integrated into the Egyptian community that this connection has been lost? The narrator wastes no time in making it clear that Moses identifies himself with Israel. Repeated reference is made to "his" "people, kinfolk" (see 4:18), as he comes to the defense of a fellow Hebrew. This identification is also shown in the following ways:

41

Moses Embodies Israel in His Own Life Experience

Moses (1) enters into conflict with the Egyptians, (2) becomes the subject of a murderous edict of Pharaoh (1:22 catches up to him), (3) has to "flee" (see 14:5) from Egypt to the wilderness, where he encounters God at Sinai, and (4) testifies to having been (become) a sojourner in a foreign land.

The last is climactic in the narrative by virtue of its position and as direct speech. It is the only statement of Moses regarding his relationship to Israel. The "foreign land" may be purposely ambiguous, both Midian and Egypt. The word *ger* ("sojourner") is used for Israel in Egypt (22:21; 23:9; cf. Gen. 15:13; Deut. 23:7). Moses' status as an Egyptian (cf. 2:19) means that he must move away from Egypt to be able truly to know the Israelites' sojourning experience. Moses gains this identity as a sojourning Israelite in Midian. Life in the wilderness also enables him to see more clearly who he is; so shall it be for Israel. The wilderness, ironically, becomes a more hospitable place than Egypt, as it will for Israel.

In a number of ways, then, Moses both *relives the fate of his people and anticipates their near future.* He becomes one of them by virtue of his own experience.

Moses' Action Anticipates/Foreshadows God's Action

1. Moses *"sees"* Israel's oppression (v. 11). This language is used of God in 2:25; 3:7, 9; 4:31; 5:19; "to see" means to strike a responsive chord. Moses is no disinterested observer and, having seen (as God will see) Israel's oppression, takes the initiative to do what he can about it.

2. Moses *"strikes"* the Egyptian. Moses' first "seeing" is an Egyptian (not necessarily a taskmaster) beating a Hebrew, with death-dealing blows. Moses responds in kind, shown by the use of *nakah* ("strike") in both verses. "Striking" may or may not be fatal (cf. 21:12–21), but Moses' response in kind suggests that the Egyptian had fatally beaten the Hebrew (or was bent on doing so). Moses made sure he was not being observed, an action that establishes premeditation and the absence of impulsiveness (hiding the body shows a concern for secrecy).

42

This action of Moses is often judged to be excessive ("an angry young man"). It is important to note, however, that *nakah* is also used of God's actions toward the Egyptians (12:12, 13, 29; 9:15; cf. 3:20; 7:17, 25). When God "strikes," the result is often death. If it is argued that Moses was impetuous, the issue of excessiveness is simply left hanging until God becomes the subject of a "striking" that leads to death. The use of the same verb suggests that Moses' action was not considered inappropriate by the narrator (cf. Acts 7:23–29), but it anticipates *God's* rather than Israel's activity. Moses introduces a new level of resistance into the conflict with the Egyptians. Some progression is evident as one moves from the midwives to the women in 2:1–10; the latter are more pro-active, though both are nonviolent and defenseless. This move from nonviolence to violence by stealth (short of open revolution) may be related to the changing nature of the Egyptian oppression. Beating people to death seems to call for more active resistance. An intensification of response *by God* will now be evident in the plagues, climaxing in the slaying of the firstborn. In effect, Moses' response is a form of capital punishment and may anticipate 21:12 (cf. 21:20; Lev. 24:17).

3. Moses *"saves"/"delivers"* the daughters of Jethro and provides water for them. When the shepherds drive the women away *(garaš,* cf. Gershom) as Pharaoh will drive Israel away (6:1; 10:11; 11:1; 12:39), Moses "helps" (v. 17, *yaša*ʿ) and "delivers" them (v. 19, *nasal*). This language is used for God's salvation (14:13, 30; 15:2) and deliverance (3:8; 6:6; 12:27) of Israel, especially in the Midianite setting of 18:4, 8–10. Both the narrator and the Midianite women use this language; with the latter it functions as witness. The fact that the deliverance involves the drawing of water also points forward to the provision of water for Israel in the wilderness (17:1–6).

4. Moses *confronts a wrong* (2:13, *raša*ʿ). Just as Moses confronts the Hebrew who wronged another, so God through Moses will confront Pharaoh. Ironically, Pharaoh will admit that he is in the wrong (9:27), while the Hebrew does not.

Moses' Action Anticipates Issues Facing a Leader in Israel

43

In verse 13 the narrator moves Moses to an intra-Israelite dispute. Issues of justice must be faced *within* the community of faith as well. This will constitute a major area of responsibility for Moses. His question, "Why are you striking your 'neighbor' "? is certainly intended to relate to 18:16, where Moses is engaged in resolving intra-Israelite disputes among "neighbors." But Moses' authority to intervene in this dispute is challenged. The accuser becomes the accused. Though an Israelite, he is not recognized as a judge over "us" (=Israel?). This relates ahead to the refusal of the Israelites to listen to Moses (6:9–11; cf. 4:1) and to disputes concerning Moses' authority (5:21; 14:11–12; cf. Num. 16:12–14). They would rather serve the Egyptians! As the Hebrew accused Moses of trying to kill him, so also would the Israelites in the wilderness (16:2–3; 17:3–4). This language also anticipates questions regarding Moses' judgments in 18:13–26. In a more general way, it anticipates conversations between God and Moses regarding his abilities to assume the call.

The "priest of Midian" (Reuel/Jethro) and his daughters appear without introduction. There is an ironic relationship between this story and the preceding one. Moses is not welcome in the Israelite community, but here Moses is shown considerable hospitality by *strangers* (anticipating chap. 18), even being given a daughter for his wife (though he has not one word to say!). Israel does not appreciate his acts of justice on its behalf; the Midianites welcome it. Israelites engage in accusations of Moses; the daughters of Reuel publicly sing his praises. Those who stand within the community of faith are abusive; those without faith in Israel's God exemplify genuine relationships. This is continuous with the actions of Pharaoh's daughter; the involvement of non-Israelites again demonstrates the importance of creation theology. Also, Moses' marriage to Zipporah integrates an "outsider" into the community. Israel is not a generically pure community; its leaders extend the family to include others.

Yet these actions of Moses, while anticipatory, are also inadequate. A personal sense of justice is not adequate for the mission God has in mind. Moses must have a word to speak and he cannot accomplish the salvation of Israel on his own; God will have to become directly involved. These two themes will become especially prominent in what follows.

44

The *common issue for Moses in each of these episodes is justice* (cf. Acts 7:26–27). Three types of injustice—experienced by three types of victims and perpetrated by persons from three different peoples—are challenged:

	Injustice	*Victim*	*Oppressor*
2:11	beaten (to death)	slave	Egyptian (master)
2:13	wronged	neighbor	Hebrew (equal)
2:17	deprivation	woman	Nomads (male)

The range of concern is striking: no matter the victim or the oppressor or the type of injustice, it must be taken up and strong effort made to bring it to an end. Moses does not articulate these matters (cf. 4:10!), and his motives are unstated. But his actions do speak, and actions are often louder than words. Moses' sense of justice transcends boundaries of nationality, gender, and kinship. He is not indifferent to evil by whomever it is perpetrated or whoever the victim might be. He demonstrates a concern for life, especially the life of the weaker members of the society, and an intolerance for abuse exercised by the strong. Also evident is the courage of Moses, risking his own life, a characteristic needed for action on behalf of those suffering injustice.

Moses' sense of justice has been learned, not from his Hebrew heritage, but from his *Egyptian upbringing* (cf. Acts 7:22!). This is a significant testimony to God's work in creation among those outside the community of faith. This, combined with the absence of God talk in the narrative, again roots this perspective, this activity, and these personal characteristics in a theology of creation. There the value of human life and the giftedness of individuals are given special prominence, becoming the basis for actions taken on behalf of others. By his actions Moses furthers the creational work of God in giving life and blessing. To say that "there is very little here of the hero of faith who decides for God" (Childs, p. 43) is to miss this point. Moses' sympathies for those less fortunate and his active response on their behalf anticipate God's will as expressed both in saving action (14:13, 30; 15:1–2) and in written statute (22:21–27). Once again, an ethic grounded in a theology of creation serves as an important basis for both redemption and Torah.

The New Testament has two considerations of this narrative (Acts 7:23–29, 35; Heb. 11:24–28; cf. Childs, pp. 33–42).

45

Acts focuses on this narrative because of Moses' experience at the hands of his kinfolk, part of a history of rejection climaxing in Jesus (vv. 51–52). Extending the anticipatory mode of the narrative, the rejection of Moses anticipates the rejection of Jesus. Hebrews takes a different tack, using Moses and his faith in the midst of suffering as an encouragement to faithful readers in comparable life circumstances. Moses "suffered abuse for Christ" (cf. 10:33). If cast in terms of its Old Testament context, Moses' ill-treatment would be considered parallel to God's suffering (Exod. 2:23–25; 3:7). Moses shares in the suffering of God (which, from a New Testament perspective, included the second person of the Trinity).

The story ends on a note of uncertainty. Will Moses and Israel get together again? Will Moses fulfill the promise shown in this activity? Can salvation come from the wilderness?

Exodus 2:23–25
When Kings Die

These verses inform the reader about what is happening back in Egypt and with God: "Meanwhile, back in Egypt. . . ." The verses are not an inconsequential notice, however. The events narrated in chapter 3 are able to happen as they do only because of what these verses report. Every change in government brings changes in various spheres. Hearing that the king of Egypt has died, the reader is led to expect changes for the better for Israel. But we are told nothing of the new king here. The narrator delays noting that he is less oppressive (4:19); he must want another matter to receive more attention here.

The development reported in Egypt is that *the people are now crying out.* The fourfold reference to Israel's "cry" and twofold reference to bondage in such brief notice catch the reader's attention. The words are piled up as they were in 1:13–14, this time with "cry" language. This is the first mention of Israel's crying out (in fact, the first as subject since 1:7). This is testimony to a change on the part of the oppressed; they now engage in public outcry and name their oppression for the slavery it is. This makes a difference in the character of their situation. It also has an effect upon God's possibilities within that context (cf. below).

The narrator now brings God into the heart of the story. Israel's "cry" is not salvific, no matter how heartrending it may be. If life is to be possible again, God will have to become involved. But *what is happening with God* is not yet knowledge available to those crying out; that will come first to Moses in the following story. This *report* concerning God will there become the *word of God* to Israel (cf. 6:2–9).

While God was mentioned in 1:15–22, and has by no means been uninvolved, the divine activity has been unobtrusive. This text signals a change in the portrayal of that God. The change in Egyptian kings must not be separated from this. The narrative ties these changes together; the one provides the occasion for speaking of the other. Theologically, changes in the world affect the way in which God can be spoken of in relationship to that world. Even more, changes in the world can affect the way in which God is active in that world. For example, it is not only Hosea's talk about God's judgmental activity but also the actual nature of divine activity that is related to the ways things are in the world of his time. God becomes active in judgment in a way that God had not been previously because of what Israel and the surrounding world had become.

Thus the death of the king in Egypt provides possibilities or opportunities for God that were not available heretofore. There is a kind of "fullness of time" at this moment that will enable God to be active in a new way in the world and for Israel. *The long period of waiting in Egypt, then, has been due not to some divine quietism but to God's waiting for the right configuration of human and natural events to put a new level of activity together with respect to this situation.* (God's waiting for the course of human affairs is also suggested by Gen. 15:16.) One cannot help being reminded of another, later period of seeming divine inactivity, a waiting for the "fullness of time" (Gal. 4:4).

The various words for crying out are commonly used in Old Testament lament literature, particularly the laments of the Psalter. In times of distress or disaster, the community gathered in worship and voiced its laments to God (e.g., Joel 2). A common liturgical pattern—lament, petition, assurance of salvation, thanksgiving—has informed the structure of the next chapters. The lament and petition formally begin here, the word of salva-

47

tion follows in chapters 3—6, the act of salvation is then detailed in chapters 7—14, and chapter 15 constitutes the Song of Thanksgiving after the deliverance at the sea.

Israel's cry "came up to God" (3:9). This phrase does not tell us whether the prayers were directed to this God (3:6 assumes a knowledge of the God of the fathers; cf. Deut. 26:7; two texts report idolatry in Egypt, Josh. 24:14; Ezek. 20:7-8). The phrase only means that these cries were now, in view of the changed circumstances, able to be attended to by God in a way that had not previously been the case. The nature of this attention is detailed in four succinct sentences, with God (rather than a pronoun) repeated as the subject:

> God *heard* their groaning
> God *remembered* his covenant with Abraham, Isaac, and Jacob
> God *saw* the people of Israel, and
> God *knew* [translations add various objects not in Hebrew]

These four verbs summarize the changed situation with God:

1. God heard *(šama'):* This is not a reference to newly sensitive divine ears, as if God had not heard their cries before. It has the sense of "to take heed of; to hear and respond to" (as in 3:7; 6:5; cf. Gen. 16:11; Ps. 31:7; 145:19).

2. God remembered *(zakar):* This does not refer to a jogging of the divine memory, as if God had forgotten promises made. To remember is to be actively attentive to that which is remembered (6:5; cf. Gen. 8:1); it is a divine sense of obligation to a prior commitment. The specific promise remembered is most clearly noted in Gen. 17:4-8 (cf. 26:3, 24; 28:15), especially the divine assurance: I will be your God (3:12; 6:7). The promise of a land is also in view (6:4). God's remembering always means action that will affect the future.

3. God saw *(ra'ah):* As noted at 2:11, this does not refer to eye contact. It is to begin to move toward the other with kindness or sympathy (3:7, 9; 4:31; cf. Gen. 31:42).

4. God knew *(yada'):* Again, this is not simply a matter of "head knowledge," as if God gained some new information or insight into what is happening. It is to so share an experience with another that the other's experience can be called one's own. While the verb does not have an object in Hebrew, the

48

object in 3:7 could well apply here: God knows their sufferings.

These verbs show that God has a new "point of view" with respect to the situation. The context has changed among both Egyptians and Israelites such that God's creational intentions for the world can now take a new turn. God can move forward with respect to the divine purposes in new ways. Israel is to be the object of God's special care; this action is grounded in God's prior relationship with the ancestors of this people.

This brief narrative ends by putting a question in the reader's mind: What will God do? What will happen now?

PART TWO

Moses and God:
Call and Dialogue
EXODUS 3:1—7:7

The story of the call of Moses has long fascinated the community of faith, particularly the burning bush. In my mind's eye is a composite of numerous efforts by Bible storybook artists to depict this incident in full color. As is so often the case, however, the picture stays in the memory but the content of Moses' encounter with the divine remains hazy. Yet, remembered pictures can occasion further inquiry.

This part of Exodus is framed by an extended call narrative (3:1—4:17) and a restatement of that call (6:2—7:7). Between these two sections is a report of Moses' return to Egypt (4:18–31) and an initial confrontation with Pharaoh which fails, intensifying the bondage of the people (5:1—6:1).

A typical call narrative includes these elements: (1) theophany, or divine appearance (vv. 1–4a); (2) introductory word (vv. 4b–9); (3) divine commission (v. 10); (4) objection (v. 11, cf. chart); (5) reassurance (v. 12a, cf. chart); and (6) sign (v. 12b). Other call narratives with a similar outline include those of Gideon (Judg. 6:11–24) and Jeremiah (Jer. 1:4–9). The conversation between God and Moses expands upon this basic form. Given these commonalities (and others), it is reasonable to conclude that Moses' call is portrayed in terms of a prophetic paradigm. Moses is called to be *a messenger of the word of God;* canonically, he is the first such person to be so called. The messenger of the Lord commissions an earthly counterpart.

Characteristic of the entire section is an *ongoing dialogue*

51

between God and Moses, interrupted by a visit to Pharaoh during which God is silent. The eight objections of Moses and God's responses thereto might be outlined as follows:

Exodus 3:1—7:7

Objections of Moses	God's Responses
3:11—*Moses* expresses his unworthiness for such a task	3:12—God assures Moses that *God will be with* him
3:13—Moses does not have enough information about God	3:14-22—God provides name: *I will be whom I will be*
4:1—The *people* will not listen to Moses or believe him	4:2-9—God will provide signs so they will believe
4:10—*Moses* is incompetent	4:12—*God will be with* Moses' mouth
4:13—*Moses* asks God to send someone else along	4:14-16—*God will be with* Moses' mouth and Aaron's

Renewal of objections after "false start"

5:22-23—*God* has failed to follow through on promise	6:1-8—Wait and see; God will fulfill God's promises: *I will be your God*
6:12—Combination of *people, Pharaoh,* and *Moses* as factors	6:13-27—God repeats the commission (+genealogy)
6:30—Repeat of two parts of 6:12: *Pharaoh and Moses*	7:1-5—Pharaoh will not listen anyway; Aaron will be Moses' prophet

This dialogue is theologically significant. The recognition of holiness (3:6) does not lead to passivity in the presence of God. Disagreement, argument, and even challenge play an important role. The divine holiness is of such a character that it invites rather than repels human response, inviting Moses into genuine conversation. God does not demand a self-effacing Moses but draws him out and works with him, "warts and all." The oft-noted speech disability of Moses adds an ironic twist to this point. It is not only a human being who challenges God; an inarticulate one does so, and holds his own!

52   Indeed, it is Moses' persistence that occasions a greater fullness in the divine revelation. Human questions find an openness in God and lead to fuller knowledge. God thus reveals

himself, not simply at the divine initiative, but in interaction with a questioning human party. *Simple deference or passivity in the presence of God would close down the revelatory possibilities.*

Even more, God treats the dialogue with Moses with integrity and honors his insights as important ingredients for the shaping of the task. God has so entered into relationship with him that God is not the only one who has something important to say. God will move with Moses, even adapting original divine plans (the role of Aaron; see at 4:10–17) in view of Moses' considerations. *God's way into the future is thus not dictated solely by the divine word and will.* God places the divine word and will into the hands of another for him to do with what he will. That is *for God a risky venture, fraught with negative possibilities.* God will now have to work in and through Moses' frailties as well as strengths. This will mean something less than what would have been possible had God acted alone; God is not in total control of the ensuing events.

From another perspective, this section witnesses to God's initial lack of success in persuading Moses to take up his calling. All of God's persuasive powers are brought to bear on Moses and he remains unconvinced for some time. God's best efforts do not meet with instant success. Hence, in 4:10–17, in the face of Moses' resistance, God must resort to plan B, calling Aaron to be Moses' voice. Obviously, God is not delighted with this option; in fact, God is angry. But God goes with what is possible; using Aaron is now the best option available to God. God always aims for the best in every situation, but God must often work with options that are less than the best (witness Aaron's failure in chap. 32). God often has to accept what people do with the powers they have been given.

Exodus 3:1–6
Curiosity and Call

God chooses a mountain in the wilderness named Horeb ("wasteland") as the place of revelation. Moses' encounter with God takes place far removed from the sights and sounds of the religious community. There is no temple nearby where he might expect a divine appearance, no sign that this is a holy place. Unlike the owner of the sheep, Moses is not a priest or a prophet; it is an ordinary, everyday journey for him with no "religious" intentions. The setting is the wilderness, and Moses' vocation is mundane indeed (see Gen. 46:34; Num. 27:17; Ps. 78:70–71). Yet it would not be the last time that God appeared to shepherds in a wilderness with an announcement of peace and goodwill. It would not be the last time that God chose *a nontraditional, nonreligious setting for a hearing for the word.*

The character of this event is noted before any dialogue ensues. Initially, the reader knows more than Moses: what is happening in Egypt and with God, that Moses is at the "mountain of God" (cf. 18:5), that it is a messenger of God who appears to him "in" (*not* in the form of) a flame of fire from within the bush (cf. Acts 7:30), and that the messenger is in fact God (see the move from v. 2 to v. 4). The reader is an observer as Moses comes to know these things as well.

The shift in point of view among narrator, Moses, and God helps resolve some of the tensions in the narrative. The narrator informs the reader of *Moses'* initial perception: a bush burning but not consumed (v. 2*b*). This is different from the reader's knowledge: not a burning bush but a flame of fire from the midst of a bush that was not consuming it (v. 2*a;* cf. the distinction in Gen. 18:1–2). The narrator then gives Moses' personal response to this sight (v. 3 is interior monologue): he turns aside to see why the bush was not consumed. He was not frightened or repelled by the sight but drawn toward it, though not for religious reasons; Moses is simply curious. But God makes use of human curiosity for his own purposes. *Curiosity leads to call.* It is only when God sees (v. 4 is God's point of view) that Moses actually moves to satisfy his curiosity that God calls to him; it is only as Moses allows himself to be drawn into the sphere of the unusual sight that communication takes place. The narrator, in turn, refines the nature of the sight for the reader; the messenger is now called Yahweh and God.

While the word spoken is the focus of the theophany, the sight seen is not simply an accessory to the word. *Sight plays an important role* in Moses' hearing (words for seeing occur ten

54

times in 3:1–9); there would have been no hearing if the sight had not been attended to. There is a greater intensity of presence for the one who appears to speak, with greater directionality and potential effectiveness for the word spoken. Appearance makes a difference to words. For God to assume the form of a messenger renders the personal element in the divine address more apparent. More generally, this not only speaks about God's relationship to the world but has implications for human life. Such "visible words" affirm that the word of God is not simply for minds and spirits. Moses' response could not be simply to believe or to speak. Moses is called also to act, to reembody the Word in the world. Seeing adds something to hearing (see Fretheim, *The Suffering of God,* pp. 86, 101).

While the bush is a divine attention-getting device, it is not simply that. The text does not speculate as to the cause of the flame or its properties (there are parallels in the ancient Near East), but Moses thought it was unusual. The association of the divine appearance with fire in a bush is unique (cf. Gen. 15:17), but it anticipates God's appearance to Moses "in fire" at Sinai (19:18); there God spoke "out of the midst of the fire" (Deut. 4:12). The word for the bush *(seneh)* is a verbal link to Sinai. God also leads the people in the wilderness "in" a pillar of fire (13:21; cf. Num. 14:14; Deut. 1:33). This is not an ecstatic vision into an otherworldly sphere; nor is it simply an "inward sight." While it is unusual, what is seen is within the world. As with other theophanies, *God uses nature as a vehicle for "clothing" that which is not natural.* The natural does not stand over against the divine but serves as an instrument for the purposes of God, evoking both holiness, passion, and mystery (fire) and down-to-earthness (bush). The word comes "out of the bush," from God and *from within* the world. The rabbis spoke here of a divine condescension; "God made his presence lowly" in order to give room for humankind to enter into a genuine conversation regarding the shape of the future (cited in Greenberg, p. 96).

After having looked, and learning that God is speaking to him, Moses is now afraid to look (it is not stated that Moses was afraid in other ways). He is afraid to look *at* God! There was a God to be seen (Noth, p. 38). The voice was not disembodied; the messenger of the Lord did appear (v. 2) and speak. Moses

55

knows that seeing God may mean death. This response shows that Moses is familiar with the religious heritage of his ancestors (cf. Gen. 16:13; 32:30; Exod. 33:20); it is also assumed in God's reference to Moses' own father.

Moses hides his face, but certainly not for long. For the next few chapters, Moses and God engage in what can only be called *a face-to-face encounter* (cf. Num. 12:8), during which Moses is anything but deferential. God's word to Moses is of such a character that it draws the other into a genuine conversation. The exchange with God moves from worshipful deference to animated dialogue (see above). Divine holiness does not inhibit human response, even on the part of one who is "slow of speech" (4:10). Moreover, the word of the holy God now articulated (vv. 7–10) bespeaks, not distance and judgment, but closeness and concern. The *holy* God enters into the suffering of the people and makes it his own (3:7). As in Hos. 11:9 and Isa. 12:6, God is "the Holy One *in your midst.*"

The emphasis throughout is on *the divine initiative.* It is God who confronts Moses and calls him to a task. Moses does not prepare for the encounter, nor does he seek it. He is surprised by what happens. Yet it is nowhere suggested that this is a "radical break with the past" for Moses (contra Childs, p. 73). In view of chapter 2, God picks a *known* entity, a person with gifts who is not afraid to enter into the kind of activity that God has in mind. The giftedness that Moses brings to this moment is not negated. To the contrary, God's creative work in Moses' life to this point has shaped a human being with endowments suited for the tasks ahead. While the specific encounter with God brings new insights and a changed direction for life, an informed creation theology will affirm many continuities with Moses' past.

This ground is now holy because of God's appearance, not because it was already holy. There is no holiness inherent in the place as such, no natural sanctity, but that which is not holy now becomes so by virtue of the divine purpose for the place (not just the divine presence). That which is an ordinary part of the natural order is sanctified, set apart for special use by God. This setting apart was not only for this occasion but also for the future. God's appearance to Moses establishes Sinai/Horeb as a

56

sacred place (cf. 3:12; Gen. 28:16–17). God draws a particular plot of ground, an aspect of the creative order, into a new sphere of relationship; nature too is affected by and serves as an instrument for the divine presence and purpose. Because of this change in the character of the place, Moses is asked to follow the custom of removing shoes to show respect (cf. Josh. 5:13–15).

One word to Moses is the divine self-identification: "I am the God of *your* father" (his own father; cf. 15:2). God specifically ties into the faith of Moses' own family. Moreover, the naming of the patriarchs demonstrates a continuity *in God* between Moses and his ancestors. This is God's story as well as that of Moses' family; the promising aspect of *the divine story* now begins to take the shape of fulfillment in this word to Moses. The reference to the patriarchs harks directly back, not simply to the Genesis narratives, but to 2:24, where the promise is given center attention. This self-identification will also occur in the narrative that follows (3:15–16; 4:5; 6:3, 8) in order to stress the importance of the divine promise in any interpretation of these events. Moses is not yet apprised of the fact that God has this promise in focus, but the reader can anticipate what is to follow. This is the *God whose promise means taking sides with oppressed Israel.* This is the God who hears and remembers and sees and knows. The connection with the name Yahweh (vv. 2, 4, 7, the first usage in Exodus) is made from the narrator's point of view (though not yet for Moses). The revealing of the name Yahweh in the following verses is the God who is to be identified with the God of Moses' own family. God's history with Israel is of one piece.

Exodus 3:7–12
The Sending of Moses

The exchange between God and Moses continues. Between 3:4 and 4:17, God speaks to Moses thirteen times. Moses responds to God in each instance, six times in a nonverbal way (3:6; 4:3, 4, 6, 7, 18; cf. 4:20). The responses of Moses range from initial deference (3:4, 6) to immediate obedience (4:3–7) to questioning or demurral (3:11, 13; 4:1, 10, 13). The latter prolong the conversation considerably. For all the power that God has at the divine disposal, Moses is not overpowered.

For Moses to respond to God in such a way reveals some very important things about both *God and Moses.* Moses' struggle is real, revealing both a lack of personal ambition and a capacity for leadership; Moses can be bold and perseverant in the face of powers beyond his own. God's responses reveal one who takes Moses' concerns with utmost seriousness and with uncommon patience. God does not understand that Moses is a slave to the divine will; God does not demand a self-effacing Moses. Greenberg (p. 94) says it well: "Those who are brought close to God retain their integrity even in moments of closest contact. They are not merely passive recipients, but active, even opposing respondents. There is true address and response, genuine give and take. The human partner has a say in shaping the direction and outcome of events." (See at 3:1—7:7.)

Many suggest that this section consists of a composite of two sources, the primary evidence for which is the apparent doublet in verses 7–8 and 9–10. While this is a possible explanation, the text is not only coherent in its present form, it is most appropriate theologically: neither God (v. 8) nor Moses (v. 10) acts alone in bringing Israel out of Egypt. God acts in and through the work of Moses (as well as the natural order). The activity of both is crucial for what is to happen. God takes the initiative, invites Moses to be sent before Pharaoh, and sets the agenda, but God *needs* Moses as an instrument in and through whom to work (as generally in the Old Testament). No wonder God goes to great lengths to enlist Moses in this endeavor; *gifted human leadership in this matter is necessary.* And so, on the far side of the exodus, the people recognize the duality of this activity on their behalf: "they believed in the LORD and in his servant Moses" (14:31).

Moreover, verse 8 (and not v. 10) includes a reference to the land of Canaan to which God is bringing Israel. The act of salvation is not simply being removed from the oppressive situation. It is also the gift of a land, a new place for life and blessing. *God's redemptive acts lead to a new creation,* to that which is "good and broad," filled with milk, honey, and other wonderful

58

things, and capable of supporting all the people mentioned! God will not leave Israel in a halfway house, redeemed but left in a chaotic wilderness. Deliverance for God is finally not only *from* something, it is *to* something, enabling the people to move from redemption to creation. This gift of land is in fulfillment of the promise given to Abraham (Gen. 15:18–19); its boundaries are essentially those of the Davidic empire (cf. I Kings 4:21). This is not utopia, but God's *historical* goal is a *creational* end. They are on their way to "the garden of the Lord" (Gen. 13:10).

How, then, might verses 7 and 9 be related to each other? Verse 9 focuses on the cry of the people and their oppression, repeating but one of the verbs in verse 7 with God as subject— seeing. Moreover, verse 9 begins with a phrase that is designed to move the matter to a conclusion: "Now, behold . . . ." As such, it brings the nub of the matter directly to the attention of Moses, who in verse 10 is asked to become directly involved. Verse 9 thus repeats the central matter of concern as a specific preface to God's request of Moses. Because I, God, have seen, you, Moses, are sent to do this task. God's seeing leads directly to Moses' sending. Moses is sent because God has seen.

Verses 7–10 are similar to 2:24–25 but constitute an important advance in the narrative. While 2:24–25 is the narrator's report concerning what God is doing, 3:7–10 is the direct speech of God. This, the first word of God in Exodus, is *programmatic;* it both sets all that follows into motion and reveals the kind of God it is who acts in the narrative to follow. This divine word to Moses is marked by a sixfold use of the first person singular, making it sharply clear that this language comes directly from God's own heart and will. Also, the twofold reference to "my people" at the beginning and at the end of this speech shows the personal character of God's relationship to these "children" (v. 10). God's relationship to this people is not established at the Red Sea or at Sinai; they are "my people" for God before any of these events takes place. *The divine election of this people is already in place* at the start of this narrative, rooted in the relationship between God and Abraham, Isaac, and Jacob (v. 6).

Three of the verbs with God as subject are repeated from

59

2:24–25 (see, hear, know), with a closer specification as to just what it is that God sees and knows. God *truly* sees (the infinitive absolute intensifies the verb) their affliction. God knows their sufferings. For God to "know" the people's sufferings testifies to God's *experience* of this suffering, indeed God's *intimate* experience. God is here depicted as one who is intimately involved in the suffering of the people. God has so entered into their sufferings as to have deeply felt what they are having to endure. God has chosen not to remain safe and secure in some heavenly abode, untouched by the sorrows of the world. God is not portrayed as a typical monarch dealing with the issue through subordinates or at some distance. God does not look at the suffering from the outside as through a window; God knows it from the inside. God is internally related to the suffering, entering fully into the oppressive situation and making it God's own. For God to *know* suffering is, to follow the metaphorical grain, to allow suffering to enter deeply into the divine being. In a later prophetic vision, we will again hear of one who is a "man of *sufferings,* and *knowing* grief" (Isa. 53:3). (See Fretheim, *The Suffering of God,* pp. 127–137, 56–66).

Yet, while God suffers with the people, God is not powerless in the face of it. However much God's work may be complicated by it, the actual situation does not finally define what is possible for God; God is never stymied or immobilized by the engagement with suffering (see Janzen, p. 230). In fact, the divine suffering is in itself a powerful force, focusing the divine energies on the situation. While the verb "remember" is not repeated from 2:24, God's activity of delivering the people and bringing them from one land to another constitutes a closer specification of what is involved in the divine remembering. God moves in to deliver, working in and through leaders, even Pharaoh, and elements of the natural order. Whatever will be said later in Exodus about the means of God's delivering activity, before it all stands this word about a suffering God. This is an important qualification of one's affirmation of divine sovereignty in the narrative.

The frequent reference to Israel's cry to God and its hardships serves to intensify the oppressive nature of the situation, as does the fourfold reference to Egypt. The Israelites' situation is of such a depressed character that they cannot deliver themselves; God must do for Israel what it cannot do for itself. But the goal is not reform, to make life more bearable in Egypt. It is removal from the situation. This makes it clear that God chooses Moses for activity in the *sociopolitical* arena; this is no ecclesiastical office to which Moses is called, at least as commonly defined!

Especially to be noted is the recurrence of this language in 22:21–27, where conclusions are drawn regarding Israel's *and God's* relationship to other oppressed persons. Israel's historical experience decisively informs the Torah which is to shape its daily life. Israel is not to be like Egypt; Israel is not to oppress others. As God related to the people of Israel, so are they to comport themselves in a like situation. God's activity becomes a paradigm for Israel; its life is to be lived in imitation of God. As God was compassionate toward the oppressed, so is Israel to be compassionate. As God truly entered into the suffering of the people and made it his own, so also is Israel to engage in an *internal* relationship with those who suffer. In even more striking fashion, *God binds himself to the Torah!* If the oppressed cry out, God will surely hear (22:23, 27). God's hearing of the cries of the oppressed is an *ongoing divine event;* God will not be indifferent to them. What God does on Israel's behalf is not something unique to the chosen people; God so relates to oppressed peoples whoever they may be. Israel does not have a monopoly on oppression or on God's compassion. God knows the sufferings of all.

In verse 11 Moses responds to God's invitation: Who am I to bring Israel out of Egypt? Moses' "Here am I" (3:4) has become a "Who am I?" Initial readiness turns into reluctance once the task has been outlined (cf. Judg. 6:15). How typical a human response this is! This is the first of eight objections Moses brings before God (see above). God replies (v. 12) in language that is both clear and enigmatic. What is clear is that God will be with Moses in all that he undertakes. Moses is assured of a constant divine presence; in all that he does he will not be left to his own resources. His "I" will be accompanied by the divine "I"; his "Who am I?" will be undergirded by the God who knows who he is. This gives Moses possibilities he would not have in himself. The verb used (*'ehyeh*) will be used again in verses 14–15; it anticipates the giving of the divine name. What is enigmatic is the meaning of the sign, that is, a happening of some sort that will assure Moses. Even though he has not re-

61

quested it, God responds to an unspoken need. The apparent meaning is that a future event, namely, Israel's worship of God at Mt. Sinai, will provide Moses with this assurance. What has puzzled interpreters is how an event so far in the future, indeed on the far side of what Moses is asked to do, can function as a sign for Moses.

Moses' question of competence is answered simply with the assurance of divine presence; Moses will not have to act alone. The sign then moves beyond Moses' question to an unspoken issue: Is it God [the "I" is emphatic] who has sent him? It cannot be made absolutely clear in advance that God is the one who stands behind this call to action. It will become clear to Moses that God has sent him only when all this has been accomplished and Moses stands with all Israel (the "you" is plural) and serves God at the very place at which they are now standing. God's assurance of being with Moses is as much as Moses can know at this moment. But when these events have taken place, God's presence will be seen to have been effective and Moses will know that it is indeed God who stands behind the commission (see I Sam. 2:34; Isa. 37:30 for other signs to be realized only in the future; Childs, p. 57).

Exodus 3:13–22
What's in a Name?

Moses continues the conversation with a question. His Who am I? now becomes a Who are you? Yet it is not a question of suspicion or hostility; it is a question that is open to the future ("if I"). Human openness is met by divine openness. The question draws forth God's name from God himself. Moses' asking leads to insight. *Human questioning leads to fuller divine revelation.* God thus reveals, not simply at the divine initiative, but in interaction with a questioning human party. God's approach to Moses invites such questions; in this way, what God reveals is related to what Moses believes he needs to know in order to do what he is called to do. God's revelation is thereby tied directly to the human situation. Both God and Moses recognize that God is not demystified through further understanding. In fact, the more one understands God, the more mysterious God becomes. God is the supreme exemplification of the old adage: The more you know, the more you know you don't know.

God's commission is that Moses go to *Pharaoh.* Moses understands that this entails being sent to Israel. But Israel has not acknowledged his leadership; he in fact may be a stranger to most. Hence the importance of going to the elders first (v. 16). Moses' question is natural: Will the people listen to him? The name of the God for whom he speaks will establish his credentials. For this purpose the divine self-identification given in verse 6 is insufficient. The assumption seems to be that, if Moses has been commissioned to bring the people out of Egypt, Moses should have a divine name commensurate with this new development in God's relationship with Israel. God's double command (vv. 15–16) that the new identification be repeated to the people shows its importance.

Exodus 3:14 is one of the most puzzled over verses in the entire Hebrew Bible (see at 6:2–3; Childs, pp. 60–70). The name given, *'ehyeh 'ašer 'ehyeh,* consists of the repeated verb "to be" *(hayah),* in the first person singular plus the relative particle (actually, Yahweh is a third person form). The most common translation is that given in the NRSV, "I AM WHO I AM." Other translations include: "I will be what (who) I will be"; "I will cause to be what I will cause to be"; "I will be who I am / I am who I will be." The last-noted seems to be the best option, in essence: I will be God for you. The force is not simply that God is or that God is present but that God will be faithfully God for them.

The use of the same verbal form in 3:12; 4:12, 15 (cf. 6:7; 29:45) suggests this. God will be God with and for the people at all times and places. The formulation suggests a divine faithfulness to self: wherever God is being God, God will be the kind of God God is. Israel need not be concerned about divine arbitrariness or capriciousness. God can be counted on to be who God is; God will be faithful. Israel's own experience with God in its history will confirm the meaning of this name. Israel both understands its history from the name and the name from its history. *The name shapes Israel's story, and the story gives*

63

greater texture to the name. At the same time, there are stakes in this for God; God has to live up to the name (see Janzen, p. 235).

The "translation" LORD (capitalized thus in RSV and NRSV) is something of a problem in this day of feminist concerns, and rightfully so. LORD wrongfully suggests that the name has a masculine identification. LORD obscures the fact that Yahweh is a name and not a title or an epithet. The use of LORD is based on the *post*-Old Testament Jewish practice of reading *Adonai* ("Lord") for Yahweh—followed by the LXX's *kyrios* (to facilitate this reading, the vowels for the Aramaic word meaning "the Name" have been superimposed on the consonants for Yahweh in the Hebrew text). In view of this concern, it could be argued that we ought simply to transliterate what the *original* Hebrew was thought to be: Yahweh (to transliterate the present form, "Jehovah," does not represent any known pronunciation). This would be consistent with the way in which every other name is handled in the versions. An alternative would be to follow the New Testament practice of using "God" (followed in this commentary in most contexts).

Some scholars suggest that God's response is a refusal to give the name, out of a belief that knowing the name gives some control over the one named: in effect, I am who I am and it is not your business to know my name. This, however, is a counsel of despair. The fact that the name Yahweh is immediately used in apposition to the God of your fathers in verses 15–16 suggests a more positive meaning. It is difficult to believe that the thousands of uses of Yahweh in the Old Testament are only a testimony to God's holding back his name. There is, of course, a lack of final *definition* in the name Yahweh. But, as with all names, this is simply to recognize the limits of drawing inferences from a name regarding the nature of the one whose name it is. Names are never fully revealing of nature.

What does *divine name-giving mean* for Israel? It is God who gives the name; God is not named by others, unlike people or other gods. Though not fully revealing, the name gives some insight into God; the giving of the name is thus a revelatory act. Naming entails distinctiveness; it sets one off from others who have names, including gods. Moreover, anyone whose name is known becomes a part of the community that has names; God

64

thereby chooses to join the historical community. Even more, to give this name with reference to the God of the fathers ties this God to a certain history. God's own history is thus integrated with the history of this people. The statement (v. 15) that this is to be God's name for all time makes two points: it speaks not only of what the people are to do but also of a divine commitment to being a part of this people's history. The God who goes by this name will participate in their story forever (see 33:19; 34:6).

Giving the name entails a certain kind of relationship; it opens up the possibility of, indeed admits a desire for, a certain intimacy in relationship. A relationship without a name inevitably means some distance; naming the name is necessary for closeness. Naming makes true encounter and communication possible. Naming entails availability. By giving the name, God becomes accessible to people. God and people can now meet one another and there can be address on the part of both parties. Yet, because name is not person, there remains an otherness, even a mystery about the one who is named.

Naming also entails vulnerability. In becoming so available to the world, God is to some degree at the disposal of those who can name the name. God's name may be misused and abused as well as honored. For God to give the name is to open himself up to hurt. Naming entails the likelihood of divine suffering, and so this act of name-giving is decisively continuous with 3:7: "I know their sufferings." This shows why there is a commandment regarding the name of God (see at 20:7; 6:2–3).

The various repetitions of verses 14–17 suggest a composite text, yet a certain coherence exists. The three different introductions suggest a special emphasis on each separate statement. The first simply gives the name to Moses; the second picks up the people's question more fully and ties the name to Moses' commission; the third takes the question one step farther and ties the name to the God of their fathers. This repetitive, rhetorical movement thus climaxes in the declaration to the people that Yahweh is their God, and this God has sent Moses. What is to be spoken to the elders (cf. 24:1) extends the entire statement. Moses is to say that God has "appeared" to him. Both the word spoken to Moses and the sight he has seen are important (cf. Gen. 48:3; I Kings 11:9–10). An appearance of God must

65

have been thought to carry more weight with the elders than just words. Appearance makes a difference to words; it is a more convincing word as a result and should help establish Moses' credibility.

This repetitiveness serves to draw out the divine reply to Moses and to focus the attention of the reader on each part. Each statement is fuller than the last, gradually building up to what God is now intending to do (v. 17). This last statement is, in turn, a summary repetition of what God originally said to Moses in verses 7–8, with one basic difference—the language of promise. What God announced to Moses is now to be promised to the people. Moses is to be the bearer of new possibilities in what would appear to be an "outless" situation. This is carried out in 4:30–31.

The next section (vv. 18–22) is a sketch of the future from God's perspective. In view of what happens, however, this is not an absolute statement about the future. God assures Moses that the people will listen to him. But, while true of 4:30–31, it is not true of 6:9 (see at 4:8). God also announces that Moses and the elders are to bring a message to Pharaoh. Yet the elders are never said to go with Moses to Pharaoh. Apparently, in view of 4:29 and 5:1, Aaron replaces the elders. This is an important observation for understanding the God of the narrative and the shape of the future subsequent to a divine word. Events subsequent to God's statement about the future occasion a change in the way things proceed. When Moses continues to object to the divine commission, *God adjusts to new developments* and appoints Aaron to stand with him (4:14–15). The future is thus not locked in by a word that God speaks (on God's foreknowledge being less than absolute, see at 4:1–9).

The message that God asks Moses to bring to Pharaoh is modest indeed (see 5:1–3; 8:27). This may be a ploy to get out of Egypt, with the understanding that the people will never return; God often has to work in and through human frailties. It is more likely an initial negotiating stance, however. God knows that Pharaoh is the kind of person who will be stubborn and will not let the people go unless compelled to. Only when God has worked wonders will Pharaoh let them go. Yet the initial statement to be delivered to Pharaoh suggests the possibility that Pharaoh might be persuaded otherwise. This is how Moses understands things, given his concern that Pharaoh will not listen to him (6:12, 30). Pharaoh could conceivably let the people go short of being forced into it. Thus the contemplated use of force, though almost certainly necessary, would not have to be used (see also at 4:8–9, 21–23).

At three points, therefore, verses 18–20 function in a way not unlike some prophetic oracles (cf. Isa. 38:1–6). *Future events may necessitate a change in the divine way into the future.*

Verses 21–22 look forward to the end of the contest with Pharaoh. The Israelites will gain favor in the eyes of the Egyptian people and will collect many valuables from them on their way out of the land. The Egyptians are not portrayed as gullible; rather, God has been at work among them so that they genuinely view Israel with favor. Yet this text contains a number of ironic images: the Israelites will receive the rewards of their slave labor—the poor and the rich will change positions (see Deut. 15:13–15; I Sam. 2:7–8); rather than being victims, they will be victors and this is their "booty"; the Egyptians respond to Israel with charitable deeds in the face of all the havoc visited upon Egypt. In the end, Egypt rather than Israel will be left destitute, in a land where milk and honey no longer flow. We learn from 11:2–3 and 12:35–36 that this is in fact what happens, though not in some automatic fulfillment of this word (cf. Gen. 15:14) but in response to the people's obedience of Moses' directive (12:35).

Exodus 4:1–9
Moses and Magic

Moses' concerns remain unresolved. Even though God has said the people will listen to him (3:18), Moses does not think so. One of the central questions (since 2:14) has been whether Israel will accept Moses as leader. From God's perspective, this is no idle question, for God has chosen to be dependent upon someone like Moses to be his agent among the people. The acceptance of Moses by the people is crucial for what God is about. Hence, the stress on belief/obedience language in this section (4:1, 5, 8, 9, 31). Believing here has reference to a sufficient level of confidence in Moses to trust what he says and to

67

accede to his leadership (cf. 14:31). The *trustworthiness of the leader* is a central issue for any community, especially when such a one claims to speak for God.

It is striking that Moses questions a word about the future which God has just spoken (3:18). From Moses' perspective, getting the people to believe him is a more serious issue than God suggests. This implies that Moses understands that a word that God speaks about future human behaviors will not necessarily be realized. Such divine statements are open to debate. Moses makes an observation that God now needs to (and does!) take seriously because it has been articulated by one with whom God has established a special relationship. As it turns out, the people both listen (4:31) and do not listen (6:9, 12).

God does not in any way chide Moses for his response. God takes the question seriously by providing Moses with additional resources for his conversation with the people—"that they may believe" (4:5). God thereby recognizes the difficulty Moses is facing and the uncertainty of the human response. This is clear from God's statement in verses 8–9 (see below).

This exchange reveals something of the nature of God's relationship with Moses. God does not adopt a take it or leave it attitude toward what God has said. God is open to disagreement, argument, even challenge on Moses' part. God is clearly the authority, but God's approach to Moses within relationship is nonauthoritarian in nature. It is more than simply divine patience; it is an openness to consider seriously what the human partner has to say. God's way into the future is thus not dictated solely by the divine word and will. God will take into account the perspective of the human party.

This interpretation is firmly grounded in verses 8–9. God acknowledges the uncertainty of the people's response by repeatedly using conditional language. *If* they do not believe the first sign, they *may* believe the second. *If* they do not believe these two signs or listen to Moses' voice, then a third sign will be given. God is certainly aware of the possibilities of the people's response; one might even say that God, given a thoroughgoing knowledge of Israel, knows what its response is likely to be. There will be no surprises for God in the sense of not anticipating what might happen. Yet, in God's own words, God does not finally know. It is possible that some spontaneous response on the part of the people will issue in a different result from what God now sees as probable. It might be suggested that God really did know but that it was necessary, for reasons unstated, for God to put the matter this way. But such a reading would mean that God was not being straight with Moses and would place the integrity of all of God's dealings with Moses in question.

Does 4:8–9 then contradict 3:18, where God states unequivocally that the people *will* listen? No. God often makes unconditional statements about the future, especially through the prophets, which may need to be recast in view of human behaviors (cf. Isa. 38:1–6; for further Old Testament examples, see Fretheim, *The Suffering of God,* pp. 45–49). The statement in 3:18 may be considered a highly probable future, but Moses by his contribution to the discussion moves God to restate the matter with somewhat less rhetorical certainty.

As in 3:11–12, Moses does not ask for signs, but God so interprets his question. There is a certain directness in God's response. God does not tell Moses what he is about to do and delays telling him the reason for the signs (4:5). God introduces the signs in such a way that they become signs for Moses as well as for the people. In fact, the first sign sends Moses fleeing. His magician's credentials are found wanting! From Moses' own reaction, he could more readily see how the people would respond and the likelihood of their being convinced that he comes with a genuine word from the Lord.

The sign narratives sound somewhat strange to modern ears, except perhaps to persons who attend to the work of magicians. It is clear that Egyptian magicians had "secret arts" (7:11, 22; 8:7, 18) whereby they could do at least some of what God does here. Egyptian literature abounds with tales of magicians and their wonder-working powers, and the practitioners were important religious functionaries. Hence at least this *genre* of activity would have been familiar to Israel; they had some basis in their own experience in the light of which to interpret these feats. Yet they must have been unusual enough to have the potential of functioning as signs that God had appeared to Moses. God's stooping to engage in this kind of magical activity has been troublesome to some commentators, leading even to a denial that this is magic. But it is magic, pure

69

and simple. This does not reflect negatively on God. To the contrary, it reveals a God who acts in and through realities that relate to the context of which people are a part. As such, they may well serve the purpose of validating Moses as a messenger from God (as with Jesus' "signs" in the Gospel of John). In other contexts, God would use other means.

Verses 8–9 indicate that the signs would not inevitably persuade the people; they could fail in their designed purpose (cf. John 12:37). There was room for the response: "Moses is just another Egyptian magician." The effect of the third sign on the people is left open (4:9), signaling that no number of signs can guarantee a positive response. Moses' silence on this point suggests that he recognizes this. If there is uncertainty even for God regarding the response to the signs, it cannot be different for Moses! Moses will have to move ahead with the task to which he is called, knowing that a positive response cannot be made certain in advance.

Signs may dazzle, but they may not lead to belief. To paraphrase Luke 16:31, "If they do not hear Moses . . . , neither will they be convinced" if water turns into blood (see Mark 8:12). Belief cannot be compelled by evidence or external signs, no matter how unusual. This may lie behind the remarkably brief notice of the doing of the signs (4:30). The people do believe, but we are not told how many signs Moses performed (at least two) or the degree to which the signs affected this outcome or even whether they were necessary for such a result. Later the people do not listen to Moses (6:9, 12). It should also be noted that Pharaoh was unconvinced by the same signs (7:13–14).

Finally, the close connection between these signs and the plagues should be noted. This is seen in specific matters (staff/snakes; leprosy/boils; water/blood), their ominous character, their relationship to the realm of nature, and the fact that both are called signs ('ot). As such, these signs relate beyond the Moses/people relationship to later activity in Egypt. One might speak of Moses' education in sign performance for later usage, but even more evident is the tie between believing and a theme of the plague cycle: "that you may know" (7:17; etc.). This invites one to observe that the line between signs used to foster belief and signs as a portent of judgment is very narrow indeed. Unbelieving Israel and unbelieving Pharaoh are not very far from each other. Signs may in fact harden one in unbelief, only to function as portents of the consequences of unbelief.

Exodus 4:10–17
Moses and His Mouth

Moses responds with still another objection. This time the focus is on his own abilities; he is ineloquent, "slow of speech and of tongue." This is likely a speech impediment, as the concentration on physical disabilities in verse 11 suggests. This has been exemplified in his conversations with God; if he had been more eloquent, he would have been able to convince God that he was not the man for the task!

But God will have none of it. God's response consists of two, seemingly contradictory parts. First, verse 11 speaks of God's creative activity in the gestation process. Through a series of rhetorical questions, God himself states that the human mouth and other senses, including Moses', are a divine creation. These questions do not deny the point of Moses' objection (or v. 12 loses its force). God simply accepts that Moses has a speech problem; in fact, God has been involved in this physical development (cf. below on divine agency).

Second, verse 12 speaks of God's providential activity in the life of Moses. Whatever the case may be regarding God's creative activity, God will be with him and teach him (not determine!) what to say. In essence, then: God knows Moses' speech abilities well, but God still calls Moses to this task, because God is able to work even with the ineloquent in bringing the word of God to others. God, then, does not correct Moses' speech difficulties; there is no divine surgery in view here. Rather, God works in and through real human impediments to further the divine purposes. A constant reality for God!

This encounter raises a number of theological issues. First, it reveals something significant about *God's calling to "ministry."* God does not call perfect individuals to leadership positions among God's people. God calls people to tasks with, as they say, "warts and all." It is not the case, however, that human giftedness is irrelevant to God, as if everyone could do equally

71

well in any calling, simply because God is able to work in and through them (contra Durham, p. 51; Sarna, p. 61). The gifts that people have do make a difference to God and to God's ability to use them. God's activity in the lives of individuals does not override whatever gifts they may have, so that God does whatever God wants done regardless (the persistence of Moses in raising objections demonstrates this). God has discerned that Moses has genuine gifts for leadership, and hence God has chosen him. Moses also has a speech impediment, but God will be able to work through him in spite of this difficulty. Theoretically, then, Moses' objection would not be irrelevant, but in this case it is beside the point. God knows perfectly well what Moses' gifts are and has still chosen him. This is continuous with God's earlier use of women (see at 1:15–22; 2:1–10) and illustrates God's ways of choosing what is weak in the world to shame the strong (I Cor. 1:26–29). In this sense, Moses' ineloquence is turned into an asset.

Second, the *issue of divine agency* is raised. It is not uncommon for scholars to interpret such texts as if Hebrew thought were ignorant of secondary causes, ascribing all human conditions directly *and fully* to divine activity; God is the absolute cause of every event. But, while viewing certain texts in isolation might lead to such a conclusion, a contextual reading makes another interpretation more probable. Verse 11 certainly affirms divine agency in the creation of human beings. God's creative work is such that they will have certain features and senses; God does not remove himself from responsibility for a world in which such things happen. God is the creator of human beings with their diverse gifts.

The text does *not* say, however, that this divine activity is *individually applied,* as if God entered into the womb of every pregnant woman and determined whether and how a child would have disabilities. This is a general statement that the world is so created by God that such things will happen. Moreover, the text does *not* say that God is the *sole* cause of all such developments. The confession of God as creator does not entail such a conviction. It is not necessary for God to say that nondivine factors have been involved in such human developments. That is not the point being made. It is only necessary to establish that the creative work of God is of such a nature that these things occur. We know from other texts of a duality of divine/

72

human agency in such matters (e.g., Ps. 139:13; Gen. 17:16; cf. Fretheim, *The Suffering of God*, pp. 71–78).

Moses does not argue with this divine response, but he does not acquiesce either. Yet his response is different; he has run out of specific reasons to give for not assuming this responsibility, at least for now. He simply pleads with God to send somebody in addition to (or instead of, so NRSV) himself. God's response is different, too. God has been willing to work through all the specific objections Moses has articulated, but when that has been done and Moses still refuses to assume the task, God becomes angry. Every objection has been taken seriously and God has shown that none of them are finally valid. One would now have expected Moses to agree to the task. But it is as if all the objections raised were not genuine issues for Moses; when all is said and done, he simply does not want to do the job, or at least do it alone. In the face of all of this, one can understand the divine anger.

From another perspective, we have witnessed God's lack of success in persuading Moses to take up his calling. All of God's persuasive powers have been brought to bear, and Moses still is not convinced. God's anger is related not simply to what precedes, however, but also to what follows. In the face of Moses' reply, God must resort to plan B. It is clear that God would have preferred not to take this step; if Moses had agreed, this next suggestion would not even have been made. Using Aaron as one who could speak on behalf of Moses is, for God, not the best way to complete this mission. Obviously, God is not delighted with this option. But God goes with what is possible; using Aaron is now the best option available to God. Yet Moses remains central in God's purposes.

This provides a likely explanation for Aaron's diminishing role in the narratives that follow. The plan outlined for him in 4:15–16 is not carried through the narrative. Moses ends up speaking on his own, and Aaron is finally nowhere to be seen in the climactic events of chapters 13—14, including the conclusion in 14:31. Moses gradually works himself into the role that God originally intended. Hence, plan B turns out to be an interim measure. Once again God adjusts to circumstances and in view of Moses' own development returns to plan A.

73

We have here a clear illustration of how God's possibilities are related to what God has to work with in the world. God has determined to work in and through people in bringing Israel out of Egypt. Given that decision, God must work with what is available. God's best option in this situation is the choice of Moses alone to carry out that task. Given human intractability in the person of Moses, however, God resorts to other options. God always aims for the best in every situation, but God must often work with options that are less than the best (judgment perhaps being the most obvious). God often has to accept what people do with the powers they have been given, even to resist God's efforts to persuade. The upshot of this is that God's effectiveness in and through such human instruments is less than what would have been the case had God chosen to use power alone or had been successful in the first attempts to convince Moses. In this divine revision of the situation, with Aaron now centrally involved, Moses has the same relationship with God as originally envisaged. But a third party has now been called to do what Moses was initially commissioned to do. And, as with any third party situations, there are more possibilities for failure. As will be seen, Aaron does not always live up to his calling (e.g., 32:21–24). Might the contest with Pharaoh have gone differently if Moses had willingly agreed to God's initial request? It is likely that this helps explain some of the unusual steps God takes with Moses in the narrative that follows (e.g., 4:24–26).

At the same time, the choice of Aaron witnesses to the fact that God is not finally stymied by human intransigence. God is able to take what is now available in the human situation and work with that. Aaron's special gifts now come into play. Aaron can speak well. Moreover, he is eager to see Moses again; his relationship with Moses is such that they should be able to work well together.

God then outlines the nature of their relationship. Moses is still to be the primary recipient of God's word and will; Aaron is subordinate to Moses. God will teach Moses, Moses shall pass that on to Aaron, and Aaron shall in turn transmit that. God himself will be involved in this passing on. God will not leave a word with Moses and then leave the scene. As the prophet is the "mouth of God" (Jer. 15:19), so God will be with Moses' mouth. God will be attentive to the passing on of the word from Moses to Aaron and from Aaron to Israel and Pharaoh. Yet Moses "shall be to him as God" (cf. 7:1). As God does with the prophet in "putting words in his mouth" (Jer. 1:9), so Moses will

74

be to Aaron. One must not weaken this so as to say only that Moses is to God what Aaron is to Moses. In some sense the word of God becomes so embodied in Moses that in and through what Moses says (and does!) *God* himself becomes active in that situation. Aaron becomes *Moses'* prophet (7:1; for a comparable function for the Levites, see Lev. 10:11).

How the word of God is understood to function lies behind this exchange. There is no word of God to human beings apart from the words and other symbols by which people communicate. There is thus no pure, unmediated word of God. Yet the finite is capable of the infinite; human words can bear the divine word. Moses/Aaron are messengers of that word, but they are no more divine typewriters than are the prophets, into whose mouths God also puts the word. One cannot finally sort out the divine word from the human word; they are bound up together in every reported word of God. But the word, nevertheless, is called the word of God.

But even if Moses will not speak, he is still called to act. And so God asks Moses to take his staff to do the signs when he returns to Egypt (4:17). The staff as an extension of the hand (cf. 9:22–23; 10:12–13) is a symbol of Moses' authority and a surrogate for the divine hand (7:5; "staff of God," v. 20), that is, an instrument in and through which God works. This section ends with Moses' silence. There is nothing yet indicating what Moses will do with this latest divine word. The reader is left to wonder. The interpreter must not take the reader off the hook (contra Noth, p. 47).

Exodus 4:18–31
God Seeks to Kill Moses

This transitional section is highly episodic, with logical and temporal relationships quite uncertain (perhaps because of a composite text). It seems best to understand the present text as a circling around the subject, viewing this transition from Midian to Egypt from various angles. It is typical of transitions that ambiguities and uncertainties abound, and in this case issues of life and death compound the complexity. The various vignettes, so filled with ambiguity, serve to highlight this, intensifying the fact that there are momentous matters at stake here, for both God and Israel.

The long dialogue between Moses and God has apparently ended. The last speech has been God's, spoken in anger. We are left wondering what Moses' response will be. He asks leave from Jethro to see whether his kinfolk in Egypt are still alive, a startling request. God's entire conversation has assumed that there are Israelites to bring out of Egypt! This suggests some mistrust on Moses' part, some uncertainty about the call of God. If they're all now dead, there is no call to heed!

God seconds Moses' decision to return to Egypt (4:19), seemingly reassuring him (but see at 4:24): those who sought to kill him (2:15) are now dead. This change in the Egyptian situation presents *God* with some new opportunities (see at 2:23), not possible with a death threat against Moses. So Moses packs up his family and heads back to Egypt. Taking the "staff of God" indicates an openness to the divine commission, but the absence of direct speech to this effect is striking.

God now expands Moses' commission beyond speaking (3:18): the wonders God was to do with *the divine hand* (3:20) are now put in *Moses' hand* to do before Pharaoh (not just Israel). In this formulation it is once again evident that God will act in and through what Moses both says and does (see at 3:8, 10). These signs (cf. v. 17) are more comprehensive than in 4:1–9. The phrasing "See that you perform" suggests that it is not yet clear what Moses will do. God also announces a new level of divine involvement in the situation. Moses is to work the wonders, and God ("as for me, I") will harden the heart of Pharaoh so that he will not let the people go (see at 7:3). This should further assure Moses of the depth of God's involvement in what he is being asked to do.

A number of theological matters should be given attention.

1. Especially to be noted is the *complementary character of the divine activity and the human activity.* Both Moses and God are to do and say certain things, working together in this confrontation with Pharaoh. *God's activity of hardening is thus not independent of Moses' activity.* God has chosen to act with intensity in these matters, but not alone; Moses is given considerable power. Stress upon this complementarity is important for Moses' continuing consideration of the commission. Moses can be assured of the likely success of this venture.

76

2. There is *no divinely determined future* (see at 7:2–5). Verse 23 as usually translated (cf. RSV), "and I say to you . . . , 'if you refuse to let him go,' " is something of a problem. The NRSV translation refers ahead to the end of the plague cycle (cf. NEB): "I said to you. . . . But you refused to let him go; now I will kill your firstborn son." The difficulty with this is God's telling Moses so far in advance what he is to say. But with either translation this is a projection of the basic scope of what is to come. Yet, as in 3:18*a*, this would be a divine expectation on the basis of present knowledge, an expectation that may or may not come to pass (in fact, Moses does *not* speak these words to Pharaoh in chaps. 11—12). The fact that Moses speaks in the subsequent narrative as if this were not a foregone conclusion suggests some such interpretation (e.g., 6:11–12). The absence of any reference to timing or frequency also indicates some open-endedness in the statement. It is not irrelevant that the first reference to the divine hardening occurs at 9:12. There is also no indication that these will be the *only* significant factors giving shape to the future, even if God's hardening of Pharaoh's heart may finally be the decisive factor.

The implied conditionality in the statement about Pharaoh's *refusal* in 4:23 is thus genuine (see at 7:2–5). While the shape of the future is probable (as with prophetic oracles), it is not finally certain that this will include the killing of the firstborn. It is possible that at some point short of that Pharaoh will stop refusing, and/or God will stop hardening, and Pharaoh will let the people go. There is therefore in the final analysis *an openness to the future* in 4:21–23.

3. The *parental image for God* has a special rhetorical power in verses 22–23. A central question for Exodus has been, Whose child is Israel? God's claim: Israel is *my* firstborn (not only) child, not Pharaoh's (see 3:10). Israel is here "brought into the closest and dearest relation to God" (Driver, p. 31), with all the intimacy a parent-child relationship implies. This image is developed by the prophets, particularly in passages involving pain and suffering (e.g., Jer. 3:19; 31:9, 20; Hos. 11:1–9). As in 3:7, God as parent enters deeply into the suffering of the children and claims them for life and freedom. This claim is institutionalized in the rite of the firstborn (see at 13:1–2). The particularly poignant point is the exact parallel drawn between God's firstborn and Pharaoh's (all Egyptian firstborn are in view). It may be that in order to free the one, the death of the

77

other will be required. At this stage, the violence is contingent on Pharaoh's refusal, but the explicitness of this violent response from God is troublesome to many readers. We will return to this (see at 12:29–36), but from this point on, the reader is invited to reflect on the story from the perspective of this potential violence.

"The LORD met him and tried to kill him." The reader has not been prepared very well for this statement. It seems designed to send one scurrying back into the previous verses to see whether the eyes had skipped a sentence or two. There one finds that *Pharaoh* "sought to kill Moses" (2:15). Also, God told Moses it was safe to go back to Egypt, for those who had sought to kill him were now dead (4:19). It turns out that the way was not safe at all—from Pharaoh perhaps, but not from God. With nary a word of explanation, the narrator reports that God confronted Moses and his family in the middle of the night and "tried to kill *him.*" The reader can be forgiven for wondering what is happening, even though one quickly learns that Moses is not killed. Apparently there is a matter between Moses and God that has not yet been resolved. The narrator seems to be silent regarding God's motivation, though it may be hidden in the difficulties; hence one should be careful not to appeal too quickly to God's mysterious ways.

The history of the interpretation of this brief passage could be described as a diligent search for that motivation. It is not often in the Old Testament that God acts in such ways without some notice of motivation (cf. II Sam. 6:6–8). This research has been complicated by numerous difficulties within the text itself, for example, the antecedent of the pronouns is uncertain, and the "blood-bridegroom" (or "blood-circumcised one") reference is quite opaque. It is not my purpose to review that wide-ranging research but to lay out some possibilities for interpretation within the context of the book as a whole. I make one textual decision: in the absence of any unequivocal indication as to who it is that God tries to kill, interpretation should leave the matter open, moving with both possibilities, Moses and his (presumably firstborn) son (see Kaplan). While most scholars think the object of God's action is Moses, his uncircumcised son would also be endangered in view of Gen. 17:14. If it is also the case that Moses had not been circumcised, and that the circumcision of his son was transferred to him by the blood, there is a

78

fluidity of reference between Moses and his son that is difficult to sort out.

It is important to note that God "tries" to kill; this softens the divine action (cf. Gen. 38:7, 10). What does it mean to say that God only seeks and does not make a "direct hit" (on God's seeking, cf. Judg. 14:4)? The means that God uses is not stated, but God leaves room for mediation, allows time for Zipporah to act, even implicitly invites it. It is therefore not to be understood that Zipporah thwarts a single-minded divine intention for death; rather, she moves into the temporal spaces allowed by God's seeking. The divine move is thus a threat, not an attempt to kill that God fails to pull off.

God "let him alone," immediately and without a word. The action of Zipporah therefore is not effective in and of itself. God *decides* to let Moses live. The blood is thus not magically conceived, efficacious apart from the divine decision. What Zipporah provides is the *occasion* for the divine action. Her action does affect what God does and is thus a powerful testimony to the importance of human activity in God-human relationships, but the ground for the divine decision remains wholly with God. Whatever the ground (mercy?), it constitutes a recognition that the situation is now such that the mission that God is about with Moses can proceed.

The opening chapters of Exodus often *foreshadow* later passages, as has been noted. This narrative technique is also important here (see Greenberg, p. 117). The application *(naga',* "touch") of passover blood to the doorposts saves the Israelite firstborn from the judgment of God (see 12:13, 22–23). Here too, the touching of blood to Moses'/his son's—the latter is a more exact parallel—feet is an action that protects him from the ominous activity of God. Moses/his son thus endure a life-threatening experience which Israel will later have to undergo, in connection with which the effectiveness of blood in preserving life is demonstrated. This may also anticipate the atoning value that blood has in the sin offering. There is life in the blood (see Lev. 17:11). The throwing of blood upon the people to seal the covenant may also be noted (24:8). If this is a parallel, the sealing of the relationship between God and Moses may be in view here. The mediation of Zipporah is then parallel to the mediation of Moses.

Another foreshadowing may be in view, which also relates

79

to the immediately preceding context. Verses 22–23 have just highlighted the issue between God and Pharaoh in terms of firstborn sons. God is about the business of saving God's firstborn, Israel, from Pharaoh, and this finally necessitates killing Pharaoh's firstborn. Immediately following this, the just-saved firstborn of Israel are consecrated to God (13:1–2, 11–16). It will be noted that Israel's firstborn are understood to be redeemed by the death of the Egyptian firstborn. In this text, then, Moses (as the embodiment of Israel as God's firstborn) or Moses' firstborn son—and this parallel once again works best with Moses' son—is placed at risk. The firstborn, including Israel's, belong to God and are to be consecrated to God. Without redemption, their life is to be returned to God. Here the circumcision of the son becomes the means by which Moses' firstborn (or Moses as firstborn) is redeemed through blood and consecrated to God. Without circumcision Israel's sons are cut off from God's people (Gen. 17:14; see Josh. 5:1–9). The firstborn sons of Israel, too, must be redeemed through blood, the blood of circumcision. Or, just as Moses was saved by the blood of his firstborn, so Israel would be saved by the blood of the Egyptian firstborn.

The one responsible for the application of the blood, as well as the interpretive word, is Zipporah, whose role is often downplayed by commentators. Once again it is a woman who, by her quick-wittedness and insight, saves Moses. She stands in the train of the midwives, Moses' mother and sister, and the daughter of Pharaoh. Moses owes his very life to a series of actions by women, two of them non-Israelites. While Zipporah's Midianite heritage may be of some consequence here (see 2:21; 18:2), it is not noted by the narrator in this passage. Zipporah is important in her own right. She is the only one named. She is the only active person in the passage, in both word and deed. Given what God is about here, that action is not without risk to her own life. Moreover, she knows what is called for to save Moses/Moses' son in this situation. The difference between Zipporah and the other women is that, while they saved Moses from Pharaoh, she saves him/his son from God—here the parallel works best with Moses. She thus plays the role of mediator between God and Moses, anticipating the very role that Moses will later play on Israel's behalf (especially in chaps. 32—34). As Zipporah saves Moses from the wrath of God, so Moses will save Israel. Moses is thus revealed as one who does not himself stand without need of mediation with God. However much Moses reaches heroic stature in his later activity, he himself is shown here, right before he embarks on his mission, to be vulnerable and in need of a mediator in his relationship with God. And it is a non-Israelite woman who provides that mediation, saving Moses from sure death.

But why is it that God takes such strong measures here? It has been suggested that this text is parallel to Genesis 32 (Jacob's wrestling with God). This is a time of testing in which Moses is prepared by God for the hard tasks ahead. He now can face any foe, no matter how hostile. Probably so, but not in isolation from the above-noted value as a sign. This is a divine demonstration of the seriousness of the matter upon which God and Moses are about to embark: a life-and-death struggle in which Israel's very life will be imperiled. That Israel or Moses will emerge unscathed is not a foregone conclusion. Israel will be maximally dependent upon God's decision and action on its behalf, yet Moses' own obedience is integral to the divine mission. Moses' continued resistance to the divine call, occasioning God's wrath (4:14), and his failure concerning circumcision are signs that do not bode well for the future. This multivalent vignette is thus a *sign* of what is at stake in all of that which is to follow. And, once again, it is a woman whose mediation shows the way in responding to the divine expectations for Israel's participation in these events.

God speaks for the first time to Aaron, asking that he meet Moses in the wilderness, at "the mountain of God" (where Moses received the word). God adds his request to a decision which God knew Aaron had already made on his own (4:14). This direct divine speech places Aaron's decision within a divine perspective. Aaron's motivation to meet Moses was informed by issues of family and friendship; he wanted to see Moses. God's explicit involvement means that there is a new purpose for this meeting. But God's decision is not unrelated to Aaron's motivations. As is often the case, God picks up on quite ordinary human affairs, not least the joy that people have in one another (4:14), and makes use of them for more specific divine purposes. In fact, what such human relationships have become contributes to the use God is able to make of them. God's purposes are less well served when human relationships are not so positive. Aaron greets Moses as a long-lost relative.

81

The narrator now reports in very sparse language, with no direct speech, the encounter with the people. For the first time it is clear that Moses takes up the commission to which he has been called. Given Moses' tacit acceptance, the narrator moves quickly through it in order to get on with the central events. Aaron speaks *all* the words (and, perhaps, does the signs—the pronoun is unclear) which God gave to Moses.

In response to these words and deeds, the people believe, that is, they believe that what he has said is the truth. But the people not only believe, they worship. Their worship is said to follow specifically upon their hearing of one particular word. It is a gospel word—God's having seen their affliction and becoming active on their behalf—that occasions their worship. It is not the signs that prompt this activity but the specific promise inherent in God's involvement. The next time the people worship, it will be upon deliverance from death on passover night (12:27). The next time they believe, it will be on the far banks of the sea (14:31). This verse thus pushes ahead to the full realization of this word of God and ties passover and sea crossing together.

Exodus 5:1—6:1
Oppression Revisited

Moses and Aaron finally arrive in the court of Pharaoh. Moses is no stranger to that scene, but the narrator makes no connections with that earlier experience. We learn from 5:23 that Moses thought this would be a brief encounter, that God would quickly deliver Israel. Moses soon learns otherwise. Pharaoh refuses to accede to his request. Israel's sufferings are intensified, and Moses and Aaron come under fire from their own people. Moses responds with complaint and accusation: God, why did you ever send me? Pharaoh has done evil to (NRSV, mistreated) Israel. But Moses' basic issue is with God: God has done evil to (NRSV, mistreated) this people and has not delivered them. In spite of this charge, God responds with the assurance that the situation is soon to change, all for the betterment of Israel's situation (6:1).

The narrator portrays these developments largely through a series of dialogues at various levels. The exchange between Moses/Aaron and Pharaoh proceeds through 5:5, after which Pharaoh assumes center stage. God's involvement returns to an unobtrusive mode. Pharaoh intensifies his demands and places the blame on Israel's own leaders. The conversation moves up and down the chain of command between Pharaoh, his task-masters, and Israelite foremen, back to Moses and Aaron, and finally to God. All but one of the participants in the drama have their say—Pharaoh, Egyptian slave drivers, Israelite foremen, Moses and Aaron, and God; only the people are silent. They are addressed (5:10, 13), but their response remains unspoken. The narrator, in the only fully indirect report in the entire narrative (5:12), speaks of the effect of these new demands on them. These direct speeches, enclosing (5:12 is in the middle of the narrative) the silence of the people, are deafening. The narrator thereby speaks volumes on behalf of the people. This combination of verbosity and silence demonstrates both the intensity of this development in the people's situation and the personal suffering they are having to endure.

Repetition is also important to the narrator. The language of serving occurs seven times in 5:9–21, all with Pharaoh as object. This recalls the repetitions of 1:13–14 and the theme, *Whom shall Israel serve?* In 4:23 God had made it clear that Israel was to serve Yahweh; Pharaoh here counters that claim. This sets the stage for what follows. Whose claim will win out, Yahweh's or Pharaoh's? Moses continues to reiterate Yahweh's claim in the face of Pharaoh's opposition; Pharaoh will finally admit Yahweh's claim in 12:31 (with preliminary admissions in 10:8, 24). This suggests that *one of the key functions of chapter 5* in the larger narrative is to set this issue unmistakably before the reader.

Once again it is literature from the oppressed themselves that helps us understand this narrative (see Croatto). It is unfortunate that this chapter tends to slip by readers so quickly. It provides a picture of the depths of Israel's situation and the ruthlessness of oppressive systems. Scholars have shown this depiction to reflect accurately Egyptian slave labor organization (even pictures from Egypt are preserved), but establishing historicity is not the narrator's concern. While God's deliverance appears all the more needed and welcome in the face of

83

such harsh treatment (another purpose of chap. 5), it is important not to take away the force of the oppression with a "pie in
the sky by and by" point of view. Or with this view: the oppression is all part of a larger divine plan. No, God enters in on the
side of the disadvantaged because God does not want this situation *at all.*

The story is best heard by viewing it from the *various aspects of the oppressive system.* With great forcefulness, the
narrator pictures "the utter sense of helplessness before the
highly organized machinery of the system" (Childs, p. 106).
"The Pharaoh has all the astuteness of the experienced oppressor" (Pixley, p. 32). His is a pyramidal system whereby the few
benefit from the labor of many. By depleting the energy of the
oppressed, the threat of organized resistance is lessened. Peti-
tions and demands are dismissed out of hand; giving in at any
point is a sign of weakness. Any sign of resistance occasions a
tightening of the grip. The oppressed must learn that their
well-being depends exclusively on Pharaoh's goodwill; don't
mess with the system. Get them to thinking that things could
never be better than they are. As they say, don't bite the hand
that feeds you. Help them see that those who claim to be their
liberators are actually making the oppression much worse than
it would otherwise be! How successful the oppressor Pharaoh is
in fostering this view can be seen in the people's later complaints in the wilderness: they never had it so good as in Egypt
(14:12; 16:3)!

The Pharaonic charge that this request comes because the
people are lazy is typical of oppressors: "You are lazy, you are
lazy" (5:8, 17). The people are actually not oppressed; they are
inherently lazy and resort to the charge of oppression so that
they do not have to work so hard. The point is to transfer the
problem from the oppressor to the oppressed. By ascribing to
the oppressed a character flaw, one is then relieved of any
burden of responsibility for their "fate." Or, the problem is
ascribed to a faulty work ethic; their values regarding work are
obviously not what they ought to be. Their increase in numbers
and their insufficient production yields show that they are not
laboring as they ought; make them work longer hours. Time off,
for religious observances at that, can only distract them from
their work. Think of the number of work hours that would be
lost! Production schedules take priority over any other con-

84

cerns, not least religious ones. And don't bother to introduce production line improvements that may ease the burden or promote well-being. In fact, take away some of what they have: gather your own straw for making bricks, but keep up the production schedules! The key is to keep them so busy that they do not have the time or the energy for complaints or rebellious thoughts, "lying words."

Moreover, the oppressors prey on the oppressed by soliciting persons who are willing to serve as foremen, actually collaborators who help create internal divisions among them. Hebrews who have "sold out to the system" are turned against Hebrews. These foremen provide fellow Hebrews "with walking examples of their 'opportunity to improve their standard of living' by accepting the system of exploitation, and participating in it, according to the oppressor's rules" (Pixley, p. 33). If complaints are spoken against them, they simply relay them to those working, so as not to jeopardize their soft jobs. And when the foremen do bring complaints to Pharaoh, they end up buying into *his* explanation of things and lay it back on the people once again (5:15–19). They turn to their own leaders as the source of the problem, laying the blame on them, thus saving the energies of the oppressors in keeping control (5:20–21). Then Moses turns right around and blames it on God! The oppressive system has worked its worst. God is as much to blame as Pharaoh. It is not far to a point of view that suggests that the people must deserve their lot, for God lies behind it. Martin Luther King, Jr. *(Where Do We Go from Here? Chaos or Community* [New York: Harper & Row, 1967], p. 124) puts it this way: "The Pharaohs had a favorite and effective strategy to keep their slaves in bondage: keep them fighting among themselves. The divide-and-conquer technique has been a potent weapon in the arsenal of oppression. But when slaves unite, the Red Seas of history open and the Egypts of slavery crumble."

With this basic sense of the nature of the oppression in mind, its force might best be gained by *retelling the story*.

Surrounding this oppression are encounters of Moses with Pharaoh and with God. Each has a special theological force. In the encounter with Pharaoh, Moses and Aaron immediately and succinctly launch into the purpose for the visit. The introduction, "Thus says the LORD," places the confrontation in a prophetic mode; the reader is invited to draw parallels with the

85

later prophets' words to kings. They report what God told Moses to say in 3:18, but with their own twists. Their tone is demanding rather than properly deferential and gives no indication of a time limit. Pharaoh responds in kind, in language remarkably similar to Moses' own questions in 3:11–13. He does not know Yahweh; hence there is no reason to let Israel go. He not only does not know, he does not care to know.

Who is Yahweh? Ironically, Pharaoh gets the question right. This question will go ringing through the pages that follow. Pharaoh's (and the Egyptians') knowing is a divine goal (cf. 7:17; 8:10, 22; 9:14, 29; 10:2; 11:7; 14:4, 17), at least in part fulfilled in 9:27; 10:16; and 14:25. As we have seen (1:8), knowing has an effect on doing, and Pharaoh's not knowing Yahweh has disastrous results on God's creation. Even more, a goal of the narrator is the *readers'* knowing. The readers are invited, not to assume that the answer to Pharaoh's question is clear, but to build up an answer as they read and ponder and explore the nuances of the narrative. The very name of Yahweh, "I will be who I am," promises that the identity of this God of Israel will become more fully known as events unfold, both to Israel (10:2) and to Egypt.

Moses and Aaron respond with little creativity: a nearly verbatim quotation of 3:18. Perhaps they think their lack of success is due to their failure to speak God's word exactly. Yet they again add a twist of their own, "lest he fall upon us with pestilence or with the sword." They exaggerate God's words, perhaps in the hope that the Pharaoh would be more responsive to such rhetoric (he would lose his slaves!).

Pharaoh does not even bother to respond directly this time. He accuses Moses and Aaron of distracting the people from their work by blabbering on about pilgrimages. He commands that the labor be made even more difficult and intense. The slave drivers continue to press the people to fulfill their quotas, even beating the Israelite foremen for not seeing that the people do their work. The foremen bring their complaints directly to Pharaoh, suggesting that the fault lies with his own slave drivers. But Pharaoh will have none of it. He responds with a "Thus says Pharaoh" (an ironic use of the messenger formula of 5:1) by stressing his original order and sharply attacking the people for laziness. Pharaoh will not be dissuaded from his oppressive policies. The foremen fare no better than Moses and

86

Aaron had. Who will be able to stand up to this tyrant? This scene prepares the way for 6:1—Yahweh is able.

The foremen take their complaints to Moses and Aaron; indeed, their complaints turn into sharp accusations. They call upon God to judge them, because this venture threatens the entire Israelite community. Justice calls for Moses and Aaron to suffer the consequences of what they have done. The leadership of Moses and Aaron is in jeopardy. Pharaoh has succeeded in sharply dividing the Israelite community. Their worry about a sword from the Lord in 5:3 is now a sword from Pharaoh. Will God's sword or Pharaoh's prevail?

Moses takes the foremen's accusation to heart and continues in the same vein in a *complaint to God*. Moses is quite disenchanted with his task, but he is not willing to shoulder the blame for the lack of results. The blame lies squarely on God, perhaps for not anticipating these developments in the statement to Moses in 3:18–19 (this leads one to suggest that these developments may at that point have been an improbability to God). Two dimensions of these verses call for discussion.

1. One key word here is "evil" *(ra'),* a word just used to refer to the people's plight (5:19). Evil is anything in life that makes for less than total well-being; it is often used with God as the subject, particularly in judgmental situations (cf. Jer. 26:3). Moses uses the same phrase to refer to both God and Pharaoh: both of them are responsible for this evil the people are suffering, each in his own way. Moses is right in saying that both are responsible; if God had not sent him to say what he did, this would not have happened. This is an excellent text for seeing the multiple agency of God and human beings at work in a given situation. Both God and Pharaoh have been active in their own ways as to lead to this single result: evil is being done to Israel. What Moses has forgotten, however, is that he also is a causative factor at work in all of this. Moses was God's instrument in bringing the word; he too "has done evil to this people." Moses should have learned this from the foremen (5:21); they had it right at that level. But God's judgment was not in order; in fact, God was an agent in this matter, too. This is ultimately a recognition that deliverance from evil may entail the experience of even more evil. Overcoming oppression is a matter for struggle, *even for God.* Evil will not give up without a fight; God cannot wave a magic wand and make it all go away

87

in an instant; protracted conflict is inevitable when evil is so deep-seated. The way from death to life will pass through many a Gethsemane.

2. The focus of Moses' complaint is the question Why? Why has he been sent to be God's emissary? Why—and here Moses no doubt gives voice to the people's complaint as well—why has God done this (to "your" people; cf. 32:11–13)? Moses, of course, knows at one level why he has been sent. What he does not understand is why this particular effect had to occur; this episode has only delayed the deliverance. God does not chide Moses for his hard questions. God receives them for what they are: complaints at a difficult moment in life. God simply responds by assuring Moses that his purposes are on track. In fact, the antagonists in this struggle are now firmly set, given Pharaoh's outright refusal. Pharaoh's time is coming. Even more, the people's deliverance is coming. God's resolve is clear; Israel will be delivered. In fact, Pharaoh himself will send, indeed drive, them out with a mighty hand. Pharaoh's own experience of the mighty hand of God (3:19) will in effect pass through him to deliver the Israelites.

Exodus 6:2—7:7
Commission Reaffirmed

There is general agreement that the section 6:2—7:7 is a Priestly version of the call of Moses. Essentially the same components of a call narrative are present as are in 3:1–12: divine encounter, commission, objection, and reassurance. The differences that exist suggest that the narrative has been made to fit the interests of this context and has a new function.

Moses is newly presented with a double commission, to speak to Israel (6:6–8) and to Pharaoh (6:10–11); this order is reversed from chapter 3 (cf. 3:10 with 3:14–17), though the order of execution remains the same (4:30; 5:1). A redactional summary of the commission (6:13, read "Thus," NRSV) clarifies that Aaron retains a role (though only Moses spoke in 6:9). Moses' twice-noted objection to the commission to go to Pharaoh (6:12, 30) is interrupted by a lengthy genealogy. In God's reply, Moses' relationship to Aaron is given a new level of significance and the word to Pharaoh is more sharply stated.

Three structural questions are raised by these notations: Why a reaffirmation of Moses' call? Why a twofold commission to Pharaoh and objection? Why the genealogy?

The Reaffirmation of the Call

Reaffirmation is needed because of important changes that have occurred with Moses, the people, Pharaoh, and God.

Moses. The restatement of the commission is most decisively determined by the objection raised by Moses in 5:22–23, especially the question: "Why did you ever send me?" This question betrays a crisis of call in view of the failures of Moses' first visit to Pharaoh and the division among Israelites engendered thereby. Also, Moses has not appropriated very well the word of God in 3:18–20, which would have helped explain Pharaoh's refusal. A return to basics is called for. But Moses not only needs reassurance, he must also be more explicitly committed to God's call. There never was an unambiguous acceptance the first time around (cf. 7:6).

The people. Their negative response to Moses reveals a "broken spirit" (6:9); they are in desperate straits. This is powerful testimony that the ability to hear the word of God can be adversely affected by the conditions in which people live (food, clothing, housing, sanitation, oppression). Until the conditions are bettered, the good news of God cannot break through into the minds and hearts of the people. Hence no further attempt is made to speak to the people until the very eve of liberation (12:3). Their future must come from outside themselves.

Pharaoh. The note in 4:19 held out some promise that the new Pharaoh would be more accommodating to Israel. But chapter 5 reveals that this is not the case; in fact, he intensifies their oppression. A different approach to Pharaoh must be taken from that outlined in 3:18–20 (e.g., not just "wonders" but acts of judgment, 7:4).

God. God is shown to be responsive to these changing circumstances and personal considerations. God may need to be clearer with Moses that Pharaoh will not listen to him (7:4) or

89

that what Moses is to say is "commanded" (7:2, 6), not open for revision (cf. 3:18 with 5:1–3).

The Repeated Commission to Pharaoh with Moses' Objections

Structurally, a genealogy is inserted in the middle of this conversation; the redactor, when picking up the narrative again, restarts it at an earlier point in a slightly abbreviated form (cf. 6:11–12 and 6:29–30). Moses did not object to the commission to the people, as he had earlier (4:1). He moves immediately to speak God's word to them (6:9), for his prior experience had been positive (4:30). It is thus ironic that Moses' prior objection proves to be on target this time (6:9). Moses' objection comes only after the commission to *Pharaoh* (6:12) and that in view of the negative response of the *people* (not Pharaoh's earlier response!). "Uncircumcised lips," a vivid way of describing dysfunctional speech, is the stated problem. But, given the similar objection in 4:10 and the arrangements with Aaron, this repeated objection is difficult to understand. Moses apparently has not been pleased with the arrangements with Aaron; Moses alone spoke in 6:9. Even though God is teaching him what to say (4:15), Moses understands his own role to be inadequately delineated.

God reiterates Moses' relationship with Aaron in somewhat different terms. God had earlier said that Moses would be as God to Aaron in speaking with the *people* (see 4:16); here Moses is to be as God to *Pharaoh* and Aaron would be his prophet. The point is similar, but the emphasis is quite different: here Moses' relationship to Pharaoh is highlighted. Moses stands as an authority above Pharaoh; his word to Pharaoh *is* the word of God. But, even more, all that he is in word and deed will be God embodied before Pharaoh. Hence Aaron will not simply be his mouthpiece but will be his prophet. The word *of Moses* which he speaks has the same authority as the word of God's own prophets. That word will come to prevail even over such a powerful tyrant. About this, Moses should have no doubts.

Especially to be noted is how God gives up sole rights to the word "God," giving it to one who is not God. This is a striking form of *divine self-effacement,* in which the achievement of the

90

divine purpose is allowed to be clothed in human form. God deigns to be embodied in Moses before Pharaoh. In and through what Moses says and does in what follows, God himself is present and active. In Moses, God's work will be done.

The Genealogy

The genealogy links Moses and Aaron with the twelve sons of Jacob in 1:1–4 (enclosing the intervening material) but concentrates on Levi. As such, it serves a credentialing purpose, demonstrating that both Moses and Aaron (especially) have the appropriate priestly lineage to serve as divine emissaries. After Moses' and Aaron's failures with Pharaoh and with the resultant identity issues, in view of the accusations of some Israelites (5:20), and Aaron's latecomer status, it may have been thought important to inform the questioning reader. Chapter 6:26–27 stresses that God addressed both Moses and Aaron and sent them on this mission. There may also have been a revisionist history at work on behalf of Aaron that prompted this insertion. Aaron's (but not Moses') descendants are named, including one grandson (Phinehas, see Num. 25:10–13); this links the Aaronide priesthood with the exodus. From another perspective, the genealogy links up with 2:23 and contributes to the theme of the fullness of time (see at 7:7). The Christian will be reminded of a comparable interweaving of genealogy and story of another savior of Israel (Matt. 1). Many details in the genealogy remain puzzling, not least how the four generations from Levi to Aaron jibe with the 430 years of 12:40.

The Gospel of the Exodus

We need to give special attention to 6:2–8. Verse 3 is often discussed at length. It sounds as if God had not made himself known to the ancestors by the name Yahweh. But if so, how is one to explain the fact that Yahweh commonly appears in Genesis (e.g., 15:2)? Scholars have usually concluded that this is evidence for originally separate sources now combined into one narrative: one source (J) used Yahweh from Gen. 4:26 on; the other sources (P here; E in 3:14–15) believed that the name Yahweh was revealed to Moses for the first time. The latter is

91

commonly believed to be historically accurate, though uncertainties abound as to the origins of the name Yahweh.

This is a plausible resolution, but what does one make of the text now that it has been combined with the J materials (see also at 3:14–15)? The likeliest interpretation is that a new name, or, better, a new import for an old name (which had no special distinctiveness?), is revealed in view of these major new developments in God's relationship to Israel. It is by the name Yahweh that the God of these events is to be addressed and revered. Yet, because Yahweh is the same God that was active among the ancestors, it would be legitimate theologically to use it in those narratives (so J), even though historically it would be anachronistic.

In 6:4–8 is an especially forceful statement of what God purposes to do on Israel's behalf. It is difficult to imagine how *the gospel of the exodus* could be stated more effectively. The promises of God stand out so clearly. God had established a covenant with (=made a promise to) the ancestors. One aspect of this promise was the gift of the land of Canaan; another was: "to be God to you and to your descendants after you" (Gen. 17:1–8). These promises God now remembers (cf. 2:24), that is, moves actively to fulfill them on behalf of an Israel groaning under the weight of great oppression. Once having uttered them, God has obligated himself; God is, according to Kierkegaard, "imprisoned in his own resolve" until they see the light of day.

The promises of God are introduced, punctuated (6:6–7), and concluded with the most common divine self-identification in the Old Testament: I am Yahweh (creating a chiasmus for this section). It will be used often in later texts (e.g., 12:12; 15:26; 20:2; cf. Ezek. 20:5–6). Walther Zimmerli *(I Am Yahweh* [Atlanta: John Knox Press, 1982], pp. 1–28) has shown that this formula bespeaks divine authority, often accompanying divine acts of self-revelation in which God's commitment to Israel is emphasized. With these words of authority and commitment, past promises are linked to present deeds. This God will not fail or forsake "my people." *There is a divine restlessness and relentlessness to be about the promises.* In the face of all obstacles, even Moses' or Israel's faithlessness, God will be faithful.

92

This promise of God (note the numerous uses of the divine "I" and the strongly personal tone) has these components:

1. God would liberate the people from their oppression. Three action verbs are used: God would *bring them out* from under the oppression; *deliver* them from servitude; and *redeem* them (a "rescuing kinsman," vindicating the rights of one wronged). These are not finally separable divine activities; they are an articulation of the meaning of salvation using a wide range of applicable vocabulary, in the manner of songs and hymns. God's acts of salvation thus have a quite this-wordly orientation and cannot be disengaged from social and political realities from which people often need to be delivered. At the same time, they cannot be so restricted; the issue at stake in these events is finally cosmic in scope.

2. The people would come *to know* (see at 7:5) that Yahweh is their God in experiencing this divine activity. Knowledge of Yahweh is in fact available to Israel. Yahweh is one who can be known within relationship. God does not want to keep people ignorant of who God is or what God is about in the world.

3. God would bring the people into the *land promised* to their ancestors and it would be their very own. This is not a temporary place; it is given for taking root and growing up; it is a place they will be able to call "home." Moreover, it is not a spiritual realm; it is a decisively earthly reality. This is a recognition that matters of place are integral to human well-being, in whatever age. The language of salvation can never be divorced from such creational time and space.

4. The centerpiece of this promise is: "I will take you for/as my people, and I will be your God." This could suggest that Israel is not yet "my people." It has been common to understand this phrase as pointing forward to the covenant at Mt. Sinai (Childs, p. 115; Durham, p. 79). This is unacceptable. Israel has already been identified as "my people" (3:7, 10; 5:1; cf. 5:23) and will be many times in the plague cycle (7:4, 16; 8:1, 20–22; 9:1, 13, 17; 10:3–4). This phrase occurs only in the first half of Exodus (finally in 22:25) in the Pentateuch (except Lev. 26:12). There is thus a special emphasis on Israel's status as God's people during the Egyptian sojourn. "I will take you as my people" is thus best understood with Deut. 4:20, 34 as God's taking Israel out from among the Egyptians (cf. Deut. 30:4; Ezek. 36:24; 37:21).

Moreover, "I will be your God" has its roots in Gen. 17:7–8 as part of the everlasting covenant to Abraham and "your de-

93

scendants," and hence understood to include Israel of the Egyptian sojourn. This refers to God being God for them in these events in fulfillment of the Abrahamic promise (6:4–5; Gen. 17:8 uses the phrase comparably concerning the land; Exod. 29:45 with the tabernacle). The phrase "You shall know that I am the LORD" has reference to the plague account (see 10:2). Every phrase in 6:6–7 is thus part of a series of God's actions *in Egypt,* enclosed by that reference in verses 6*a* and 7*b*. In this context the stress would be on Israel as *God's* people rather than Pharaoh's people. It remains to be seen what the covenant at Sinai means in view of this reality.

The *message that God conveys to Moses* in 7:2–5 is theologically complex and deserves special attention. It is largely a composite of previous divine words to Moses (3:18–20; 4:22–23; 6:6–8), but there are some new twists.

1. There is no talk of a three-day journey into the wilderness. It is an unambiguous word: let my people go from Egypt. While the "three days" appears in the conversation with Pharaoh (8:27), no one—not even Pharaoh—now thinks that that is really an issue. Pharaoh's negativity has prompted a divine decision that is nonnegotiable and not open to gradualist possibilities.

2. The Egyptians will come to know that Yahweh is God. This is in part a response to Pharaoh's claims (see at 5:2), but all Egyptians are in view (see 14:4, 18); indeed, the entire world is (9:16; cf. 8:22; 9:29; Isa. 45:6). The cosmic scope of these events will receive attention throughout. This knowing (= recognize as God) is related to two aspects of these events (7:5): God's acts of judgment against Egypt and God's liberation of Israel. Thus, both negative and positive notes introduce the plagues and are carried throughout the narrative. The reader must be attentive to both.

Positively, the recognition of God as Lord on the part of both Israelite and non-Israelite worlds is boldly stated in the midst of the plagues: "so that my name may be declared throughout all the earth" (see at 9:16; cf. Ps. 96:3). Even Egypt is opened up to the vista of new possibilities entailed in such a declaration (see Isa. 19:23–25). This means that, while the focus of the exodus is on the deliverance of Israel, its *public* character witnesses to God's *creational* purposes for the entire world. Israel's liberation moves toward the fulfillment of God's pur-

94

poses in creation. God's activity on behalf of Israel is for the sake of the world! There is thus a fundamental *mission orientation* to the entire plague cycle.

Negatively, *public* acts of judgment are in view. What Pharaoh and the Egyptians have done to God's work of life and blessing in the world will not be overlooked. God will not be indifferent to evil. Acts of cruelty and ruthlessness, which bring people to the brink of despair, must be brought to justice and publicly exposed for what they are, so that the world will know that such anticreation deeds will not be tolerated. Indeed, unless there is judgment, the creation that God intends will be turned into chaos. For Egypt and others to know that Yahweh is God is to recognize that God will be about preserving the creation, of moving resolutely against all those who are antilife and antiblessing. Thus, for example, the hardening of Pharaoh's heart must be viewed in *creational* terms. Moreover, the relentless, seemingly arbitrary prolonging of the plagues must be related to this wider *public* impact, so that the world may know. The reference to other nations hearing of God's deeds (15:14–16; cf. 18:1, 8–12) focuses at just this point—they may well be next on God's agenda for wiping out the evils of the world.

Hence the *public character* of these events is of the utmost significance. In particular, the *cosmic* character of the divine activity in the signs and wonders testifies that this God is the God of all *creation*. The concern stretches far beyond this historical moment for Israel; the future of the creation is at stake. We have seen the importance of this theme in earlier chapters but largely in terms of the hidden activity of God. The unobtrusive divine activity will not do for this time and place, however. God's activity must be done, not secretly or quietly, but openly, with loud drums and ringing shouts of joy. It must be done in this way so that the peoples of the world will hear and come to know.

3. Pharaoh will not listen to Moses, but in time he will let Israel go (see NEB on 7:2). God ("As for me, I") will play a part by hardening Pharaoh's heart and working signs and wonders. Moses ought not be discouraged at Pharaoh's refusals. They will not be a sign of God's impotence; rather, God will use the impasse for *public* purposes, taking even Pharaoh's refusals and weaving them into a plan for Israel's liberation.

95

INTERPRETATION

Exodus 7:6, like 7:3–5, is in effect an advance notice: Moses and Aaron will do just as the Lord commanded them to do. From the narrator's perspective, this shows a more conclusive positive response on Moses' part to the divine commission than was the case before. Before a new round of conversations begins, the reader is assured by the narrator that Moses has now moved beyond any objections and is prepared to do God's bidding. Once again it is shown how important it is for God's purposes with Israel that the human beings chosen by God be maximally responsive to that call. The notice about the ages of Moses and Aaron seems innocuous, but it serves to mark that point in their lives where their role as servants of God in this momentous endeavor can go forward without further ado. When this is tied to the genealogy a note is sounded that we have "the right people in the right place at the right time" (Durham, p. 81). But it also hooks back to the last such reference in 2:23. There we spoke of a "fullness of time" regarding these developments. This note is another signal to that end. The drama is ready to unfold.

EXCURSUS:
The Hardening of Pharaoh's Heart

In the interpretation of this theme, the tendency has been to push the issue to one side or the other: either God has determined Pharaoh's behaviors and is in total control of events leading up to the exodus; or, Pharaoh's freedom of will is intact until the end. I wish to argue for a mediating position, namely, a limited determinism of Pharaoh's behaviors that emerges in the course of the conflict. More generally, one could contend that, as with all of God's enemies (15:6–7), Pharaoh is *ultimately* doomed to fail in his efforts to keep Israel enslaved. Such an outcome would be *anticipated* in chapters 3—7. (Cf. the articles by Gunn and Wilson.)

A few details. Ten times God is the subject of the hardening, as is the case with Pharaoh and his heart. Three verbs are used: (1) *kabed* ("to be heavy")—normally Pharaoh is the subject, God only once, 10:1. It is used of bodily organs when they are

96

not functioning properly (cf. 4:10). The heart, the seat of the mind and the will, is no longer *as* responsive or resilient to outside influence, hence stubborn, obstinate. This verb is used positively of God being honored in 14:4, 17–18. It is ironic that Pharaoh's hardening leads to God's honoring. The defeat of the hardened oppressor brings *public* honor to God. (2) *hazaq* ("to be strong")—both God and the heart of Pharaoh are subjects. Positively, the heart is firm, unswerving in its purpose. Negatively, it is stubborn and ought to be changed. Again, it is Pharaoh's "strength" that enables God's hand to be shown as strong (13:3, 9, 14, 16). In Ezek. 2:3–5; 3:7–11, Israel, though stubborn, has the option of hearing or refusing to hear. (3) *qašah* ("to be hard")—both God and Pharaoh are subjects. This root is used elsewhere for Israel as a stiff-necked people (32:9; 33:3–5; 34:9; cf. Ezek. 2:4; 3:7). Pharaoh does not have a monopoly on hardheartedness (on the larger semantic field of stubbornness, see Jeremiah below).

It is often noted that the pentateuchal sources use this language differently: in the older sources, Pharaoh is the predominant subject; in the Priestly source, God is. It is impossible to determine, however, whether this distinction was clear in the original form of these sources. In the present redaction they have been mixed and interact with one another; this is the only certain form of the text we have.

Hardening occurs five times *while* the effects of the plague are still present (7:22; 8:19; 9:7; 9:12; 10:27?), four times *after* the plagues have been removed (8:15, 32; 9:34–35; 10:20). Only in the latter had Pharaoh asked Moses to entreat the Lord to remove the plague. Pharaoh responds in this way even when creation is made right once again. This makes the anticreation character of his stance clear. Because hardening is a creational matter, it is a fitting correspondence.

It is important to note that an act of hardening does not make one totally or permanently impervious to outside influence; it does not turn the heart off and on like a faucet. This may be illustrated by God's hardening of the heart of Pharaoh's servants (10:1; cf. 9:34). In view of this, their response in 10:7 is striking. Though God's hardening has occurred, they see the negative impact on Egypt, are open to a different future for Israel, and urge Pharaoh to change his ways. Hardening is an act that occurs again and again in the texts. Yet, as in recurrent

97

instances of callous-making of any sort, there will be a buildup of hardness or imperviousness over time. That must be the import of the continued references to hardening. Hence the effect of hardening at the beginning of the plague cycle is different from its effect at the end.

Childs (pp. 170, 174) worries about "psychological ploys. . . . Attempts to relate hardness to a psychological state . . . miss the mark." Indeed, Pharaoh's obduracy cannot simply be explained as due to his state of mind. Yet divine activity is directly related to psychological effects concerning Pharaoh's decision-making powers. Human patterns of thought and will may in time become irreversible through continual refusal to respond to God's word. At the same time, God bears responsibility for keeping the word of God coming on and on. Hence no interpretive attempt should be made to get God off the hook. A psychological/theological split here ought not be tolerated.

That both God and Pharaoh are subjects of the hardening is important. Pharaoh as subject actually counts for something; decisions he makes are related to *his own* stubbornness. The agonizing of Pharaoh gives evidence of internal decision-making processes. *God as subject intensifies Pharaoh's own obduracy.* While initially this does not result in a numbing of Pharaoh's will, it begins to have that effect as events drive toward final disaster. Both need to be said: Pharaoh hardens his own heart, and so does God.

It is important to note that, in the plague sequence, God first becomes the subject of hardening in 9:12 (sixth plague), and Pharaoh is the last subject in 9:35 (seventh plague). The references to God's hardening before the sequence begins (7:3; 4:21) only promise future action; 9:12 begins to fulfill that word. This progression is certainly not accidental. Each refusal makes it easier for Pharaoh to refuse the next time. More and more, the end becomes a certain matter. As Pharaoh's resistance progresses, God's hardening enters the picture; then, after the loop back to Pharaoh's own resistance in 9:34–35, God becomes the sole subject. Not only is that "loop back" true to human psychical behaviors, it shows that God's hardening activity, once begun, does not immediately control the situation.

98

We have seen in a preliminary way that there is an openness to Pharaoh's future (see at 4:21), but how is that related to the hardening theme? Other factors need to be considered.

The word "refuse" *(ma'an)* bears closer examination. This verb occurs six times in the narrative (4:23; 7:14; 8:2; 9:2; 10:3–4). In three instances, conditional language is also used (8:2; 9:2; 10:4; and also 8:21; cf. 4:23 RSV), always in speeches given by God to Moses to deliver to Pharaoh. This "if" language is problematic if only a negative decision of Pharaoh is possible. That is, if God says "if," such language conveys to Pharaoh (and to Moses) that his "refusal" is only a future possibility, not a certainty (see Isa. 1:19–20; Jer. 38:21). But if, in fact, Pharaoh's "refusal" is a certainty, then to hold it out as a possibility is deceitful. The use of "if" language by God also implies that God's foreknowledge of Pharaoh's decision is not absolute at that point (see at 4:1–9).

In 8:2; 8:21; and 9:2, Moses is to speak the "if" language to Pharaoh; if Pharaoh refuses, the plague will be forthcoming. In each instance, however, the plague is sent without a report of Moses' delivering that word to Pharaoh or Pharaoh's refusal (8:6; 8:24; 9:6). The narrative is telescoped, with Moses' speech and Pharaoh's refusal assumed; as 7:6 states in advance, Moses in fact did tell Pharaoh as God commanded. That these are genuine conditionals and genuine refusals can also be assumed from the one time the refusal speech is actually delivered to Pharaoh (10:3–4).

In 10:4 God tells Moses to visit Pharaoh but without telling him what to say (10:1), though God has hardened Pharaoh's heart. Then Moses and Aaron go to Pharaoh, and, for the first time, the conditional language is reported. It seems clear that God's hardening in 10:1 does not predetermine Pharaoh's (or his servants', 10:7!) response. Having just heard the reference to divine hardening, Moses and Aaron use the language of refusal twice, including the conditional sentence. If Moses and Aaron understood the divine hardening to predetermine Pharaoh's refusal, then their use of conditional language was both deceitful and pointless. They understood that the divine hardening did not foreclose either of the two possibilities for Pharaoh and his servants inherent in the "if" language. The divine hardening did not override Pharaoh's decision-making powers. Hence, divine hardening, though it has an impact on Pharaoh's decision, does not yet preclude either possibility.

Moses' perceptions of what God has said are important for this issue elsewhere in the narrative. In 6:12 (cf. 6:30), Moses objects because Pharaoh will not listen. But the reason given is not related to what God has done or will do; it is his ineloquence (to which God replies, 7:1–2). The implication is that, if he were eloquent, Pharaoh might respond positively to what he has to say. Moses says this even though he has heard God's word of 4:21. In other words, Moses must have thought it possible that Pharaoh would let the people go.

In three instances (plagues three, six, and nine) a different pattern prevails. God tells Moses to send the plague without going to Pharaoh. It is reasonable to suppose that the Pharaonic hardening, just reported, leads directly to the plague. That two of these cases follow the *removal* of the plague, and the other God's protection of Israel's cattle, reinforces the anticreation stance of Pharaoh. While the plagues are not a judgment specifically for the hardening, Pharaoh's obduracy exacerbates the pattern of refusal which keeps the judgments coming.

Regarding the divine speech in 7:3–5, it is important to note that the previously noted conditional refusal passages all occur *after* this statement. Thus this passage should be consonant with the above discussion (assuming coherence in the final redaction). God responds to Moses' twice-voiced concern about Pharaoh's not listening: Pharaoh will not listen anyway, even though God performs many wonders. Then God will lay his hand upon Egypt and bring out the people with acts of judgment (it is noteworthy that the specificity of 4:23 is lacking here).

The future does seem to be laid out here in a rather determined way. But there are two major points of uncertainty. First, there is no reference to timing or frequency regarding God's and Pharaoh's activity, just some future time. There is time for all kinds of things to happen, including wonders, divine hardenings, and Pharaonic refusals.

Second, God's statement concerning Pharaoh's refusal to listen is not an absolute statement about the future (see at 4:1–9). This is suggested when it is said upon Pharaoh's not listening, "as the LORD had said" (7:13, 22; 8:15, 19; 9:12; cf. 9:35—after the seventh plague God's hardening takes over). This phrase is used only with reference to Pharaoh's—human— behaviors. If God's statement is not absolute, then this phrase is used to show that in each instance God's word is on target. Matters have progressed *as God thought they would.*

100

The considerable range of correspondence that exists between Pharaoh's sin of oppression and the plagues (see Part Three) shows that the latter are destined for Egypt according to an act-consequence schema. They are judgments for Pharaoh's death-dealing behaviors. Moses' announcement is comparable to the preaching of the prophets, who warn of judgment already on the horizon; but, if repentance is not forthcoming, they announce its inevitability. It may be that Pharaoh's positive response to the word of God could break the schema and Egypt escape one or more plagues. Finally, however, there is a growing sense that the full force of the judgment is inevitable (see below).

The beginning of God's hardening (9:12), and its constancy from 10:1 on, parallels this growing inevitability of the full force of the judgment. As these points *the divine hardening itself participates in the judgment* which is to come; in fact, it may be said that God's hardening activity gathers momentum and drives the judgmental events toward their disastrous end. To use other words, God's hardening of Pharaoh's heart is an aspect of the larger judgmental picture. While we might want to use stronger language for God's involvement, Ps. 81:11–12 captures its force quite well: "But my people did not listen to my voice; Israel would have none of me. So I gave them over to their stubborn hearts, to follow their own counsels." God's activity makes Pharaoh's own obduracy of such a character that he is driven to the point of no return.

There is a limited kind of deterministic language that one can use at the end of the narrative. It is not unlike a boat on a fast-moving river, headed for a gorge or a waterfall. As often in history, human decisions and other factors can bring human affairs to a point where there is no turning back, no possibility of getting the boat to the shore before it goes over the waterfall. In such cases, history's possibilities are inexorably narrowed to a single one (cf. apocalyptic). Deterministic language can be used to interpret such moments; but it is not a determinism that was in place from the beginning, as if the trip over the falls were always the shape of the future, but only in the sense that there may come a moment when in fact that plunge is inevitable.

This can profitably be related to passages in Jeremiah and Ezekiel that speak of the fall of Jerusalem in comparable terms; as the end nears, even repentance cannot stop it from coming

101

(cf. Jer. 4:28; 15:1–9; 16:12; Ezek. 7:1–9). This pattern is also present in Jeremiah's use of the language of stubbornness (6:28; 9:13; 11:8; 13:10; 18:12). God's work through the prophets may lead to repentance, but in its absence that very work makes the stubbornness more obdurate (see II Kings 17:14). God becomes involved in the very sin and rejection of the people. In such situations, the continued divine involvement has the effect of intensifying the sinful behavior of the people, driving it toward its fullest negative consequences as it goes crashing through the gorge. Life then becomes possible only on the far side of the judgment (cf. Deut. 32:36).

This point is not reached with Pharaoh at least until after the eighth plague, as the references to Pharaoh's sinning show. Both Pharaoh *and narrator* use the common language for sin in depicting his behavior (9:27, 34; 10:16), that is, as personally willed actions which stand against the will of God. Sin is taken seriously here as Pharaoh's own willful conduct, as one would also describe his sin of oppression against Israel.

It should be noted that these events would not redound much to the glory of God if it were only a matter of God's outwitting a windup toy. If Pharaoh is an automaton, a "puppet in the hands of God," then God is not shown to be much of a God at all, a divine objective in the narrative. The reality of the conflict and the power of evil are important matters if the divine name to be declared is one that will in fact "get God honor and glory" (14:4, 18) among the nations. God's struggle with evil is real; God does not rid the world of evil with a flick of the wrist. There will be genuine conflict in moving a people from bondage to freedom; the pharaohs of this world do not give up easily.

God's relationship to Moses should be related to this issue. In both cases, God struggles with the human will; there are a number of parallels in their different contests with God. God is clearly not in absolute control of Moses. For all of God's powers, Moses is not easily persuaded to take up his calling. In fact, God resorts to a backup plan in providing Aaron to stand with him (see at 4:14). God relates to Moses in such a way that his will is not overpowered. There is no reason to deny that this is God's way with people more generally. At the same time, Pharaoh is guilty of violating God's order in a massive

102

way; his genocidal behavior might even be described as Hitlerian. Hence one ought not simply conclude that God's ways with Pharaoh can readily be transferred to others. Yet, even though Pharaoh is an embodiment of the forces of chaos, he remains a human being whose own will contributes to the shaping of his future.

PART THREE

The Plagues

Exodus 7:8—11:10

An Overall Perspective

Considerable effort has been expended trying to determine *the structure of the plague narrative*, but with little success. Durham's comment is worth noting: "Formulaic patterns can easily become as wildly speculative and as absurd as fragment-hypotheses" (p. 96). We do not have "carefully controlled variations of several themes and forms, but a series of somewhat haphazard variations on a single theme, all drawn to a common general form from at least several circles of tradition" (p. 117). It may be said that this somewhat controlled haphazardness corresponds to the nature of the material.

That there were varying traditions is evident from a comparison with Psalms 78 and 105; they witness in different ways to a seven-plague tradition. Source analysis has discerned three interwoven strata in chapters 7—11, though the extent of their representation is disputed. The J account was most extensive, with seven plagues and the basics of the structure as we now have it. The present text, the only certain form of text we know, will occupy our attention.

Regarding internal structures, the following observations may help the reader be more discerning. It is commonly thought that the plagues become increasingly more serious and unpleasant, more and more a threat to Egypt's well-being, beginning with annoyances, moving to disease and damage, and finally to darkness (= uncreation) and death. Or, there is a certain logic to five groups of two in terms of content (Nile, insects, diseases, damage, darkness/death); or, three groups of three in terms of setting (Pharaoh approached early morning outside—plagues 1, 4, 7; at the palace—plagues 2, 5, 8; and not at all—plagues 3, 6, 9), climaxing in the death of the firstborn. In some arrangements, the rod contest in 7:8–13 is considered the first plague (the firstborn deaths stand climactically outside the series). In such an ordering, Aaron's staff becomes the instrument in the first four, Moses' hand/staff in the last four, and God more directly in the middle two.

In terms of *agency*, God is explicitly active in only six plagues (1, 4, 5, 7, 8, 10). Aaron/Moses are involved in three of these in a dual role (1, 7, 8), and alone in plagues 2, 3, 6, and 9 (see 7:1!). In the summary, however, only the agency of Moses and Aaron is acknowledged (11:10; cf. 4:17), as only God's was in the introduction (7:3). In the four cases where the plague is removed (plagues 2, 4, 7, 8), a dual role is again evident as God did "according to the word of Moses" (8:13). In the eighth plague, a third agency (wind) is active in both execution and removal.

These complex interrelationships suggest that, while they are *God's* signs and wonders, one must speak also of the activity of Moses and Aaron with respect to each. Both God and human beings are agents. Moses and Aaron would not be effective without God's power working in and through them, and God is dependent on Moses and Aaron, working in the world through that which is not divine. Both God and Israel recognize this dual agency (3:8–10; 14:31).

The *most basic perspective* within which the plagues are to be understood is *a theology of creation*. Scholars have shown that, in Israel (and the ancient Near East), the just ordering of society—as reflected in its laws—was brought into close relationship with the creation of the world. A breach of these laws was a breach of the order of creation and had dire consequences on all aspects of the world order, not least the sphere of nature, threatening life with chaos. There is thus a symbiotic relationship of ethical order and cosmic order.

Seen against this background, Pharaoh's oppressive, anti-life measures against Israel are anticreational, striking at the point where God was beginning to fulfill the creational promise of fruitfulness in Israel (Gen. 1:28; Exod. 1:7). Egypt is an embodiment of the forces of chaos, threatening a return of the entire cosmos to its precreation state. The plagues may thus be viewed as the effect of Pharaoh's anticreational sins upon the cosmic order writ large. The remainder of this section will seek to spell this out.

In terms of language, three words deserve special note. The "serve" theme continues throughout, climaxing in Pharaoh's own command: Go, serve the Lord (12:31). Two other words are used over fifty times each: *kōl* ("all") and *'eres* ("land, earth"). While used in every plague, there is an explosion in their use as one moves into the seventh plague. This is an extravagance of language, perhaps a failure of language: every tree, all the fruit, no one can see, not a single locust, the whole land. Everything is affected or nothing. A hyperbolic way of speaking has taken control of the narrative. These outer limits of language match and convey the content of a creative order breaking out of its normal boundaries. As such, this language serves a theological purpose.

In terms of the history of tradition, this language is most strongly evident in the judgment oracles of the prophets (particularly Ezekiel) in which the entire natural order is caught up in the devastation (cf. Jer. 4:23–26). In the New Testament, the book of Revelation makes much use of the plague tradition. This text has a dramatic form that finds no real biblical parallel; the closest is the flood story, another ecological disaster—see the use of *kōl* in 7:21–23. At one level, the language is to be taken literally (otherwise the theological point is lost); at another level, the highly stylized form may reflect the dramatization of an experience of ecological disaster. Connections can be made between 10:2 and the retelling notices in 12:26; 13:8; and 13:14 associated with ritual. *A dramatized reading in a cultic setting* is a possibility.

Common parlance refers to these events as plagues (i.e., a blow or stroke), but the narrative itself uses the language of "sign" (*'ot;* 4:17; 7:3; 8:23; 10:1–2) and "portent (wonder)" *(mopet;* 4:21; 7:3, 9; 11:9–10). The meaning of "sign" in this context is a specific word or event that prefigures the future by the affinity of its nature (cf. I Sam. 2:34; Jer. 44:29; I Kings 13:2; II Kings 19:29). As signs/portents, their intent is not finally to leave observers with mouths open in amazement. Having gotten peoples' attention, they point toward a disastrous future, while carrying a certain force in their own terms. They are both acts of judgment in themselves and point toward a future judgment, either passover or sea crossing or both. Each of the signs must be examined in these terms (see the exposition on each sign). Generally, it may be said that the plagues are *ecological signs of historical disaster.* They function in a way not unlike certain damaging ecological events do today, portents of unmitigated historical disaster.

The above-noted usage of *'eres* ("earth, land") provides one clue to this focus: What is happening to God's earth/land? While it centers attention on the land of Egypt, the entire earth is also in view. The "knowing" texts, theologically so important in the cycle, are concerned with earth/land: God is Lord in the midst of the earth (8:22); there is no God like Yahweh in all the earth (9:14); the earth is the Lord's (9:29; cf. 19:5). So also is the central verse, 9:16: so that my name may be declared throughout all the earth. For the sake of the mission of God, there is a concern for the earth.

We have seen that God's liberation of Israel is the primary but not the ultimate focus of the divine activity. *The deliverance of Israel is ultimately for the sake of the entire creation.* The issue finally is not that God's name be made known in Israel but that it be declared *(sapar)* to the entire earth (9:16; cf. Ps. 78:3–4; Isa. 43:21). God's purposes in these events is creation-wide, for all of the earth is God's. It is to so lift up the divine name that it will come to the attention of all the peoples of the earth (cf. Rom. 9:17). Hence the *public character of these events* is very important.

To put this in different words: In order to accomplish God's mission in the world, that world must be teeming with life. If Pharaoh persists in his antilife policies at precisely that point at which God has begun to reactualize the promise of creation (1:7), then God's very purposes in creation are being subverted and God's mission is threatened. God's work in and through Moses, climaxing in Israel's crossing of the sea on "dry land," constitutes God's efforts to return creation to a point where God's mission can once again be taken up.

In view of this overarching creational theme, the plagues need more detailed attention. They are most fundamentally concerned with the natural order of things, God's nonhuman creation. Each has to do with various phenomena of the natural order. The collective image presented is that the entire created order is caught up in this struggle, either as cause or victim.

108

Pharaoh's antilife measures have unleashed chaotic powers that threaten the very creation that God intended.

Those elements of the nonhuman order that are on the *victimizing* side are all out of kilter with their created way of being. They all appear in distorted form. Water is no longer water; light and darkness are no longer separated; diseases of people and animals run amok; insects and amphibians swarm out of control. What must the numbers have been when every speck of dust in the land became a gnat (8:18)! What size must the hail have been to "shatter every tree" (9:25)! And the signs come to a climax in the darkness, which in effect returns the creation to the first day of Genesis 1, a precreation state of affairs. While everything is unnatural in the sense of being beyond the bounds of the order created by God, the word *hypernatural* (nature in excess) may better capture the sense. The plagues are hypernatural at various levels—timing, scope, intensity. Some sense for this is also seen in recurrent phrases to the effect that such "had never been seen before, nor ever shall be again" (10:14; cf. 10:6; 9:18, 24; 11:6).

Regarding the *victims* of the plagues, scholarly attention has tended to focus on the effects of the plagues on human beings (a typical anthropocentrism). But in every plague there are devastating effects upon the nonhuman—water, the land, various plants and animals, even the air. The stress on the word "all" serves to show that nothing in the entire nonhuman order escapes from these ill effects. Even more, the effects (like the causes) are hypernatural. The hail strikes down *every* plant and shatters *every* tree. Boils break out on every beast and human being. The locust devastation is such that "not a single green thing remains" (10:15), and not a soul can see the land. Except in Goshen, where the hypernatural extends in the other direction, with not a single cow dying from plague, not a single swarm of flies, not a single hailstone falling, and the pitch-black darkness stops dead in the air precisely at the border. The exemption for Israel participates in the uncharacteristic, hypernatural behaviors of the natural order.

This means that attempts to see these signs as *simply* natural occurrences are far removed from the point of the text. The continuity with the natural is sufficient to show that it is creation that is adversely affected. Their sequencing does have a certain naturalness to it—frogs leaving bloody water, flies drawn to piles of dead frogs, and so forth. But these continuities really serve this purpose: to show that the elements of the natural order are *not* what they were created to be and to do. Their "behaviors" break the bounds of their createdness. It is a picture of creation gone berserk. The world is reverting to a state of chaos. It is a kind of flood story in one corner of the world, that corner where God's creation purposes were beginning to be realized.

The theological grounding for the plagues is an understanding of the moral order, created by God for the sake of justice and well-being in the world. Pharaoh's moral order is bankrupt, severely disrupting this divine intent, and hence he becomes the object of the judgment inherent in God's order. A key word is *šepeṭ*, acts of judgment (6:6; 7:4; 12:12; Num. 33:4; cf. Ezek. 30:14). God sees to the moral order of things, enabling the effects of Pharaoh's sinfulness. Such judgments are not imposed on the situation from without but grow out of, have an intrinsic relationship to the sinful (or to the good) deed.

Correspondence thinking between deed and consequence is prominent. It is sharply evident in 4:23: God's judgment of death on Pharaoh and the Egyptians correlates with that experienced by Israel at their hands. Other verbal and thematic correspondences are: (1) The extended oppression of the Israelites and a prolonged oppression of the Egyptians by means of the plagues. (2) The losses experienced by the Israelites—general well-being, property, land, life—and those felt by the Egyptians. (3) Israel's bondage and its ill effects upon their personhood and the hardening of the Egyptians' hearts (14:17), an experience of enslavement. The "broken spirit" (6:9) of the Israelites that prevents them from hearing the good news and the hardening of Pharaoh's heart that inhibits his hearing the word of the Lord. (4) The indiscriminate death experienced by Israelite babies at the hands of a Pharaoh bent on genocide and the death of Egyptian firstborn. (5) The "cry" of the Israelites in bondage (3:7, 9) and the "cry" of the Egyptians (11:6; 12:30). (6) The cosmic sphere in which the plagues function correlates with the creational sins of Pharaoh so central in the narrative. He has been subverting God's creational work. So the consequences are oppressive, pervasive, prolonged, depersonalizing, heart-rending, and cosmic because such has been the effect of Egypt's sins upon Israel and the land.

110

In those instances where God removes the plague the appropriate language is that of re-creation. God overcomes the chaos and returns those elements of the natural order to a closer semblance of their created scope and intensity. These become anticipatory of God's re-creational activity and are also played out in the gifts of water and food in the wilderness. In some cases the sign of judgment is retained. For example, the phrase "Not a single locust was left in all the country of Egypt" (10:19) is certainly intended to connect with "Not so much as one of [the Egyptians] remained" (14:28). Here, re-creation entails ridding the world of the perpetrators of evil. As it was with flies and locusts, so it will be for Egypt.

God is portrayed in these texts as active in judgment, that is, in the interplay of Pharaoh's sin and its consequences (though not without mediation), but in effect God gives Pharaoh up to reap the "natural" consequences of his anticreation behaviors (hardening of the heart being one). God's seeing to this order is not a passive "letting it be," but God does function within certain limits provided by that order. The plagues are *not an arbitrarily chosen response* to Pharaoh's sins, as if the vehicle could just as well have been foreign armies or an internal revolution. The consequences are cosmic, because the sins are creational. God thereby acts to reestablish the *rightness* of the created order (ironically confessed by Pharaoh himself in 9:27, *ṣaddîq*). The divine power over all forms of Pharaonic power is demonstrated through the moral order for the purpose of re-creating justice and righteousness in the world order.

The sin-consequence schema is not understood in mechanical terms, however, as if all of these results were inevitable and programmed to occur within a certain temporal and causal frame; there is a "loose causal weave" in the moral order. Pharaoh was given opportunity to break into the schema, to turn the situation around. Note also the warning in 9:19–21, where the "fear of the word of Yahweh" provides relief from judgment, mitigating the effects and the sense of inevitability (cf. 10:7). God himself enters into the prolongation of the consequences (see 9:16) for the purpose of mission. But, finally, in the face of resolute refusal, the only way into the future was for God to drive the consequences to their deepest level. 111

More generally, such a correspondence at the cosmic level is reflective of the symbiosis between the human and the nonhuman orders commonly observed in the Old Testament, from Genesis 3 on (e.g., Hos. 4:1–3; Jer. 9:10–16, 20–22). Also to be noted is that the combination of plagues and judgment is a feature of many prophetic texts. One need only cite those which have to do with oracles against Egypt by Ezekiel (Ezek. 30:13–19; 32:2–8; 38:19–23) to find parallels to this tradition (more are cited in the discussion of individual plagues). The fall of Jerusalem is in effect a time when Israel also becomes the recipient of plagues (see Deut. 28:27–29; Exod. 15:26).

In this ecological age we have often seen the adverse cosmic effects of human sin. Examples of hypernaturalness can be cited, perhaps not least in the mutations occasioned by ecological disasters and the use of atomic energy. The "nuclear winter" presaged by many is often depicted in plague-like terms. The whole creation groaning in travail waiting for the redemption of people needs little commentary today (Rom. 8:22).

This perspective suggests that talk of "miracle" is of marginal value in interpreting these narratives, unless its meaning can be confined to the wonder-full things which God accomplishes. The hypernaturalness which we have seen is by definition unusual but fits within the categories of judgment and moral order. The complexities of the divine, human, and cosmic interaction in the narrative cannot all be factored out, but the upshot of the entire experience for Israel is that God has been at work in their lives for good and that through what God has done they have been freed from enslavement to evil.

God's immediate goal is to get Israel through the waters of chaos, enabling them to walk on the "dry ground" of creation. Hence the creation themes will become prominent once again as God works his cosmically re-creative deed (see at 15:1–21; see Fretheim, "The Plagues as Ecological Signs of Historical Disaster").

Exodus 7:8–13
On Swallowing Rods and Egyptians

The encounter between Pharaoh and Moses/Aaron in 7:8–13 is sometimes considered formally to be the first plague.

There are some structurally common elements that suggest this (cf. v. 13), but its scope and effect are very limited. It is more likely a preface to the plagues, setting the stage for what follows and providing some interpretive clues.

(1) It sets the hardening of Pharaoh's heart in place. The plagues follow from Pharaoh's initial refusal and begin (7:14) with the recognition that Pharaoh is in a stubborn mode. (2) It puts the staff front and center as the instrument for God's activity through Moses and Aaron. The staff takes on a virtually sacramental status in these texts. (3) Pharaoh himself ironically requests a wonder. God has only to give him what he asks for. He will live to see many more! (4) Pharaoh asks, again ironically, that Moses/Aaron establish their credentials. They will more than "prove themselves" over the days to come establishing with clarity that Yahweh stands behind all they do. (5) The "wisdom" character of what follows is established with the activity of the "wise men" (cf. 1:10). Whose wisdom regarding world order will prove to be superior? Ironically, all that the magicians can do is make matters worse: more snakes, more bloody water, more frogs! This is also established as a battle of wills. Whose will will come to prevail?

The important hermeneutical clue to what follows is found in the sign character of what happens, particularly the swallowing of the magicians' staffs by Aaron's. This does not represent Aaron's superior power to do magical tricks! Only indirectly is it concerned with God's power. This act functions as a sign of things to come in a very specific way: the fate of the Egyptians at the Red Sea. The only other use of the verb "swallow" *(bala')* in Exodus occurs in 15:12, where it refers to the swallowing of the Egyptians in the depths of the earth beneath the sea. This results from God's "stretching out his right hand," a reference to the staff (see 7:5; 14:16).

That the word for serpent is here different from that used in 4:3 supports this interpretation. *Tannin* is a much more terrifying creature than any snake. A closer look at the symbolism shows this to be an *ironic reversal.* The staffs of the magicians also become *tannin.* Aaron's *tannin* swallows theirs. Elsewhere, this word refers to the chaotic forces that God defeated in the exodus (see at 15:1–21; Ps. 74:13; Isa. 51:9). Even more, it is used elsewhere as a symbol for the Egyptian Pharaoh (see Ezek. 29:3–5; 32:2; and for Babylon as a swallower of Israel,

113

Jer. 51:34); God is imaged as a fisherman who will catch him and give him to the animals for food. Here God turns the tables, using a dragon to swallow up the chaos monster.

The seemingly innocuous reference to snake swallowing is thus an ominous sign for Pharaoh: it is a signal of his fate. This connects with the pervasive creation language of the text; God defeats chaos and reestablishes the creative order.

Exodus 7:14–25
Whose Blood in the Water?

The highly symbolic character of the sign in 7:8–13 invites the reader to be alert to ways in which it will be paralleled in the following narratives. How do they function as portents of things to come for Egypt?

The episode begins with a summary of 7:13, except that it is divine speech. God tells Moses what the narrator has just told the reader. Pharaoh's refusal to let Israel go is a product of his stubborn will. Moses is to go to Pharaoh as he walks by the river, a reminder of Pharaoh's daughter (2:5). Moses was found at the end of her walk, too, only this time Moses will shape the future of Pharaoh's household, not the other way around. The staff will provide some strong symbolism for the occasion; he was just "swallowed" by it. Pharaoh's "not heeding" (v. 16) is parallel to the Israelites in 4:8–9: if they did not "heed" the initial signs, they would get a sign involving the Nile and blood. That sign involved only a small amount of water, but this one will include all the water in the Nile! The Nile shall become blood and stink from dead fish (see Isa. 50:2), as the land will later (8:14).

The repetition of "The LORD said to Moses" (7:19) suggests that the announcement of the sign to Pharaoh had taken place. Aaron is to stretch out his hand/staff over all the waters of Egypt, even water in barrels, pots, and wells, so there will be "blood throughout all the land of Egypt" (vv. 19, 21). The oscillation in the text between the Nile only and water everywhere emphasizes the comprehensiveness of the effects of Aaron's striking. Doing this in Pharaoh's presence makes the origin of the sign clear. This plague is unusual in that it reports the actions of Aaron and God in nearly identical words (7:20, 25): Both struck *(nakah)* the Nile, but only Aaron is said to strike the *water.* The use of the same verb is intended to indicate that both were active in bringing about this effect; the actions of both were necessary for this one result. Though God's action is primary, Aaron is the one through whom God works. God has chosen not to act directly or alone. The staff, called the staff of both Aaron and God (4:20), is the point where these two powers meet. It thus has a kind of sacramental character; it is a visible, tangible instrument for use by a human agent in and through whom God chooses to work.

At the same time, this act is not especially extraordinary, for the magicians replicate it by their "secret arts." The question of who is sovereign is left unresolved. That is not the point to be made here. For the magicians to have unbloodied water to change suggests that the first wonder was immediately reversed, only to be repeated by the magicians. Hence, ironically, it is the effect of *their* work that makes for continuing problems (7:24). Generally, however, the occasional discontinuities in these stories is an invitation to think in less literal terms and more in "sign" terms.

The point of the sign is to be found in the repeated phrase, "There was blood throughout all the land of Egypt." One immediately thinks of the waters of the Red Sea flowing with the blood of the Egyptians. Or, of 12:30: "There was not a house where one was not dead." God had smitten "all the firstborn in the land of Egypt" (12:29). The irony of the tenth plague is that those who have the sign of the blood do not have blood shed, while those without blood do. At that time, "the blood shall be a sign for" Israel (12:13). In this wonder, however, the blood throughout the land serves as a sign for Pharaoh and the Egyptians of water becoming red with their blood. In 11:6, the cry of the Egyptians is as extensive as the blood. Ezekiel 32:6 is startling: "I will drench the land [Egypt] even to the mountains with your flowing blood; and the watercourses will be full of you." Ezekiel will also use the word "fish" to refer to Egyptians, and the death of "all the fish of your streams" (29:4–5). These references show that this sign was more than just a bloody mess, a lot of dead fish, and a headache for waterworks personnel. It

115

was an ominous sign for Pharaoh, but it didn't sink into his consciousness (7:23). The use of "smite" *(nakah)* in 7:17, 25 also points forward to its use in 12:12–13, 29 (cf. 8:12–13; 9:15).

The ultimate purpose of the sign is so that "you shall know that I am the LORD" (7:17). Pharaoh is looking into the face of historical disaster. The sign is a means by which Pharaoh's potential future could be integrated with his knowledge of God. God asks that Israel be liberated from oppression to "serve" Yahweh; Pharaoh insists that Israel be enslaved to him. Pharaoh needs to recognize that this is an issue with cosmic implications. As Ezek. 29:3 puts it, Pharaoh said, "The Nile is my own; I made it." God's action should show Pharaoh that the land of Egypt, its water, and its people are neither his creation nor his to do with as he pleases. But if he insists, there will be blood throughout the land.

Exodus 8:1–15
The Land Stank

The image of 8:3–4 is extraordinary: frogs in your house, in your bed, in your oven, in your pots and pans, and jumping all over you! Everywhere, in everything! The image is both humorous and grotesque; it conjures up one messy situation. As with other early signs, it is not calculated to hurt or kill people but to make life genuinely unpleasant. Pharaoh is given the chance to avoid the mess, but he refuses.

Aaron stretches out his rod, and frogs "cover the land of Egypt." But, as before, the magicians duplicate the effort. Irony and humor pervade the scene. Twice the number of frogs! Pharaoh's own servants make an already unpleasant situation that much worse. In an effort to make a point against Israel and its God, Pharaoh doubles the trouble.

For the first time, we see some change in Pharaoh. His magicians can bring the frogs on, but they cannot get rid of them. Pharaoh asks Moses to entreat Yahweh (cf. Isa. 19:22), using the name for the first time, recognizing that it is Yahweh with whom he has to do. If God removes the frogs, he will let the people go. Moses accepts a seeming disadvantage; Pharaoh should tell him when to pray. Pharaoh applies the pressure: Tomorrow! This gives Moses the opportunity to make an unusual response. In effect: Israel's God will respond according to Pharaoh's own schedule! But the purpose for God's accommodation is made clear: that Pharaoh may know that there is no God like Yahweh. This is an advance from the last "knowing" passage (7:17). God will do this in order that Pharaoh can come to know not only that Yahweh is God but that Yahweh is incomparable.

God responds "according to the word of Moses" (cf. 8:31; Num. 14:20); the frogs die. This phrase helps assess the relationship between God and Moses. Usually, of course, people do according to the word of God. But here God responds specifically to Moses' wishes. It is as if God thinks: If Moses, with whom I have established a special relationship, believes that this is an important thing to do in this situation, I will do as he says. The frogs were not zapped into thin air; they died, and everybody had to pitch in and pile up the carcasses. Then the narrator adds a seemingly extraneous comment: "and the land stank." This phenomenon has had an adverse effect upon the natural order of things. But when Pharaoh saw that the frogs had died, he went back on his word and would not let the people go.

The sign value of this wonder for Pharaoh may be focused at three points. The verb *nagap* ("to smite," 8:2) is not used again until chapter 12 (a cognate in 9:14 may refer to chap. 12). It is used three times for the smiting of the firstborn (12:23, twice; 12:27; cf. 12:13—noun; Josh. 24:5). This is a strong word, often meaning a fatal blow and used in contexts of divine judgment (Isa. 19:22; Ps. 89:23). It is anomalous that the narrator, out of all the plagues, should raise the specter of fatal blows in connection with frogs. It is, again, an ominous sign, a sign of something more deadly that could be on the horizon. Also, one cannot help thinking that the stinking of the land would constitute something of a sign for Pharaoh. In the last plague, the death of so many children and animals (12:30) would have created a comparable problem for Egypt. And the picture of all the Egyptians piled dead on the seashore (14:30) creates a similar image. Pharaoh's own nose should tell him that something is amiss here. Perhaps the phrase "covered the land of Egypt" (v.

117

6) also portends an ominous future, looking to the waters of the sea which "covered" the Egyptians (14:28; 15:5, 10; cf. Ezek. 30:18).

Exodus 8:16–19
From Dust to Dust

Gnats are pests. If they are mosquitoes (the translation is uncertain), even more so. Egyptians would have been familiar with the problem, if not to this degree. Again, this sign is a matter of discomfort. But the point goes beyond discomfort to being a *sign of human mortality and abject humiliation.*

This is the first of three signs where no request is made of Pharaoh and no warning given him. This suggests that it is a direct response to Pharaoh's failure to live up to his word. Aaron is told to strike "the dust of the earth" with his staff, that there might be pestering gnats throughout Egypt. Aaron did so, and "all the dust of the earth became gnats throughout all the land of Egypt." The reader is left with the image that there was no dust left in the entire country! This unusual image once again suggests that this is a sign.

The key word for the sign here is the repeated word "dust" (*'apar*), the loose topsoil. "The dust of the earth" has been turned into gnats. Dust is that from which human beings have come and to which they return upon death (cf. Gen. 3:19; Eccl. 3:20; Job 4:19; 10:9; Ps. 104:29). In fact, it can refer to the grave or the nether world (Job 17:16; 21:26; Ps. 22:29; Isa. 26:19). The image thus suggests the end of the Egyptians; they will be no more, for their source and goal have been taken away. It is also an image used to speak of the humiliation of those who oppose the God of Israel, including the kings of the earth (Isa. 26:5; 41:2; 49:23; Micah 7:17; Job 40:13; Ps. 72:9). Dust is the creation of God (Isa. 40:12; Prov. 8:26), and in this sign God displays control of it. But its use as a prominent image of human mortality and humiliation is a sign which Pharaoh ignores at his peril.

118

The magicians finally meet their match. Their report to Pharaoh is simple and straightforward: This is the finger (working through the staff?) of God. Israel's God has now bested them, and they respond in recognition of this fact. Indeed, it is a *public* testimony that this is the work of God. But Pharaoh will have none of it and pursues his stubborn course. There is no indication that the dust is returned to normal. Gnats seem now to be a way of life.

Exodus 8:20–32
The Land Is Ruined

The flies now join the gnats—swarming flies at that. This is an insect infestation of some consequence. Yet life and limb are still not threatened. It is basically a nuisance, particularly in a day before insect repellents and screen porches! Yet, the text says, "the land was ruined" (v. 24). Again, the unusual language suggests its sign character.

The beginning of the narrative sounds a number of familiar strains. Every person and place in the country is affected. Homes are infested, but so also is the "ground" *('adamah)*. This word joins others (earth/land; dust; country) to stress the cosmic dimensions of the sign; the land comes under attack and "mourns" (cf. Hos. 4:3). Animals, plants, and trees will soon join those affected. In this plague and the next, Moses' instrumentality is not mentioned (but see 11:10).

There is one exception. Israel, its people, animals, and land (Goshen), are singled out. From this point on, Israel is explicitly or implicitly said to be excluded from the signs' effects. This represents an intensification of the struggle; it "ups the ante" for Pharaoh (see his concern in 9:7). It demonstrates in a new way who is in charge of this situation. A new "knowing" comment is introduced at just this point (8:22): "that you may know that I am the LORD within the earth/land" (the ambiguity of the reference—Egypt or world—must be retained). For the first time, the knowing is associated with the distinction between Israel and Egypt. Israel's God is not one who stands afar off, dealing with the world in general terms. God is involved in the very midst of the life of the *entire* earth (see 9:14–16). But God too must make choices; here God chooses to side with the oppressed. This protection of Israel is an anticipation of their later

119

deliverance from the forces of chaos, especially on passover night.

For Pharaoh, this exclusion functions as a sign of future disaster, especially when combined with the phrase, "All the land was ruined." To have flies stopped at the Goshen border, as if by an invisible wall, should have been a sign of some extraordinariness to Pharaoh. The sole reference to "sign" within a plague sequence (8:23) at just this point supports this. The language of knowing because Yahweh makes such a distinction is repeated at 11:7. The distinction in the slaying of the firstborn is precisely the event of which this is the sign. The use of the root *šaḥat* ("ruin") stresses this; it seems much too strong to be a literal reference to the fly infestation (cf. Ps. 78:45). This word plays a central role in chapter 12 (see its use in Gen. 6:11–12 for a preflood state of affairs). In 12:13, Israel is promised that because of the blood "no plague shall fall upon you to *destroy* you." In 12:23, this word refers to the "destroyer" (NRSV) of the firstborn of Egypt. The flies that ruined the land (note the repetition in 8:24) but not Israel were an ominous sign of the destroyer that could bring ruin to Egypt. On that night "there shall be a great cry throughout all the land of Egypt" (11:6). The cry of the Egyptians corresponds to the length and the breadth of the ruination of the land. Pharaoh: are you listening?

Up to this point, Pharaoh has spoken only once (8:8). Now comes a more extensive reaction, with the flies still buzzing all around. He is not nearly as generous this time, giving Israel permission to sacrifice only if they stay in Egypt. Moses' reply constitutes an argument that Pharaoh accepts. It is not certain which sacrifices might be an abomination, but Pharaoh implicitly acknowledges the problem by saying Israel can go into the wilderness, but not very far. Pharaoh again asks Moses to entreat the Lord. Moses agrees but warns Pharaoh not to deal falsely this time (8:14). Moses prays; once again God does "as Moses asked" (see 8:13). Not one fly remains. But Pharaoh again reverts to form and does not let the people go.

As with the frogs, God's removing the flies overcomes the chaos and returns this aspect of the natural order to a closer semblance of its created scope and intensity. While this is anticipatory of God's re-creational activity, a sign of judgment is present. The phrase "not one remained" (see 10:19) is repeated

120

in 14:28 with reference to the Egyptians. God's re-creation entails severe judgment on the oppressors.

Exodus 9:1-7
Whose Livestock Die?

This sign takes a significant step beyond nuisance and discomfort. All the livestock in Egypt die of a "severe plague." The familiar approach to Pharaoh is repeated. This time a plague (anthrax?) will fall directly on the livestock, perhaps as a consequence of the previous plagues (8:18). Once again Israel is excluded from its effects; their livestock will not die. Pharaoh is given a day's notice (8:23); in the absence of a positive reply, God sends the plague. As in the previous plague, God is not said to use Moses and Aaron (though see 11:10); the plague itself is the medium of disaster. Pharaoh does not speak a word; he only seeks to determine what has happened to Israel's livestock—not one is dead. That occasions a still further extension of Pharaoh's stubbornness regarding Israel.

The sign value of this plague lies at two points. The use of the word *deber* for the plague is an ominous word (note a play on words—*dabar* ["thing"], in vv. 5-6); it is used exclusively in divine judgment contexts, whether in Israel (Deut. 28:21; Ezek. 5:12) or among Israel's enemies (often with cosmic effects, Ezek. 38:22; Hab. 3:5). The sign is concentrated on Egypt's animals (see Ezek. 32:13), not Israel's, a matter about which Pharaoh shows concern. He should begin to see that God is bringing this matter very close to home; for the first time his own possessions are affected. The force of the sign is finally driven home to Pharaoh when the death of the firstborn includes Egypt's livestock (11:5; 12:29) but not Israel's. The sign value for the reader will again be lifted up by the hyperbolic use of *"all"* for the death of the livestock.

In 9:19-21, however, God through Moses warns the Egyptians to protect their livestock from the coming hailstorm. This prompts the reader to seek to discern a nonliteral meaning for the hyperbole, thus enhancing its sign value. This passage also demonstrates the power that the "fear of the word of the

121

LORD" has. Those who do or do not "regard the word of the LORD" thereby give shape to their future. It may function as an indication of a future possibility other than disaster.

This killing is difficult for persons who have a developed ecological sensitivity or are concerned with animal rights. Slaughterhouses kill thousands of such animals daily in our culture to satisfy our meat-eating tastes, but somehow God as the subject of such killing seems wrongheaded, even cruel. It seems so "un-Godlike." Others might be troubled by the divine motivation. Why should animals be killed when people are the problem? These questions should be placed in the context of our discussion of the act-consequence schema above. The consequences of Pharaoh's sin, indeed human sin generally, are cosmic in scope and often have severe effects on animals (see Hos. 4:1–3). The symbiosis between human and nonhuman worlds has many positive aspects; here we see what can happen if human beings falter. The problem is with human beings, not with God (see the divine move to protect animals in 9:19).

Exodus 9:8–12
Signs of Mortality

The sign in this passage affects human beings much more personally and painfully than any of the signs so far. Sores breaking out all over the body have the capacity of focusing one's attention. It is a vivid reminder of one's mortality. It should function as such a sign for Pharaoh.

This sign is similar to the gnats in that God begins by immediately telling Moses to do the sign. Moses and Aaron are to take handfuls of ashes and throw them toward heaven. They will become a fine soot that settles on everything, causing open sores to break out on people and animals. These links between the nonhuman and the human are noteworthy. Standing in Pharaoh's presence, Moses does as God commands; the outbreak of boils occurs. Enter the magicians one last time; they have moved from an active to a passive stance, from sign-worker to victim. They can no longer stand alongside Moses; they can only slink away. A new level of intensity has been reached in the struggle. This is also portrayed in the fact that this is the last mention of Aaron in these events; Moses now stands alone. Moreover, this is the first time that God is the subject of Pharaoh's hardening (see excursus).

This sign has been prefigured in the sign in 4:6–7. There Moses' hand becomes leprous and then is returned to normalcy. Leprosy is mentioned elsewhere in the Old Testament with the verb used in 9:8–12, *parah* ("break out"), and is specifically connected with boils (Lev. 13:18–23). Pharaoh's situation is thus once again made parallel with the sign given to Israel (see at 7:8–13, 14–24). As the sign functioned for Israel, so also should it function for Pharaoh. As Israel believed when it observed the sign, so also should Pharaoh. This is an ominous sign of a disease that will be even more devastating for the Egyptians. While the "plague" that falls on them (12:13) is not identified, it is likely a more intensified form of that which is experienced in this plague. That the origin of the boils is furnace ash is probably intended to lift up the fiery nature of the phenomenon, a vivid image for judgment (see Joel 2:3). The power of this plague's significatory value is seen in the later recollection of "the boils of Egypt" as a possible judgment on Israel (Deut. 28:27, 60). This sign of human mortality and susceptibility to disease should have served for Pharaoh as a premonition of more severe possibilities.

Exodus 9:13–35
A Sign from Heaven

The next two wonders constitute the longest narratives of the series. This is a sign of the new levels of intensity in the struggle with Pharaoh. Much of this length is due to the extraordinary detail regarding the natural phenomena and their effects upon Egypt, its land, its animals, and its people. For the first time we are told of effects upon vegetation of all kinds; every conceivable aspect of the land of Egypt is now caught up in these signs. Even more, with the occurrence of weather-related phenomena, the entire natural order seems to be caught up in this series in one way or another. Only light and darkness seem to be untouched; that day will come, too.

The sign begins as did the first and fourth plagues, but now

123

some important sentences unique and central to the cycle are used. God says, "I will send all my plagues [blows] upon your heart." The plural for plague may be a reference to the various weather phenomena that follow, but more likely it refers to the rest of the plagues, climaxing in the final blow. These will be sent, not simply upon his people, but upon his heart (see 7:23). In effect, they are blows to the heart, which would have a hardening effect. The fourth of the "knowing" statements follows: that you may know that there is none like Yahweh in all the earth. This is similar to the first (7:17) in that knowing comes as a result of experiencing the plagues; it is verbally the same as the second (8:10), except that "the earth" is picked up from 8:22. This stresses that Yahweh is Lord of the entire earth; it is a statement of God's incomparability extended to universal proportions. All the earth is God's, as the next "knowing" passage proclaims (9:30).

The translation of the first verb in 9:15 is uncertain; "should have put forth" (so Brown-Driver-Briggs, *Hebrew Lexicon*, 774; cf. NRSV, "could") is a likely translation. The essence of verses 14–16 is: If I had not had the intention of your knowing that there is none like me in all the earth, indeed that my name be declared throughout all the earth, then I should have put forth my hand and cut you off from the earth. This is what you have deserved.

For all of Pharaoh's attempts to subvert God's intentions in creation through his oppressive actions against Israel, he deserves the death penalty. He and his predecessor have pursued a genocidal policy. There is no question of fairness in such a final verdict. If God had not seen that through Pharaoh's continued life a larger salutary purpose for the world could be achieved, God should have exacted the punishment of death. The question here is not what God *could* have done, as if God's power were in doubt, but what *should* have been done had God not had a more comprehensive purpose that his life could serve. The concern is why God has allowed this struggle to be prolonged in view of Pharaoh's ongoing intransigence. This matter is also lifted up in 9:17—Pharaoh has been exalting himself at the expense of God's people. If it were not for larger purposes that God could achieve, Pharaoh should have met his end.

124

The last clause in verse 16, though commonly neglected, is a key to the entire sign cycle. Here God's ultimate goal for the creation comes into view. In three "knowing" texts (8:22; 9:14, 30) the relationship of God to the entire earth is emphasized. Yahweh is no local god, seeking to best another local deity. The issue for God *finally* is that God's name be declared *(sapar)* to the entire earth. This verb is used elsewhere for the proclamation of God's good news (e.g., Ps. 78:3–4; Isa. 43:21). This is no perfunctory understanding of the relationship of non-Israelites to Yahweh. To say that God is God of all the earth means that all its people are God's people; they should know the name of this God. Hence God's purposes in these events are not focused simply on the redemption of Israel. *God's purposes span the world.* God is acting in such a public way so that God's good news can be proclaimed to everyone (see Rom. 9:17).

And so, given God's larger purposes in all of this, further signs will come upon Egypt. Comparative language now begins to be used: such a hailstorm has never before been seen in Egypt (9:18; see also 9:24; 10:6, 14; 11:6). It is the intensity and the incomparability of these concluding events that give them their sign value. But in a move unique to the sign cycle (9:19), God tells Pharaoh how to blunt the effects of the storm: bring the livestock into shelters. The narrator comments (9:20–21) that there were Egyptians who heeded the warning because they "feared the word of Yahweh." This is an illustration of the point just made in verses 14–16. The God of the Hebrews was making an impression on some of Pharaoh's servants; there is still some openness to Egypt's future at this point. Pharaoh and others, however, did not yet (!) fear Yahweh (9:30), and they are now portrayed in hardening terms (9:34; 10:1). But even among these there emerges a renewed level of appreciation of this God (10:7; 11:3). The God of Israel is the God of the entire world, even Egyptians, and God's activity is beginning to have an effect that is in tune with God's purposes. A later prophet will make a remarkably positive assessment of the Egyptians' relationship with Yahweh (Isa. 19:19–25): "Blessed be Egypt my people." God's work among the Egyptians in the time of the exodus has a long-term effect.

Moses is to use the staff, that hail may be brought upon the land. The weather becomes frightful indeed: the sky is filled with thunder and lightning and hail. The text brings Moses' and God's action together in a cooperative way as dual agents in bringing the hail (as in 7:19, 25; 10:13). The effect of the hail is

125

devastating, on vegetation in particular (9:25). Once again the language of "every plant" and "every tree" grabs the reader's attention; this is later shown to be hyperbolic (10:5, 12, which 9:31–32 explains only in part), but its significatory value remains. This is a sign of incredible intensity, never before experienced. Once again the people of Israel are not touched by the devastation (see at 8:22).

In response to this disaster, Pharaoh sends for Moses and Aaron. There follows a remarkable confession: I have sinned; Yahweh is in the right and I and my people are in the wrong (on the importance of these clauses, see excursus). For the third time he asks for Moses' intercession. Also for the third time Pharaoh promises that he will let Israel go. Moses will pray to God on his behalf, even though he knows that the confession does not entail that Pharaoh *yet* fears the Lord. There are no grounds for thinking that it is simply cynical—perhaps it is an act of appeasement; that it was lacking in any depth is shown by the fact that, once the storm had stopped, he "sinned yet again," hardened his heart, and would not follow through on his promise to let the people go.

The incomparability of this plague—twice stressed, 9:18 and 24—constitutes a sign of the incomparable fury of the plague of death (11:6). While the intensity of the weather also has a high significatory value, it does so because of the common associations of hail and related phenomena. They are used in two primary contexts, theophany (Ps. 18:12–13; 77:16–20) and divine judgment (Isa. 28:2, 17; 30:30–31; Ezek. 13:11–13; 38:22–23; Hag. 2:17). Hail is a powerful image of God coming in judgment, and being experienced in such an intense form would function as a sign of that to any who would listen.

Exodus 10:1–20
Driven Into the Red Sea

Usually the reference to the hardening of Pharaoh's heart occurs at the end of each sign narrative. Here it occurs at the beginning, as part of a divine word preparing Moses for the visit to Pharaoh. God has hardened not only Pharaoh's heart but that of his servants as well. This signals some new developments. God proceeds to give some reasons for this: (1) One reason is that these signs may be shown to Pharaoh and his servants. This harks back to previous statements such as 9:14–17. (2) A second reason is that this story of God's acts may be told to generations of Israelites yet to come. This theme of recounting God's deeds to children will recur later (12:26; 13:8, 14). The translation "made fools of" (NRSV; cf. NEB) the Egyptians is possible, but the infrequently used verb could just as well be translated "busied myself with" or "severely dealt with" (see NAB). (3) Another reason is that all of this is in order that *Israel* may know that "I am Yahweh." Such "knowing" language usually has reference to Egypt. But God has a mission among God's own people as well, that they may believe (an ongoing concern; cf. 4:31; 12:27; 14:31).

For the first time the reader hears of the actual reporting of God's word to Pharaoh (cf. 9:20; excursus). The sign this time is locusts. They will not only destroy everything left by the hail, they will *fill* their homes (cf. 8:21). This is certainly an ominous sign.

Though God has hardened the hearts of the servants of Pharaoh (10:1), and they themselves have done so as well (9:34), in 10:7 they echo Moses and Aaron in pleading with Pharaoh to let the Israelites go so that they may *"serve* the LORD their God." Divine hardening does not preclude their decision that Pharaoh ought to let Israel go (see excursus). They are able to see what Moses is about and are dismayed that Pharaoh cannot. Pharaoh responds by calling Moses and Aaron back. His response this time, however, stands in basic disagreement with his servants. He is less willing to let Israel go than before (9:28). Events and divine hardening have stiffened his resistance. When Moses insists that all Israel is to leave, he balks. In fact, he is adamant; they must have some evil purpose in mind. He will allow only the men to go; they must leave women and children behind, ensuring their return to Egypt. As if to demonstrate his resolve, Pharaoh drives them from his presence.

The divine response is the locust plague. The elevenfold (!) use of the word *kōl* ("all") in verses 12–15 stresses the absoluteness of the devastation left by the locusts. Given the fact that, like hail, locusts are a common symbol of divine judgment (Deut. 28:38, 42; II Chron. 7:13; Jer. 51:27; Amos 4:9; 7:1), this

127

is certainly a portentous sign. The use of the image in Joel is particularly similar (1:4, 7, 17–20; 2:9–10, 25). As with the frogs (8:6), they will *"cover* the face of the (whole) land" (10:5, 15), a portent of the waters covering the Egyptians (14:28; 15:5, 15). A sign may also be present in the phrase "No one can see the land" (10:5). When the destroyer moves through Egypt on that fateful night (12:13, 23), not seeing the blood on the doorposts means tragedy. The twice-noted incomparability language (10:6, 14) is a clear sign of the incomparableness of the final plague (see 11:6).

A sign may also be present in the causal factors at work, even more complex than in previous signs. Not only are both God and Moses involved, God also makes use of a natural phenomenon (the east wind) to bring the locusts upon Egypt. This is another signal from the narrator of events to come; in 14:21 God will also use the east wind to drive the sea back for the people of Israel. But the sign is particularly present in the language used to describe the removal of the locusts. They are driven into the Red Sea and "not a single locust was left" (10:19; see 8:31). This is precisely what happens to the Egyptians in 14:28. As it was with the locusts, so it will be with the Egyptians. The locusts and the Egyptians did comparable damage to the land; they will share a common end. The sign is thus found both in the plague and in its removal.

Pharaoh reacts once again (see 9:27) with the language of confession: I have sinned against Yahweh your God and against you. A new note is sounded with his request for forgiveness. In fact, he pleads with Moses, and for the fourth time asks him to pray to God to remove the cause of the devastation. The language indicates that the significance of the signs is beginning to dawn on him: remove this death from me. Once again Moses prays to the Lord, and again God responds positively, sending a west wind that drives the locusts into the sea (the only time God uses the nonhuman order to remove a sign). The result is complete: not a single locust remains in all the land of Egypt! Not one. But God once again works to harden Pharaoh's heart, and he did not let the people of Israel go.

Exodus 10:21–29
A Return to the First Day of Creation

As with signs 3 and 6, the ninth sign begins with an immediate directive from God. Moses acts without hesitation. This time it is darkness, but not an ordinary darkness. It is darkness that lasts three days without break. It is darkness that is palpable, which can be touched and felt. All human movement could be described with the word "grope." Like a winter whiteout, where all you can do is stay indoors for the duration of the storm, so this was a blackout, with no light whatsoever. It had nothing to do with a sun that had gotten stuck on the other side of the world; the Israelites had light where they were. It was not a continuing night; the darkness made both day and night sheer blackness.

The darkness language, anticipated in the previous plague (10:5, 15), should make its function as a sign clear for both Pharaoh and reader. The phrase "thick darkness" is used elsewhere for the devastating effects of God's judgment (Isa. 8:22; Joel 2:2; Zeph. 1:15), as is darkness more generally (Isa. 13:10; Joel 2:10), including Ezekiel's oracle against Egypt (Ezek. 32:7–8). The use of darkness with the infrequent language of "feeling, groping" is also present in such contexts (Deut. 28:29; Job 5:14; 12:25). This is perhaps the clearest judgment language yet used; it is an ominous sign indeed for Pharaoh. The narratives that follow are filled with darkness language, both with respect to the tenth plague (11:4; 12:12, 29–31, 42) and the sea crossing (14:20–21). It is the darkness of chaos, a precreation state of affairs. That is why it is the most serious plague but one. God is at work in the darkness, however, and God's new creation will burst forth in the light of day.

Pharaoh quickly responds. Once again, however, it is with a qualification: all the people can go, but the animals must be left behind. But Moses will have none of it: the animals will be needed in order to serve Yahweh, but the identity of the animals cannot be determined in advance. Once again God hardens Pharaoh's heart and he does not let the people go. This time

129

the story does not end with the hardening notice. Pharaoh reacts angrily to Moses: Get out! And you'd better be careful, for if I see you again, you are a dead man. Moses responds, his voice coated with irony: You'll get your wish (but he'll be the dead man!). This change in narrative conclusion may be intended to indicate that an impasse has been reached.

The narrative does continue unbroken into chapter 11. But that will be the final announcement for Pharaoh: the greatest blow of all is now inevitable. There is no turning back from this point. There will be no more opportunities for Pharaoh to let Israel go, except on the far side of disaster.

Exodus 11:1–10
The End Is Near

Yet one more plague. The end is near. An impasse has been reached. There is no more room to maneuver. The stream of negotiation has reached the narrows, and the waters are shortly going to go crashing through the gorge. There is no stopping things now. A final judgment will fall upon Pharaoh and Egypt.

It is likely that 10:1–4, whatever its previous history, now functions as a narrative interlude, consisting of an inner word of God to Moses. This anticipates the interludes that follow in chapters 12—15. While Moses probably intended to conclude the discussion at 10:29, it now concludes with 11:4–8.

It is commonly suggested that the tenth plague "belongs to the realm of the supernatural" and has "no grounding in natural events" (Sarna, pp. 77, 93). This view cannot be sustained. The tenth plague is another instance of what we have called the hypernatural (see above). The word commonly translated "plague" *(nega')* in 11:1 is not used elsewhere in Exodus. It is used mostly in Leviticus 13—14, where it is commonly translated "disease." We are thereby encouraged to think of the death of the firstborn in terms of this genre of event, though its timing and scope are clearly hypernatural in character. Pharaoh's response to this devastation is predictable. He will let the Israelites go; in fact, he will drive them out, leaving no one behind (see 3:19; 6:1).

130

Moses is to speak to the people and remind them (see at 3:21–22) to ask their neighbors for their silver and gold possessions (reported in 12:35–36). The narrator then comments that God had given the people favor in the eyes of the Egyptians— and hence the gifts must be genuine; even more, Moses in particular was highly regarded by every Egyptian but one, Pharaoh. This stands over against God's activity of hardening; perhaps one could speak of God's "softening" of their hearts. All of this divine activity in the plagues did have a certain salutary effect on these people (see 9:20; 10:7).

Far from being "somewhat clumsy" (Childs, p. 161), this interlude is presented to highlight one thing: Pharaoh stands alone! He is the one whose stubbornness has brought Egypt to this point. Pharaoh's own servants will come and bow before Moses (11:8)! One is prompted to wonder: If it had not been for Pharaoh, what would the effect of these signs have been? History has shown that this picture of the difference between a country's leaders and its people is not uncommon.

Following upon verse 3, a startlingly black picture is presented in verse 4. It is a word to Pharaoh of the harshest of judgments. God will go forth into the midst of Egypt (the divine means is unstated) and all the firstborn shall die, from the least of them to the greatest, human beings and cattle. Distinctions among the Egyptians will collapse; everyone will be affected, including Pharaoh himself. And there shall be a great cry *(se'a-qah)*, unique in Egypt's history. It was last heard among the Israelites under Egyptian bondage (3:7, 9). Once again God will make a distinction between Israel and Egypt. Israel will be so protected that not so much as a dog will growl at them. This distinction is something that Pharaoh will "know." God is one who makes choices, who makes distinctions. The Egyptians are chosen because of what they have done to the Israelites, indeed to the creation. God has begun to fulfill the blessing of Gen. 1:28, and this creating must be protected from the anticreation forces of the world. God will move with a liberated people in extending this creative activity to the entire world.

In response to this great tragedy, *all* of Pharaoh's servants will tell Moses to take his people and leave Egypt. Ironically, the Egyptians themselves take up Moses' call to let the people go. Pharaoh's silence in the face of this announcement is deafening. Yet he is the one who will in fact order the people out (12:31–

131

32); in the light of the event itself, Pharaoh will assume this responsibility. Having made this announcement, Moses leaves Pharaoh's presence in great anger. He cannot be angry at the permission to leave Egypt. He must be angry at the fact that everything has come to this. God in effect confirms this: Pharaoh will not listen anymore, but the many refusals and signs have served an important purpose. This is a stock phrase, a kind of refrain for this point in the narrative, rather than a reference to the last plague.

Exodus 11:10 serves as a summary statement for all the signs up to this point. The verse brings all the principals of these events together and puts forth a key aspect of their involvement. Moses and Aaron did *all* these wonders; God hardened Pharaoh's heart; Pharaoh did not let Israel go. But now things will change: Pharaoh will let Israel go.

God's implementation of this announcement is not immediately reported. It is delayed until 12:29–32. Between announcement and act comes the report of the feasts of passover and unleavened bread. This announcement closes the sign cycle, yet it anticipates the passover. Literarily, the placement of chapter 12 serves to retard the action of the narrative; the reader is kept waiting regarding the outcome of the announcements of chapter 11. But this also serves to place the actual event of 12:29–32, when it is reported, outside the flow of the story and integrates it into a liturgical context. Given this context of worship, the visitation of God among the Egyptians is given a special character, a certain solemnity, taking it out of "ordinary time and space"; it is liturgical event.

PART FOUR

From Passover to Praise
EXODUS 12:1—15:21

Introduction: Story and Ritual

The redaction of Exodus 12—15 demonstrates that liturgy is the key to its proper interpretation. The accompanying chart shows how the story line of these chapters is enclosed by liturgical material in multiple ways. The entire story is surrounded by details of the passover ritual (12:1–27a) and songs of praise (15:1–21); the two story sections individually are enclosed by matters associated with worship. One is invited, indeed compelled, to read the story *through* a liturgical lens.

It has been common to suggest that these materials were written under the influence of later cultic practice. That is to say, later practice of these rituals has influenced the way in which the narrative has been composed. To put it succinctly: liturgy has shaped literature. The most provocative formulation of this was that of Johannes Pedersen. For him, all of Exodus 1—15 is a historicization of a cultic celebration of these events in Israel's worship. While including all of chapters 1—11 in such a formulation is problematic, chapters 12—15 (and probably the plague cycle) are properly so understood (cf. Childs, pp. 195–206). Many different layers of tradition from centuries of religious practice have been integrated into the final form of the narrative. The following commonalities in the three addresses of Moses to the people regarding *future* worship practices illustrate this point.

At the same time, as noted below, *redactionally the passover is represented as shaping the event itself.* It might be noted that integrating later material into the story of an earlier period

Structure of Exodus 12:1–15:21

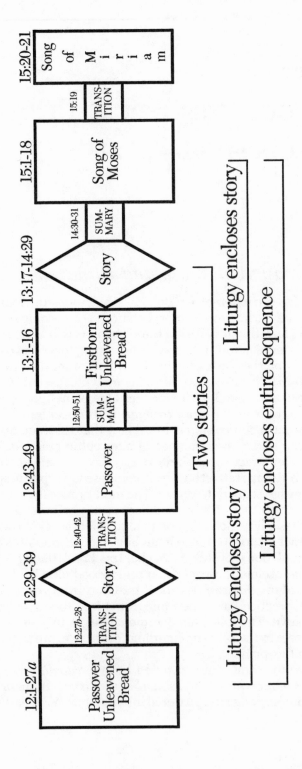

134

	Passover 12:21–27	Unleavened Bread 13:3–10	Firstborn 13:11–16
When in Canaan . . .	12:25	13:5	13:11
Promise to fathers	12:25	13:5	13:11
When children ask . . .	12:26	13:8	13:14
God's action in Egypt	12:27	13:3, 9	13:14, 16
Sign/mark	cf.12:13	13:9	13:16
Keep this service	12:25	13:5	——
Observe forever	12:24 (14)	13:10 (12:17)	——
Sacrifice	12:27	——	13:15
For/to Yahweh	12:27	13:6	13:12

is not a deception. It indicates the fundamental nature of the passover liturgy. In and through this ritual every generation of Israelites was the recipient of God's exodus-shaped redemption. In every era, Israel confessed: God delivered *us*.

First, note that the announcement of the tenth plague (11:1–8) is separated from the carrying out of the deed by extensive ritual material (12:1–27). This could be explained by the time needed for preparations, now conveyed by God. The reference to the tenth and fourteenth days of "*this* month" (12:3, 6) even suggests that those days are some time away from this address to Moses and Aaron. Yet this would necessitate no small temporal break between 12:20 and 12:21 (Moses' word to the elders to begin preparations) and telescoping the tenth to the fourteenth days of the month in 12:21. But, more important, this view fails to recognize the degree to which aspects of later celebrations have been integrated into the text; this alleviates any need to iron out temporal difficulties regarding the original event. Other explanations seem preferable for the interruption between announcement and deed.

1. This break has a literary function. It retards the action of the narrative, creating a certain suspense. The death of the Egyptian firstborn has been announced in no uncertain terms, unconditionally. Pharaoh will not be responsive in any case (11:9). The reader is poised to hear the other shoe dropped.

135

Then God launches into a detailed ordering of a festival to be celebrated. Only in verses 12–13 does it become clear how this is to be related to the prior announcement.

2. The break provides a hermeneutic for interpreting the entire narrative. As noted, ritual materials literarily enclose the events of the night of departure from Egypt (12:1–28, 43–49); both begin with the word of God to Moses and Aaron. Moreover, the summary in verses 50–51 is a repetition of the "inner ring" of the account (vv. 28, 41). This summary (which is not chronologically understood) melds the two dimensions of the text into a single whole: the celebration of the passover (v. 50) and the exodus from Egypt (v. 51). *The historical event is at one and the same time a liturgical event.* But the inclusio provided by the ritual material is the decisive interpretive factor: it lifts up the liturgical character of the event. Liturgical material flows into the event and away from it. The same is true for the resumption of the story in 13:17—14:31.

The effect of this *liturgical hermeneutic* is to place these events outside the normal flow of the story. It gives them a character not unlike that which a pageant gives the Christmas story, somewhat impressionistic or even surrealistic in relation to the actual events, beyond normal time and space. There is a certain solemnity, even mystery, about the matter; the high emotion that must have been a part of the occasion is greatly subdued. There are no pauses to savor what happened to the Egyptians; Israel, like its God, voices no pleasure in the death of anyone. Neither relish nor revelry is to be seen. Matters of detail are both heightened and diminished. Exact numbers are given at some points, elsewhere only the barest of notices. The flow is somewhat episodic, like scenes from a short play or rubrics from a liturgy. Liturgical material is incorporated here and there (e.g., vv. 34, 39, 42). Moreover, certain details take on new meaning, for example, Pharaoh's ironic comment to Moses and Aaron: "Go, serve the LORD" becomes a liturgical rubric, while "Bless me also" becomes a liturgical response.

This interweaving of story and ritual also has important theological implications (see separate sections).

Exodus 12:1–28
Passover, Past and Present

This section consists of a word of God to Moses regarding the ritual—passover and unleavened bread combined—to be followed for the deathly event to come (vv. 1–20) and a speech of Moses to the elders regarding passover only (vv. 21–27). While these accounts probably have their roots in separate sources (P and J respectively), verses 21–27 are now presented as an abbreviated report of verses 1–20. Details regarding the passover ritual can be found in Bible dictionaries and commentaries; the following comments focus on theological aspects of the narrative (on vv. 24–27, see at 13:16).

A newly liberated people will create practices and institutions that are in tune with their new status. In the case of passover, however, liturgy *precedes* the liberative event. Redactionally, the ritual is set in place before the event occurs. As noted above, story and liturgy have been so integrally interwoven that they cannot be understood properly in isolation from each other. But liturgy has not only shaped literature, it has shaped the event itself. The event takes place according to certain liturgical rubrics. The event *is* liturgy. Hence the identification of the act of God in the text cannot be narrowly associated with a historical event. Act of God is also a liturgical event (see below).

This could support the view that passover is rooted in an existing nomadic rite of passage. While this rite may be what is repeatedly mentioned by Moses to Pharaoh (see 3:18), now ironically celebrated *in* Egypt, its meaning has been transformed in view of changed circumstances. Whatever the roots of passover may have been, it has now been drawn into the heart of the liberating event itself and represented as a God-given ritual for a coming event and its subsequent actualizations.

At the same time, the meaning of passover is not completely comprehended by the exodus events. Specifically, the use of an animal and its blood carries a meaning that is not exhausted by the historical associations. Here elements of the created order, indeed the very life of creation, function as a sign of redemption. (On unleavened bread as creational, see 13:3–10.)

Unlike its function in a nomadic rite, the blood has no apotropaic role, having properties in and of itself that would automatically provide protection from an evil. What is important is the word, *the promise associated with the sign,* not the sign in and of itself (12:13). The blood is a sign "for you" (i.e., for Israel), not for God! That is, it is a sign of the divine promise: *God commits himself* to pass over the blood-marked houses. Israel can rely on God's being faithful to this commitment. A sign from the sphere of creation becomes a vehicle for Israel's redemption.

It is thus not irrelevant that the substance used is blood. The sign is not simply a "marker," as if any colorful substance that caught the eye would do (contra Sarna, p. 92). In the blood was life; it is the vitality of the living (Lev. 17:11, 14; cf. Deut. 12:23; Ps. 72:14). It is a sign of life, but not a symbol in a weak sense. The blood was the life *of creation* given for the people who lived in the marked houses. It is the *life given* that provides the life for Israel, not simply the blood as a marker of protection. The blood of creation is shed so that Israel's blood might be spared. But it has this power because of the word of God that so proclaims its significance. *God uses creation to achieve redemption.*

The hermeneutic provided by the interweaving of liturgy and story gives a further theological force to the interpretation of the passage. Childs (pp. 204–205) speaks of these texts in terms of both act of God and word of God. Event and interpretation must be kept together. True enough. But his discussion does not properly identify word of God and act of God in terms of this text. The bracketing passover material is not word of God in the sense of an interpretation of the event. Rather, the word of God (in other words, the myth) is the *story* of the event itself (in which act of God is central); this is, of course, an interpretation.

It is this story which is referred to in the request for an interpretation *of the ritual* by the children—a remarkably inclusive aspect of Israel's worship (12:27; cf. 13:8, 14–15). The passover material enclosing this text is liturgy in which the proclaimed story would be dramatized or reenacted. As such, it is *passover* which is act of God; in and through the celebration of the passover God works salvation initially, and ever anew, in the lives of the participants, (re)constituting them as the redeemed exodus community. The passover is the "LORD's passover" (12:11, 27, 42). As such, it is a sacramental vehicle for making the exodus redemption real and effective for both present and subsequent generations. When Israel reenacts the passover, it is not a fiction, as if nothing really happens in the ritual, or all that happens is a recollection of the happenedness of an original event. The reenactment is as much salvific event as the original enactment. The memory language (12:14; cf. 13:3, 9; Deut. 16:3) is not a "soft" matter, recalling to mind some story of the past. It is an entering into the reality of that event in such a way as to be reconstituted as the people of God thereby.

This analysis affects another of Childs's theological considerations, namely, his distinction between redemption as memory and redemption as hope. The dialectic present in these texts, however, is not "between the past and the future" (Childs, p. 205). It is between the past and the present. It is the question of how the salvific effect of a past event can be appropriated or realized in every new present. Liturgy, by being structured into the very story of the past redemptive event, provides the answer. The saving power of the original event is made available ever anew to the community by God's redeeming activity within the context of worship.

This understanding of passover has been integral to both Jewish and Christian traditions. The Jewish liturgy for passover (Passover Haggadah) stresses that worshipers in every celebration are actual participants in God's saving deed: God brought *us* out of Egypt. The passover also serves as important background for the New Testament presentation of the death of Jesus and the understanding of the Lord's Supper.

For the first time since 4:31, the people bowed their heads and worshiped, no doubt a service of thanksgiving for the word of deliverance. Their obedient acts of preparation follow (v. 28). This twofold response on the part of the people is not irrelevant to what follows. The deathly act that enables Israel's deliverance is God's work, but the people's response prepares the way. (On the destroyer, see below.)

139

Exodus 12:29–36
A Tragic Night, a Joyful Day

As noted, the placement of this plague in the midst of ritual considerations takes it out of the normal flow of the story, out of ordinary time and space. This gives it an impressionistic character in relation to actual events. Its somewhat episodic flow may be due to the composite nature of the text, but it also enables the narrator quickly to view death and new life from different angles of vision. The story is told in spare, straightforward language; there is no literary embellishment, no stopping to savor what happened to the Egyptians. Even with the joy associated with newfound freedom, Israel, like its God, voices no pleasure in the deaths of these persons. This gives the entire scene a certain solemnity.

Attention is here given to the two major aspects of the narrative; it is *a story of both death and new life.*

It happened in the middle of the night, when all of that world was dark. The darkness of the night matched the darkness of the deed. No household was spared, not one. Indeed, no barnyard escaped. It was a deed done while all were asleep; it was not a public execution, though the effects were public indeed. As hard as it is to say, the victims were primarily children: both boys and girls—whoever happened to be the firstborn in the family. It helps but little to say that there was no suffering; to use a modern image, it was sudden (infant) death syndrome throughout Egypt that night. One can appreciate the great cry that went up, from parents in particular, including Pharaoh himself. However much it is appropriate to speak of judgment, and Pharaoh's genocidal decision to kill all Hebrew baby boys was made not long ago (see 1:16, 22), no reader can rejoice at the deaths of children. Their lives were snuffed out because of what adults had done. It might be helpful to draw on historical parallels, not finally as a justification for killing, but as a reminder of other forms of history's violence. Perhaps carefully drawn analogies between Pharaoh and Hitler might be helpful, including the fact that American bombs killed many German

140

children, while asleep and while awake, and in strange and unpredictable patterns of locale.

It is one thing to speak of American bombs, but it seems almost blasphemous that God is the one who "drops the bomb." The text does not back off from identifying the subject of this judgment: God smote all the firstborn in Egypt from the least (this time prisoners are mentioned) to the greatest, both animals and human beings. This does not mean that God killed each of the firstborn directly, one by one (see Ps. 78:49). The text uses various words in speaking of a nondivine agent: 11:1 speaks of *nega'* ("plague"), a word often used for diseases; 12:13 speaks of *negep* ("plague"), a word commonly used for pestilence or blow; in 9:15 *deber* ("pestilence") is used, as in 9:3 for the cattle epidemic; *mašhit* ("destroyer," NRSV) occurs in 12:23, a word associated with destruction and pestilence (cf. II Sam. 24:15–16; Isa. 37:36). It is best to think of a pestilence epidemic that kills quickly. This killing of firstborn only ought not be interpreted literally (its possible historical basis is that no household remained untouched). As with the other plagues, the emphasis on "all" is intended to portray an aspect of creation gone berserk. The moral order has "boomeranged" in such a way that the order of nature (which includes epidemics) has become something it ought not be.

The language of 4:23 should be recalled. There the killing of the Egyptian firstborn is understood as a measure for measure, making the punishment fit the crime. Pharaoh had sought to kill the male children of Israel (1:22), a genocidal measure that would in time have killed off the people of Israel. So the firstborn of Egypt suffer a fate comparable—it is not genocidal—to what Pharaoh had planned and begun to carry out.

This helps answer the question, Why not just any person from every Egyptian family? It is because of the widely known understanding regarding firstborn. This would be a public statement as to God's claim over Egypt, God's authority over the Egyptian people rather than Pharaoh's. The firstborn are dedicated to Yahweh rather than to Egypt's gods (see 12:12). Given Pharaoh's attempt to claim Israel's children, this constitutes God's counterclaim at a comparable, if less severe, level. Because it is directly responsive to the type of claim Pharaoh was making, it would perhaps be a measure that would finally be convincing to him.

141

While it is still dark, in the immediate aftermath of the death of his own firstborn, Pharaoh summons Moses and Aaron. He orders them to take all people and animals, leave Egypt, and serve the Lord, as Moses has demanded. The narrator formulates Pharaoh's last words to Moses in the language of benediction: Bless me. Its tone and intent are uncertain; the narrator leaves the reader with the ambiguity. What will happen to Pharaoh? The scenario sketched out in 4:23 has become a reality.

The narrative continues in almost snapshot fashion, quickly passing by the reader various vignettes highlighting those last moments on the way to freedom. Every word should be lingered over, for freedom and new status under God are precious indeed.

The Egyptians as a whole are now said to react, and the practice of referring to the entire Egyptian people remains striking. As if in one body, perhaps thinking they will be the next victims, they hurry the Israelites out of the country. And so in haste the people of Israel take their unleavened bread (see at 12:14–20) and flee the country. The narrator only pauses to inform the reader that, in obedience to Moses, they had already asked for and received the fine possessions of the Egyptians, whose hearts had been softened toward Israel by God (see at 3:21–22; 11:2–3). And so they left the Egyptians "stripped clean" of their valuable possessions. Their status has now changed; they leave Egypt "dressed out," not as slaves, but as persons who have been raised to a new level of life by their God. Their raiment and jewelry are those of persons no longer bound but free. "You are a crown of beauty in the hand of the LORD, and a royal diadem in the hand of your God" (Isa. 62:3).

Exodus 12:37–51
Freedom and Faith

142

Verses 37–51 are a composite from various sources and probe a variety of concerns. As a consequence, the final redaction is highly episodic. It is as if every traditor through whose hands this material passed had to enter some notes on the import of this central event; the effect is to provide a number of transitions into the next section. This may be said to correspond to the transitional character of this moment in Israel's life. Issues of coherence have been particularly felt with respect to the passover section in verses 43–49. As has been noted, it is likely that the concern for enclosing the story with matters of ritual informs this particular placement. The notes that follow lift up some of the key themes.

The people are on their way. After their years of servitude to the Egyptians, freedom joins the people of Israel on the road to the Egyptian border. They were a "mixed crowd," consisting of more than the descendants of the twelve sons of Jacob. Many non-Israelites had been integrated into the community of faith, and other communities no doubt took advantage of the opportunity to choose freedom. *Freedom for Israel means freedom for others* (see 22:21; 23:9). When the people of God are liberated, not only their own kind can come along. The benefits of freedom have a fallout effect on all those with whom they come in contact, whether they are people of faith or not. So it has been throughout the centuries, often in spite of efforts by the people of God to become a community unto themselves. God's redemption is not for the chosen few; it is for the sake of all the world. Would that every community where the people of God are gathered could be called a "mixed crowd."

At the same time, there are distinctions to be made between Israelites and non-Israelites regarding passover observance (vv. 43–49). This is a feast only for the "congregation of Israel." Circumcision is the distinctive factor because that is a sign of membership in the community of faith which confesses the God of passover. This is not a new level of exclusivism but a recognition that passover is a festival for persons who have faith in this God. These others are invited to join that community by being circumcised, a sign that they have made the confession of this "congregation" their own. The experience of freedom is hereby integrated with the confession of faith in the God who liberates. Exodus and passover must be kept inextricably together if the reality of redemption is to be kept alive in the community.

Moreover, the people of God are accompanied by "great numbers" of animals; *both animals and people are liberated.* Freedom has an effect on more than human beings. This theme

143

is sounded again and again in the Scriptures (see 20:10; Deut. 5:14; Ps. 36:6; Rom. 8:22). Israel's God is one who is about redeeming the entire creation. "The wolf shall dwell with the lamb . . . and a little child shall lead them" (Isa. 11:6).

This people is a *community on the way*. They do not tarry. Opportunities for freedom must not be dallied with; one must take them and run. Even God-initiated moves take advantage of the moment; the opportunity may not come round again, even for God. And they travel light. They are not burdened by provisions that would weigh them down (Luke 10:4). Much that is near and dear to the life of bondage is to be left behind, if freedom is not to become another form of slavery.

This community of faith is *an intergenerational reality*. The number of people involved in the exodus—600,000 men plus women and children—seems impossibly high (see 38:26; cf. Num. 26:51). That would mean more than 2,000,000 people, given a typical age and sex distribution. Part of the problem is the length of Israel's sojourn in Egypt, here said to be 430 years, compared with the four generations in 6:14–25—a difference in sources that has not been able to be reconciled. Some scholars have translated the word *'elep* as "clans" rather than "thousand," hence some 600 family units (see Sarna, pp. 94–102). Others consider the number to be hyperbolic in order to make a theological point, testifying to how the people of Israel had multiplied in Egypt. While this may be so, one can be even more specific. This figure is an approximate representation of the population at the time of David and Solomon. It thus becomes a way of confessing that all Israel from this later time was brought out of Egypt by their God.

Two items can be cited in support of this interpretation. First, there is some indication that the building of the Solomonic temple was considered the end of an era that began with the exodus. The song sung at the sea climaxes with the building of the temple (15:17). Moreover, in a way unparalleled elsewhere, I Kings 6:1 takes special note of the time between exodus and temple (480 years). Further, Solomon links these two eras in his prayer (I Kings 8:9, 16, 21, 51, 53) and blessing (8:56), particularly in terms of the divine fulfillment of promises to Moses (see Deut. 12:9–11; I Kings 5:3–4).

Second, liturgical language explicitly ties the exodus generation with later ones. Each post-exodus generation is to confess

144

that their God had brought *them* out of the land of Egypt (12:26–27; 13:8–10, 14–15). The fluid use of pronouns, and the moving from past to present reference, witnesses to Israel's ever-contemporary appropriation of these events. These are words to be professed to the children "in time to come," whenever they ask. Past event and present worship are elided (see at 12:1–28). Interpreting 600,000+ as a liturgical number says that all Israelites from the time of David and Solomon had experienced the exodus. This was a saving event for them as much as for the original participants.

This section contains two transitional pieces (see chart). Verses 40–42 conclude the story of verses 29–39 but are concerned to note that it happened "on that very day"—the day of passover, the "night of vigil"; verses 50–51 conclude the entire section by integrating exodus and passover, "on that very day."

The "night of watching by the LORD" is to be a "night of vigil" by the Israelites in all subsequent generations. The word "vigil" can also have the sense of keeping watch or observing (12:17, 24). It probably has reference to God's watching over/ keeping the people of Israel on this death-filled night. This is testimony to a quiet but active bonding of God to Israel. Psalm 121:7–8 captures this point well: "The LORD will keep you from all evil; he will keep your life. The LORD will keep your going out and your coming in from this time forth and forevermore." What God has done for the Israelites is to be paralleled by Israel's careful watching/observance of the passover. *Israel's keeping remembers God's keeping.*

Verses 50–51 conclude with a reference to Israel's faithful observance of the passover and God's deliverance from Egypt. God's action is thus not separated from Israel's faithfulness. It is not that God's salvation is dependent upon Israel's obedience, however, any more than in a Christian setting salvation is made dependent upon the celebration of the sacraments. But the human activity does in fact provide for an instrumentality in and through which God works salvation. Exodus and passover must be tied together if the experience of redemption is to continue to be a living reality for Israel.

The exodus is announced in an almost matter-of-fact way in verse 51 (see 12:41; 13:18), though the sea crossing has not yet occurred. Some scholars therefore suggest that the exodus occurs at this point (see Coats, *Rebellion in the Wilderness*).

Hence the sea crossing belongs to the wilderness wanderings cycle. While this may have been true for an earlier form of the tradition, the present textual arrangement certainly incorporates the sea crossing into what is known as the exodus. While verses 29–39 report Israel's leaving Egypt, the crossing of the sea (14:1–31) reports the deliverance from the Egyptians who had pursued them beyond Egypt's borders (implied in 14:11–12). The liberation of Israel is not simply being brought out of Egypt, a matter of geographical placement; it is being delivered from the hand of the Pharaoh, the embodiment of the forces of chaos (see at 14:1–31).

Exodus 13:1–16
Body and Memory

This section seems to be a unity, though the separation of the firstborn texts (vv. 1–2, 11–16) has occasioned no little discussion. The oft-made suggestion of a deuteronomic source for much of this segment, if not all of it (and 12:24–27a), has some merit but remains problematic. The integration of story and ritual is especially to be recalled. This ritual material, combined with the song of praise in 15:1–21, encloses the story of the sea crossing and keeps the two sides of the exodus event literarily and liturgically united. We look first at leading theological themes and then reflect on certain passages and redactional considerations.

The narrator continues to focus the reader's attention on *what God has done on Israel's behalf.* Again and again the events are rehearsed and explained (vv. 3, 8, 9, 14, 15, 16), finishing with a flurry of references (and providing an inclusio with 12:51). For all that Israel is called upon to do, God's redemptive activity fills the scene.

At the same time, there is a repeated *look to the future* and the time in a new land, a place both of gift and responsibility (vv. 5, 7, 11). The *divine commitment to Israel's future* is recalled (vv. 5, 11). Israel can be assured that God will see to this commitment; God has bound himself in this regard. Yet the focus for talk of the future is not on hope; the settlement in the

146

land is considered so much a certainty that responsibilities can be delineated for the time beyond the fulfillment of promise.

The basic rhythm of the text is thus not that of memory and hope but of *memory and liturgical responsibility.* The effect of this is that the various instructions concerning future worship practices are not presented in heteronomous fashion. They are grounded in specific divine activity: because of what God has done, Israel is to respond in certain ways. Even more, the liturgical responses correspond to specific aspects of those events. (1) The consecration and the redemption of the firstborn correlate with the death/life of the firstborn on passover night. Because of the divine redemption of Israel's firstborn, they belong to God. (2) The eating of unleavened bread specifically replicates the haste with which Israel left Egypt (12:34, 39). (3) The various liturgical details of passover are also replications of the events of that original night.

While these responses are certainly vehicles for Israel's expression of *gratitude* for what God has done, the text contains no explicit language in this regard. Moreover, they are not simply means by which Israel engages in the *recollection* of the past; the memory language, explicit (vv. 3, 9) and implicit, has a deeper significance. As with passover (see 12:1–28), the concrete and replicative nature of each of the rituals indicates that they are *vehicles in and through which God effects salvation for each new generation.* The interweaving of past and present reference and the use of the pronouns (e.g., 12:27; 13:3–4, 8, 14) imply that a cross-generational experience of salvation is in view (cf. Mishnah tractate on Passover, 10:5). The direct involvement of children in each ritual (vv. 8, 14; 12:26) incorporates new generations into this saving reality. These instructions are thus given for Israel's continued life and blessing. The concern is not that God be properly thanked but that the redemptive experience be a living reality for each Israelite in every age.

An integral part of this experience is that what happens in the liturgy receive *appropriate interpretation.* Specific instruction for children is highlighted in each instance, with (12:26; 13:14) and without (13:8) their request. The interpretive word is central to the liturgical activity. Moreover, the binding of the instruction closely to one's body (vv. 9, 16) is for the sake of the word, "that the law . . . may be in your *mouth.*" The mind is

147

not a stable enough repository for this life-giving word; it is to be kept close to one's physical self (through a bodily mark, or a piece of cloth, or a container for written words). *The body is here pressed into the service of memory.* All this to assure that each generation can know that word and experience the reality to which it witnesses.

Some general comments about *the firstborn phenomenon* are in order. The first child born into a family had an important role in many ancient societies, including a special status and inheritance rights. This is still true in some modern cultures (cf. Jewish practice). In addition, the firstlings of domestic animals and the firstfruits of crops were set apart. The Israelites took over this custom and gave it a special import (see Exod. 22:29–30; 23:19; 34:19–26; Lev. 27:26–27; Num. 3:13, 40–46; 8:17–18; 18:15–17; Deut. 15:19). God was believed to be the giver of life, and the life of the firstborn was consecrated to God in gratitude. While various means were provided for their "redemption" through an offering, God used that as a vehicle to pour life back into ever new creations. Hence the law of the firstborn is an integral part of *Israel's creation theology;* by this means, God was believed to bring continued life and blessing into the community.

This practice is transposed into a new key in view of Israel's passover experience, but without losing the creational aspect. Verses 15–16 sharpen this historical connection in a somewhat surprising way. But, first, the larger context should be brought into consideration.

The material concerning the feast of the unleavened bread is placed between sections regarding the firstborn and hence is to be interpreted in terms of their consecration. It is the firstborn theme that is the decisive focus of passover night, from which the consecration of firstborn naturally follows. Unleavened bread is to be celebrated "because of what the LORD did for me when I came out of Egypt" (13:8; 12:17). The burning center of what "the LORD did for me" was the death/salvation of the firstborn, which testifies to the "strong hand" (vv. 3, 9, 14, 16; cf. vv. 8, 15) by which God brought Israel out of Egypt. Unleavened bread is thus integrated into this focus in any remembrance of that night. The common structure and themes in the three speeches of Moses (see at 12:1—15:21; 12:21–27; 13:3–10, 11–16) stress this as well. The first day of unleavened

148

bread coincides with this night (12:17, 34, 39; 13:3–4). It is likely that this was celebrated for seven days thereafter, carrying the community through the first days of liberation (hence chap. 13 has a logical placement).

Firstborn language is used in the collective sense for Israel's relationship with God in 4:23 (so also firstfruits, Jer. 2:3). This refers to the entire people as God's firstborn and hence would refer to *both male and female* (so also Jer. 31:9). This is a metaphorical use of the term, but the literal and metaphorical usages are interrelated in these texts. The death and the life of passover night also make no distinctions between male and female firstborn. This would also seem to be the case with the consecration *(qadaš)* of the firstborn in 13:1–2. This is a specific action taken on that very day, according to Num. 3:13 (and hence naturally precedes the future-oriented vv. 3–16). This inclusiveness is important when it is remembered that God's claim on Israel's firstborn constitutes a counter to Pharaoh's efforts to claim authority over *all* Israel. When Israel gets to Canaan (13:11), the inclusiveness remains (v. 12), but the practice of redemption pertains only to sons (vv. 13–16). The redemption of the sons becomes a sign for the redemption of children of both sexes.

Verses 15–16 give a special twist to the issue of the firstborn. In essence, Israel is to continue to be attentive to its firstborn because of what the *Egyptian* firstborn have suffered. Israel's firstborn are to be "given to God," but as God himself did, they are to be redeemed rather than sacrificed. But at what cost? Is it the Egyptian children? It is noteworthy that the redeemed Israelite children of passover night are not explicitly mentioned, only the sacrificed *Egyptian* firstborn, followed by "Therefore." Is it possible that the firstborn belong to God not only because Israelite children were saved but also because Egyptian children were killed? This is thus an everlasting reminder in Israel at what cost Israel's firstborn were redeemed. The death of the firstborn of the Egyptians is thus not forgotten; it is seared on Israel's memory forever. (It is doubtful that child sacrifice is in view; see Plastaras, p. 159).

149

Exodus 13:17–22
Providence and Planning

This section consists basically of the narrator's report regarding the initial stages of the people's departure from Egypt; it is drawn from at least two sources. The focus is on God's leading (note the inclusio of *naḥah* ["lead"], vv. 17, 21). We lift up some aspects of that theme.

The narrator initially discloses a previously unreported conversation of God with Moses. This indirectness enables a stress on God as a subject of the leading, though in fact God uses nondivine agents in and through which to lead. God was concerned that Israel not take the most traveled route from Egypt to Canaan, lessening the chances of encountering hostile forces along the way. The divine concern is that the people might change their mind if forced into battle, even though they were equipped to some degree. God's concern is shown to be justified, given Israel's later reaction (14:10–12).

This divine concern for Israel is important in that it shows that God must take into account prevailing sociopolitical forces as well as people's emotional makeup in charting a way into the future. One might expect that God, with all the power at the divine disposal, would not back off from leading the people into any situation. God would just mow the enemies down! No, *the human situation makes a difference regarding God's possibilities* and hence affects the divine decisions. The exercise of divine power in providential activity is thus shown to be of such a nature that it could not ignore or override whatever obstacles might come along. Divine planning in view of such human circumstances is necessary, and so God's guiding hand leads Israel on a route that has less potential for difficulty. In fact, this divine concern suggests the possibility of failure; the people could decide to return to Egypt.

This shows that, for God as well as for people, planning for the future will make a difference with respect to the shape which that future will take. Divine providence is shown not to

150

stand over against careful planning; in fact, a careful consideration of future options will be important for the kind of providential activity God is able to employ. It is also clear in this passage
that God's leading is not independent of human involvement.
While God leads, Moses does too. Moses mediates the divine
guidance to the Israelite people.

Yet Moses is not the only instrument that God uses: a pillar
of cloud by day and a pillar of cloud by night. This is probably
one pillar, showing up differently during night and day, *in*
which God was present (see 14:24). It is constantly with Israel
throughout the wilderness narratives (see 14:19–20, 24; Num.
14:14). It anticipates God's revelatory activity (19:9, 16–18;
33:9–10; cf. Deut. 31:15) and God's dwelling among the people
in the tabernacle (see 40:34–38). Cloud and fire are associated
with the divine presence elsewhere in the Old Testament (I
Kings 8:11; Isa. 6:4–6). The nature of the phenomenon is not
clear, though a burning brazier held aloft at the head of the
caravan has been commonly suggested. It is clear that such
empirical phenomena were not necessary to accomplish the
task of divine guidance (cf. Gen. 28:15). The wilderness setting
and the people's situation were such that *a tangible assurance*
of the divine presence was believed necessary. Such phenomena impress the fact of God's presence upon all the people's
senses, not just their minds or spirits. The whole person experiences the presence of God.

This section contains a somewhat curious notice for the
modern reader. Moses took Joseph's coffin along on the exodus
journey. Joseph had made an agreement with his family that his
bones would be taken back to the promised land (Gen. 50:25–
26) and buried in a family grave site (Gen. 33:19). This interest
lifts up an important stage along the way toward the conclusion
reached in Josh. 24:32 (cf. Acts 7:16). Israel's sojourn in Egypt
had begun with a conflict among the sons of Jacob, resulting in
Joseph being sent to Egypt. Joseph became the one in and
through whom God preserved alive the remnant of Israel (see
Gen. 45:5–7; 50:20). Bringing his bones out of Egypt brings
closure to the Egyptian stage of Israel's life and provides a
symbol of the fact that what began with Joseph has now been
realized in a marvelous way: Israel has been preserved alive by
God's providential activity.

151

Exodus 14:1–31
The Sea Crossing

The story of the sea crossing is a text of considerable complexity. The song of the sea in chapter 15 is likely an early poetic form of the narrative in chapter 14, and the latter is an interweaving of at least three sources. While somewhat different versions of the crossing can be reconstructed, our interpretation is based on the final form of the passage. The section of verses 1–18, concerned with preparations, may be distinguished by the inclusio in verses 4 and 17–18: the divine hardening; God gaining glory over Pharaoh and all his host; the Egyptians "shall know that I am the LORD."

As noted in the introduction to 12:1—15:21, the narrative in chapter 14 is enclosed by liturgical material. The reader moves into this chapter with the refrain of God bringing Israel out of Egypt ringing in the ears (13:3–16). One moves away from it singing songs of joy for all that God has done. This serves to tie passover and sea crossing together as a two-sided divine act of deliverance (also combined in the confessional material of 18:1, 8–11). As with chapter 12, the effect of this redaction is to make chapter 14 as much liturgical event as historical event. When this understanding is combined with the source interweaving, the effect is a concatenation of images that, as with most liturgies, do not always sit easily with one another but provide a multifaceted look at the unfathomable divine deliverance. What we have finally is an *impressionistic picture* of the crossing that is not intended to be delineated in any precise way.

It may well be the case that, at an earlier point in the history of this tradition, the sea crossing was distinct from the exodus and considered the first of Israel's wilderness experiences (see at 12:37–51). But the effect of the liturgical redaction and concomitant theological considerations (plus such continuities as the conflict with Pharaoh and the hardening of his heart) is to combine passover and crossing into an event with two phases. Liberation from Egypt can finally be confessed only after free-

152

dom from Pharaoh is a reality. The Egypt-wilderness boundary does not finally define the distinction between exodus and wilderness traditions. At the same time, as often in Exodus, narratives function in anticipatory ways, here providing continuities between sea crossing and the wilderness journey.

From a theological perspective, *the two events keep redemption and creation firmly together.* The creation theme has been prominent throughout Exodus. It is the sea crossing that lifts up the cosmic side of the divine activity, bringing God's creational goals to a climax. It is only at the sea that the forces of chaos are decisively overcome and the world is reestablished on firm moorings. To use images from the Christian tradition, the present redaction keeps cross and resurrection together. It is not fortuitous that Exodus 15 is a long-standing Old Testament lesson for Easter Day. God's victory at the sea is not simply an event of local significance, vanquishing a historical enemy, however important. It is a cosmic victory. Without it, passover is only a partial victory and Israel's liberation from anticreation forces only as far-reaching as the next major body of chaotic waters it encounters on its journey.

This issue is related to the oft-discussed identification of *yam sup* (13:18; 15:4, 22), traditionally translated as Red Sea (literally it means "sea of reeds" or, better, "sea of the end"). For various reasons (including the absence of reeds in the Red Sea) it has become commonplace to identify the "sea of reeds" with one of the smaller bodies of water in the delta region. Yet, while this phrase is so used in the Old Testament, it also clearly refers to the Red Sea proper (I Kings 9:26; Jer. 49:21; cf. Exod. 23:31). This is an instance where historiographical considerations (where did it actually happen?) and the liturgical/cosmic context may come into conflict. While it may be that the actual crossing took place in the delta region, *the context is decisive for retaining the Red Sea translation* (cf. the creedal/liturgical use in Ps. 106:7, 9, 22; 136:13, 15; Neh. 9:9). Such a major body of water best serves as a vehicle for conveying the cosmic freight of God's victory. Moreover, the nature of liturgical language (also evident in some of the details of the crossing story) is such that the images and other features of the retelling are refined to sharpen its theological import.

153

In these events, the Egyptians are portrayed as moving from frenzied activity to the profound stillness of death on the seashore. The Israelites move from fear and doubt to stillness to faith and worship. God (through Moses) moves from quiet planning to sharply focused activity to being the object of Israel's praise.

Divine and Human Preparation (14:1–18)

The narrator uses eighteen verses to set up the event at the sea. It can be approached through a closer look at the major participants and their activity.

At the divine level, continuous with 13:17–22, the narrative emphasizes *God's strategizing*. God tells Moses to turn Israel back toward the sea, near certain places of unknown location. This entails, not a return to Egypt (14:11–12), but a different route on the wilderness side of the border. The reason (a change of plans?): it would appear to Pharaoh that the wilderness had entrapped the Israelites and he could be lured into a pursuit and himself be entrapped. Once again divine planning is in view. Not just any setting will do for what God is about. God takes into account the dynamics of the situation, including military possibilities and Egyptian strategies, in planning for the next stage of the conflict with Pharaoh.

What God sees as an entrapment possibility will not be accomplished with just military maneuvers, however. God will harden Pharaoh's heart so that his planned pursuit of the Israelites will be intensified. *God's stated purpose* is remarkable in that there is no mention of Israelite liberation. The focus is on what will happen *to God* and to the *Egyptians' relationship to God*. While Israel is the immediate object of the divine activity, God's purposes are more comprehensive. God will get glory (better, gain honor) over Pharaoh and his armies (see Ezek. 28:12). The objective is to bring the Egyptians, indeed the entire world, to the point of knowing that *Israel's* God is the Lord of all the earth (cf. 14:25). The word for gaining honor belongs to the same root as one of the hardening verbs *(kabed)*. Pharaoh's hardening leads to God's honoring.

The point of the wordplay is that the defeat of the Hitlerian oppressor will bring *public honor to God*. This public honor is specifically voiced in chapter 15. God's liberating action leads to hymns of praise before all the earth. The language of praise always entails both language *to* God (adoration) and language *about* God (witness). Praise is a public activity. Initially the praise comes from the Egyptians themselves: "The LORD fights for them" (14:25). Ironically, *the Egyptian praise becomes a theme for Israel's praise.* In turn, Israel's praise in public honor of God leads to the realization of the divine objective in all of these events: so that my name may be declared throughout all the earth (9:16). Without the praise, God's victory would not become known before the world. *God's goals are dependent on Israel's praise.*

At another level, Pharaoh and his army engage in frenzied preparations and fervent pursuit of the escaping Israelites. Every chariot (fourteen references in chaps. 14–15!) and every horse/horseman (twelve times), indeed the entire Egyptian army, is thrown into the fray. Egypt devotes its brightest and best to the chase. This is no minor military maneuver from the Egyptian perspective. Yet, given God's announced involvement (v. 4), the reader knows that all this bravado will finally be in the service of Israel's God and God's mission in the world.

Before God proceeds with the hardening of Pharaoh's heart (v. 8), Pharaoh is pictured as having already changed his mind (=heart). He knows what is finally at stake here, voicing the theme recurrent from the beginning of this struggle (1:13–14): Will Israel *serve* Pharaoh or someone else? God's hardening activity does not occur in a vacuum; it is not contrary to Pharaoh's (or the Egyptians', 14:17) own general will about the matter. God intensifies a well-ingrained proclivity (Noth, p. 111: "strengthened him in this resolve"; see excursus). In effect, God uses existent human stubbornness against itself by closing down available options. Pharaoh is already engaged in an extensive mustering of his troops. He spares no cost or effort. He takes up the headlong pursuit—note the repetition in verses 8–9—of the Israelites, who were marching on in confident disregard of his activity. The language of the Egyptian pursuit is echoed in the song of victory at the sea (see 15:9): their goal has now become destruction rather than simple capture.

Between these two powers planning and struggling for preeminence stand the Israelites in fear for their lives. They know more of Pharaoh's intent than of God's. Their response is described in words reminiscent of their time in bondage—they cry to the Lord. But their cry is now channeled through Moses, and it takes the form of a complaint. They accuse Moses of

155

ulterior motives: he has brought them out in the wilderness to die. For the first time we hear of earlier complaints made to Moses: they had asked to be left in bondage because they preferred to serve *(sic)* the Egyptians (cf. 5:21; 6:9). Such service is preferable to life between the devil and the deep blue sea. At such moments, the enemy seems so near; God seems so far away. Even in the aftermath of a grace-filled experience.

This is the first of many such "murmurings," as they have come to be called, which Israel often voices in the wilderness (see at 15:24). Yet the desire to stay in Egypt, and now the urgent pleas to return there, are typical for people who have gone through an extensive period of oppression (see Freire). This dispirited and just-released-from-slavery people does not need a word of condemnation from either commentators or Moses. Moses understands this and brings a word of pure gospel to them. As in the lament psalms, Moses speaks an *oracle of salvation* to a hurting people (see Ps. 12:5), making clear the divine plan in all of this. The use of the lament at this point stresses that Israel does not have the resources for its own deliverance; it must depend upon God alone.

Do not be afraid. This first word is one commonly spoken by God in theophanies (Gen. 26:24) or to those lamenting (Lam. 3:55–60). It is a word of assurance that one's worst fears will not be realized (see Deut. 20:3–4). God is present and at work on their behalf. It is a word that is heard at a later time by a suffering Israel (Isa. 41:10–14) and comes to shepherds abiding in the field with their flocks (Luke 2:10). For the people of God in one suffering situation after another this is a word of assurance. God is on their side, at work on their behalf. They need not be afraid.

Stand firm. The people are not to flee but to station themselves at the ready. Yet they are not to fight, as the word might suggest (see Jer. 46:4), nor are they to use their armaments (see 13:19). Rather, they are to stand ready to observe the salvation that *God* at the divine initiative will work for them (see II Chron. 20:17; Isa. 7:4). They need not worry about standing up to the Egyptian army. God is about to liberate Israel from the Egyptians forever. What God does will decisively affect their "seeing" (thrice in v. 14; twice in vv. 30–31). Their perspective will now be shaped by what God does, not by what the Egyp-

156

tians do. The view on their horizon will take the shape of freedom wrought by God rather than bondage.

Keep still. This is not a word asking that the people "not move a muscle." It is not a call for passivity, as if angels will now come and carry them across the sea (see 14:15). It is a word calling for silence. What the people might have to say, whether in lament or battle cry (see II Chron. 13:14–15), will have no bearing on what is about to happen. Neither Israel's words nor deeds will add to what God is effecting on their behalf (cf. Ps. 46, highly pertinent for this setting).

At the same time, Moses is given a central place as agent for the saving work of God (14:16, 21) and is given recognition for this in later tradition (Isa. 63:12). This does not in any way stand at odds with the tradition that speaks solely of the dividing of the waters as the work of God (see Ps. 78:13; Neh. 9:11). This dual involvement was announced initially by God (3:8, 10), and it is recognized as such by the people on the far side of the event (14:31). This is consonant with God's ways throughout the Scriptures and beyond, from those who preach and teach the word of God to those who preside over the sacraments. Salvation is no less the work of God because God uses human beings (or nonhuman entities such as the wind) as instruments in and through which to work.

Salvation. This theologically charged word *(yešu'ah)* is specifically related to deliverance from the Egyptians; so, the sociopolitical dimensions of the term are present. Yet the cosmic character of the event (see 15:1–21) means that its effects are much more comprehensive. Given the pervasive effect of oppression, salvation will affect not only who they are as human beings but the entire world of which they are a part. *Salvation is at once individual, corporate, and universal.*

The Lord will fight for you. The image of God as warrior or leader in battle is a theme present in both narrative and song (see 14:25; 15:3). While this is not an especially prominent theme in the Old Testament as a whole, it plays an appropriate role in this context (see at 15:3).

After such a clear statement on God's saving work the reader is not prepared for verse 15. Moses is scolded for conveying the people's cry to God. Many scholars suggest that this belongs more properly after verse 12. In any case, the force of the divine response is that this is not a time for Moses to bring such concerns before God. God is about to act in ways that will respond to the lament. Moses must lead, not complain: telling the people what to do and extending his hand/staff over the sea.

Through the Sea to Dry Land (14:19–31)

Pharaoh and his army are in hot pursuit; the people are anxiously waiting on events; Moses stands at the ready; God has decided what to do. The stage is set for the divine victory over the forces of chaos. After a brief look at some introductory matters, we will explore the themes of the sea crossing.

The combination of various sources provides a kaleidoscope of images: divine messengers, pillars of fire and cloud, alternating light and darkness, a strong east wind, the sea cleft in two, walls of water standing up and lying down, a dry sea canyon pathway, bogged-down Egyptian chariots, a lonely human hand twice stretched out, and a shore strewn with dead bodies. It is enough to make a movie mogul's mouth water.

The liturgical use of this material may be evident in Joshua 3—4, where the Red Sea/Jordan crossings are linked by a number of common themes (see 3:16–17; 4:22–24). The Jordan River may have been used as a site for a ritualized dramatic rendering of the Red Sea crossing. The historical basis for the detail of the account cannot be determined. Tidal movements in the delta region might be a factor. One could then speak of an unusual confluence of natural and historical possibilities of which God takes advantage. At the least, it has a basis in an escape of an Israelite group from Egyptian control, an event remembered as so exceptional that only an intensified form of the presence of God could adequately explain it. Once again liturgical interests and powerful storytelling skills combine to convey *an impressionistic picture.* Trying to sort it out in a literal fashion, or suggesting that Israel considered the detail to correspond precisely to reality, is like retouching Renoir's paintings to make them look like photographs.

The events at the sea begin with *a divine initiative;* the messenger of God *in* (cf. v. 24; 13:21; see at 3:1–6) the cloud pillar takes up a position between the people of Israel and the Egyptians. God thereby works in and through the *natural entities* of cloud and darkness. The effect of this is that Israel and

158

Egypt are separated from each other by a heavier than usual darkness during the night (cf. 10:21–29).

Events continue: God acts in and through *a human agent,* Moses stretching out his hand/staff over the sea, and a *natural entity,* a strong east wind blowing all night long (note the length of time it takes; it is not a divine snap of the finger; cf. 10:13, 19). The agencies that create the path through the sea are thus threefold—divine, human, and nonhuman—working in harmony with one another. As has been the case throughout the exodus narrative, God does not work alone; God works through the instrumentality of both human and nonhuman powers to accomplish the divine purpose.

The effect is *an act of creation.* Dry land appears in the midst of chaos, just as in Gen. 1:9–10 (cf. 8:13) at the separation of waters. The divine creative act in the sphere of nature serves as the vehicle for the creation of a liberated people (note also the birthing language—path through water). Creative activity in nature enables creative activity in history. What happens in nature creates new possibilities *for God* within the historical sphere. The work of God as *creator* effects the redemption of a people. The activities of God as creator and redeemer are here integrated. The result is not simply historical redemption but a new creation. It should not be forgotten that Moses is thus to be regarded as God's instrument in creation as well as in redemption. This is continuous with the "let us make" of Gen. 1:26, where creation is shown to be a dialogical act. The extension of dominion to the human in creation is here exemplified in a specific creative act.

This creative act prompts a twofold *human response.* On the one hand, under cover of darkness, the people of Israel walk through the sea on dry land. The people of Israel are thus not passive; it is an act of faith to walk through such a sea canyon. But faith is not thereby made into a work; it is the appropriation of a gift created quite apart from their own doing. On the other hand, the Egyptians follow Israel's lead into the newly created possibilities, with chariots and all. God's creative activity, however, makes for possibilities of judgment as well as redemption. The character of the human response shapes the nature of the participation in those new realities. The anticreation purposes 159 of the Egyptians, set on the subversion of the just order of God's world and the termination of life and blessing, place them in diametric opposition to what God has newly brought into being. But, even more, God has entered into the willfulness of their intent, driving their obduracy inexorably to their final ruin (see above). In relatively straightforward moral order talk, the Egyptians' anticreation activity turns the creation against them and they suffer at its hands. God is the broker of that moral order.

As the morning breaks for Israel, the night falls on the Egyptians. God cuts off the Egyptians' participation in the new creation. The dry land is turned into a quagmire. The brightest and best of the Egyptian military become bogged down in the effects of their own anticreationism. Terror-stricken, they suddenly realize that they are in over their heads, that a power is at work among the Israelites on behalf of the creation that can turn back their efforts. They voice a public confession regarding Israel's God: Yahweh fights for them. The Egyptians now know that Yahweh is God of all the earth (see 14:4, 18). Ironically, they provide imagery for Israel to voice its own hymnic praises (see at 15:3). This language is fundamentally liturgical and creational, portraying a struggle against the forces of chaos. It has its roots in the mythic divine battle against all that is anticreation.

As in opening up the sea, so in closing it down, God works in and through human and natural agencies. They are God's agents in creational judgment as much as in creational redemption. Moses stretches forth his hand/staff over the sea once again, the Jerichoan walls of water fall down, and the dry land disappears. The Egyptians take flight right into the returning waves. They drown in the midst of a chaos of their own making. Not one remained alive. As morning breaks, the sea is calm and the shore is covered with the Egyptian dead. Chaos, in all of its creational-historical manifestations, has been overcome. But Israel walked through the sea on dry land and was safely standing on the opposite shore. God is the victor. Israel is free. The created order is once again established.

When the people see the great work that God has done, they respond in a number of ways (cf. 4:31; 12:27): they revere Yahweh; they believe in Yahweh; they believe in Yahweh's servant Moses; and they sing a song of praise to God for the life and blessing that had become theirs this day. Somewhat unsettling is the fact that the same language of belief is used for Moses as well as for God. The one who serves as an instrument of God's word and action must be trusted as one who truly represents, indeed embodies, the God in whose name he speaks. This lifts up the extraordinary importance of the leader in the relationship between God and people. But it is God alone who is revered and worshiped and to whom Israel's doxologies are sung. Without such a response, the great deeds of God would have been without a voice in the world. God's goal, to have the divine name declared to all the earth (9:16; see Josh. 4:24), would have been set back. The importance of this witness is now given prominence with the insertion of the songs in chapter 15.

Exodus 15:1–21
A Cosmic Victory

This section consists of two hymnic pieces voicing praise and thanksgiving to God for deliverance from the Egyptians, both historically and cosmically conceived. It is important not to slight either the historical or the cosmic dimension of this victory. After some introductory matters, we consider the theme of thanksgiving and explore the implications of the pervasive creation theology in the song.

1. The *two songs of praise* (Moses and the people, vv. 1–18; Miriam, v. 21) are preceded by nearly identical references to the saving act of God on behalf of Israel (14:28–29; 15:19). This highlights the rhythm of salvation deed and song of praise. Structurally, the role given to women at the beginning of Exodus (including Miriam) is here returned to and provides an inclusio for Exodus 1—15. The importance of women for the story is thus given prominence once again. In terms of the history of tradition, the Song of Miriam likely came first and the Song of Moses is an expansion of this; but both are generally recognized as some of the oldest poetry in the Hebrew Bible. In terms of the present redaction, however, the Song of Miriam functions as an antiphon, serving to reinforce the thanksgiving voiced by the people as a whole.

161

Yet Miriam's response is not simply choral. Rita Burns *(Has the Lord Indeed Spoken Only Through Moses?)* has shown that the references to musical instruments and dancing in which "all the women" (see I Sam. 18:6–7) participate allude to a more complex ritual in which *the sea crossing is dramatically reactualized.* Verses 1–21 must be seen not as isolated songs from the past but as part of a larger liturgical whole, reflecting a regular dramatization of the crossing (see at 14:19–31). Hence, 15:1–21 constitutes a parallel to the passover texts, and the two form an inclusio for the larger unit, 12:1—15:21. The stories associated with both passover and sea crossing are thus enclosed within liturgical texts. When such usage is combined with the poetic form, the result is that the images associated with the events are even more impressionistic than those in chapter 14. Attempts to reconstruct the detail of the event from this type of material are doomed to fail.

The content of the liturgical material in 15:1–21 is more wide-ranging than in chapter 14. It is often thought that it moves from sea crossing (vv. 1–12) to anticipations of the land settlement and the establishment of God's abode in Canaan— more likely than Mt. Zion (vv. 13–18). This is a natural extension in view of earlier texts regarding the land promise (3:8, 17; 6:8; 12:25; 13:5, 11). Moreover, we have noted that a number of passages link the sea crossing with that of Jordan (note the "passing over" in 15:16; Josh. 4:22–24; Ps. 114). Verses 1–18 may reflect this more comprehensive dramatic actualization of constitutive events of Israel's past.

2. We have noted that all of Exodus 1—15 is patterned according to a distress, lament, divine word and deed, song of praise structure: the oppression and cries of distress (chaps. 1—2); God's response in word (3:1—7:7) and deed (7:18—14:31); and the praise (chap. 15). This pattern is also present in its basic contours in chapters 14—15. The fearful people speak the lament (14:10–12); Moses proclaims the oracle of salvation (14:13–14); the deed of salvation follows; and the people respond with praise. The various historical recitals are also outlined in these basic terms (e.g., Deut. 26:5–11; Josh. 24:3–13), as are comparable songs in the Psalter (e.g., Ps. 32; 34). Even the prose/poetry structure, with need, lament, and word/deed of salvation in prose followed by thanksgiving in poetry, is not uncommon (Judg. 4—5; I Sam. 1—2; Jonah 1—2; Isa. 38). Claus Westermann *(Elements of Old Testament Theology* [Atlanta: John Knox

Press, 1982]) has shown that this pattern is basic to Israel's understanding of its history with God.

Characteristic of this structure is that what God has done is not rehearsed in independence from the specifics of the human situation. The acts of God on Israel's behalf are emphasized, but they are *not isolated from human experience.* Very specific human needs have been expressed to which God responds quite directly. Thus, as in this text, God does not respond to human oppression of a sociopolitical sort by ignoring those realities in the shape which God's salvation takes. God's saving acts are directly respondent to expressed creaturely need.

The songs themselves are the product of a new experience, an experience of *both* God and people as liberator and liberated. This is a new moment for God as much as for the people; God has never been such a liberator before. There is here an interresponsiveness of God and people to the reality of each other's experience. And so, just as God out of God's own experience of suffering (3:7) has responded to Israel's experience of oppression, so Israel from the midst of its own experience of freedom responds to *God's* experience as liberator.

Hence God's salvific deed is *not isolated from human response* to that divine experience. While God's work is central, the human response is not incidentally reported. If there were no human response, what God has done would not become known; it would be like a rock falling in the sea. The human response makes a difference to God (see below). That response has five facets in chapters 12—15: The people *(a)* fear Yahweh and believe in him; *(b)* believe in his servant Moses; *(c)* sing praises; *(d)* engage in rituals—passover, unleavened bread, redemption of firstborn; and *(e)* retell the story of what God has done.

This human response to what God has done has *a multidirectional character.* Response is directed to *(a)* God: faith, trust, and thanksgiving; *(b)* Israel's leadership: trust in Moses; *(c)* Israelite generations yet to come: retelling the story and reappropriating its saving power within various aspects of worship and religious commitment; and *(d)* the wider world: witness through acts of praise. The center of attention in this chapter is praise and thanksgiving, which encompasses matters from both *(a)* and *(d)* and implies *(c)*.

163

The Song of Thanksgiving constitutes praise to the God who has delivered Israel from bondage and established them in their land. As praise, it functions both as adoration and as witness, as an honoring of God and as a witness about God before all the world (see Ps. 119:171–172; Patrick D. Miller, Jr., *Interpreting the Psalms* [Philadelphia: Fortress Press, 1986]). The psalms often reinforce this double aspect of Israel's praise. Gratitude to God is directed not only to God, as important as that is; it is also to be expressed in the presence of others (see Ps. 22:22; 109:30). Gratitude is giving testimony to others regarding what God has done (Ps. 66:16; 34:11; 40:9–10). Indeed, the whole world is in view as the object of such witness (Ps. 57:9; 18:49; 22:27; 96:1–3).

Praise as glorification of God harks back to 14:4, 17–18, where God speaks of gaining honor over Pharaoh and his army. But God's gaining honor is not rooted in a divine self-centeredness, as if the glorification of God were a matter of God's basking in the applause of Israel. Thanksgiving to God is not fundamentally a matter of God taking everlasting curtain calls from an eternally grateful people. One gives honor to God, not in response to a command, but because "it is meet and right" so to do. Even more, praise and thanksgiving are finally a matter of witness before all the world. The purpose of all of God's activity remains that which was articulated in 9:16: "so that my name may be declared throughout all the earth" (on this purpose for the exodus, see also Lev. 26:45; Ps. 106:8; Isa. 63:12; Ezek. 20:9, 22; Neh. 9:10). Together then, the reasons for praise relate specifically to God for what God has done and then to God's relationship to those who do not (yet) honor Yahweh. The one always entails the other.

To speak of thanksgiving as magnifying God is to speak of that which increases God's power and renown. This means that God himself is affected by the praise, not simply those who speak praise or respond to it. God is "enthroned on the praises of Israel" (Ps. 22:3); it makes a difference to God that God is praised. For this means that God's name or reputation is enhanced within the world. What God has done reverberates throughout the earth, calling attention to this God's identity, and all that God is about in the world. *Praise enhances the attractiveness of God.* People outside the community of faith

164

may be drawn to this God when they hear all that has been done.

This larger world is clearly in view in Exodus 15. According to verse 14, the peoples of the world have already heard; the word has gotten around quickly indeed. It is as if the praise articulated in the opening verses spreads like wildfire and those who have heard can be incorporated into the song before it is finished! The reputation of Israel's God goes out ahead of Israel like a veritable pillar of smoke and fire. The Philistines, the Moabites, the Edomites, and the Canaanites are specifically mentioned (vv. 14–15). They are so impressed by the news that they can only stand by, struck dumb, as the people of God journey to take control of the promised land (v. 16). While their reaction is largely one of fear and dismay when faced with Israel's God, we will also hear in chapter 18 that the word is received as good news by Jethro.

What have the peoples of the world heard that occasions this response? The word "heard" is, of course, not shaped simply by the external features of the event. The language used to speak of the event shapes the interpretation and hence the actual experience of what happens. A simple report of a group of slaves escaping from Egypt would have put the fear of God in few, if any. But if that escape is interpreted in terms of the worldwide purposes of a Creator God who is about the business of setting a chaotic, oppressive world straight, then all perpetrators of injustice might well melt away. Only such an interpretation makes it clear *what actually happened* at the sea. What happened cannot finally be determined by the tools of historiography. The eyes of faith claim to see a greater depth *in the event itself.* The song insists that the Creator God is the decisive factor in the event, and hence *only when one hears the interpretation does one know fully what in fact one has experienced.* It is thus the event *so interpreted* that makes the word such a powerful word as it makes its way from mouth to mouth across the world.

Central to this word is what God has done to the Egyptians (v. 4). To be noted, however, is that this is the only verse in which Egypt is specifically mentioned. One can still read the Egyptians into the enemy (vv. 6–7, 9), the sea (vv. 5, 8, 10, 12), and "them" (vv. 5, 10, 12). Yet, especially in view of verses

165

13–16, the praise of what God has done has been extended rhetorically beyond Egypt to be able to be applied more generally to God's activity. The language used is typical of other hymnic pieces: God is one who shatters enemies, overthrows adversaries, and consumes the opposition in wrath. The more general language of divine activity predominates: man of war, power, strength, right hand, arm, greatness, majesty, holiness, fury, terrible, glorious deeds, wonders, guidance, redemption, steadfast love. Leave verse 4 aside, and what God has done could be made generally applicable to God's work everywhere. This is a Creator God who is at work in this way all over the world. No wonder the other nations are trembling.

An additional contribution to this worldwide perspective is the use of the *mythic pattern of chaos:* its conquest by God, issuing in the creation, the building of a sanctuary and the divine enthronement (see Miller, *The Divine Warrior,* pp. 113–117; Cross, pp. 112–144). It is clear from a variety of Old Testament texts that this language was explicitly used to speak of the sea crossing. For example:

> Was it not you who cut Rahab in pieces,
>   who pierced the dragon?
> Was it not you who dried up the sea,
>   the waters of the great deep;
> who made the depths of the sea a way
>   for the redeemed to cross over? (Isa. 51:9–10)

> You divided the sea by your might;
>   you broke the heads of the dragons in the waters.
> You crushed the heads of Leviathan;
>   you gave him as food for the creatures of the
>   wilderness.
>   (Ps. 74:13–14, NRSV)

In addition, see Ps. 18:15; 77:15–20; 106:9; 114:3–5; Isa. 63:12–13 (cf. Job 26:12–13; Ps. 89:9–10). Especially noteworthy are texts that identify the chaos monster with Pharaoh/Egypt: Ezek. 29:3–5; 32:2–8; Ps. 87:4 (cf. 89:10); Isa. 30:7 (cf. 27:1); Jer. 46:7–8. Egypt is considered a historical embodiment of the forces of chaos, threatening to undo God's creation.

This mythic pattern is clearly evident in chapter 15, though the later merging of chaos/Egypt language has not always been recognized as fully present. Part of the problem has been an unnecessary disjunction between historical and mythological realities. The Egyptian enemy is certainly historical, but just as certainly more is involved. The Egyptians are also represented as metahistorical in that *the chaotic forces of the world are concentrated there.* We have seen throughout the commentary how they represent anticreational forces. The absence of names for the pharaohs is but one small sign of this larger issue. The references to the divine judgment on Israel's gods show that the enemy and the battle are cosmic in scope (12:12; 15:11). As will be noted, traditional weapons will not succeed against such an enemy (this is also why Israel does not fight).

We shall see below that the forces God uses in the defeat of the Egyptians are nonhistorical (though they have a historical effect). It is God as creator who is fundamentally at work here. It is God the Creator who heaps up the waters and covers the Egyptians with floods, whose winds blow and whose earth (=underworld?) swallows them up, and who thereby *creates* a people (the verb in v. 16 is *qanah;* cf. NEB; Deut. 32:6; Ps. 74:2; Gen. 14:19–22). While the language of chaos may be more passive here than elsewhere, verse 8 is likely understood as a subduing of chaos, in the sense of bringing it under control to be used by Yahweh (cf. Ps. 18:15—God's anger is explicit here—a simple reference to wind will not do; 33:7). And then, in *manifest irony,* it is pressed into God's service (vv. 4–5, 10, 12) against this embodiment of chaos, Pharaoh and his host. At the behest of God, chaos swallows up its own! (as at 7:12).

The implications of this are theologically significant. Most basically, it demonstrates that the language of creation is drawn on to speak of Israel's liberation from Egypt. Historically, given the age of the text, this means that an already existent creation theology provides the most basic fund of images to speak of the meaning of these events. Redactionally, much the same thing must be said. We have seen in no little detail the degree to which creation thought pervades the early chapters of Exodus. The God portrayed has been powerfully active in the realm of nature, primarily in the stories of the multiplication of the Israelites and the plagues, and fundamentally concerned about the anticreation practices of Egypt. It is this God who delivers Israel at the sea; it is no wonder that creational categories are used to portray it. This is not to say that the events themselves do not

167

contribute important new dimensions to this existent theology. They do. The interpreter must attend to both historical and cosmic dimensions.

In a fundamental way this means that what happens at the sea is to be immediately placed in a universal framework (and is made no less particular thereby). While the mythic pattern accomplishes this, it simply provides a capstone to the imagery seen to be so dominant in the text to this point. Simple historical or redemptive (or even "typological") categories cannot, in themselves, provide such a universal perspective. Only a creation theology can do this. *It is precisely because what happens here is cosmic that it has universal effects.*

Hence all of Israel's future enemies between the sea and the fulfillment of God's promise "melt away" (vv. 13–16). After the victory at the sea, such conflicts are already settled and Israel has its land. Moreover, the enthronement of God in the promised land is an accomplished fact *already at the sea* (vv. 17–18). God *from this victory onward* "reigns forever and ever." Verses 13–18 do not look forward to the future (the tenses are best translated as past; see NRSV; NEB); there is a kind of "realized eschatology" in place here. At the historical level, of course, there are events yet to take place between the sea and the land. But that is not the basic point in this text.

Michael Fishbane's comments are helpful here (*Biblical Interpretation in Ancient Israel* [New York: Oxford University Press, 1985], p. 357):

> To the degree that the routing of the enemies and evil ones of Israel's history is typologically presented as a reactualization of a primordial cosmic event, historical redemption becomes a species of world restoration and the dynamics of history reiterate creative acts of divine power. Inevitably the status of the historical is profoundly affected. This is not to imply that the events in question lose their concrete historical facticity.... The mythic configuration of divine combat and victory provide the symbolic prism for disclosing the primordial dynamics latent in certain historical events (like the exodus), and so generate the hope for their imminent recurrence.

It is from *within* this sphere of understanding that the *"divine warrior"* references must be interpreted (15:3; actually the metaphor is simply warrior, "man of war," not "God of war"—an important difference). One must go to the mythic

168

pattern to elucidate its meaning more than to holy war traditions. There are continuities between the latter and these texts (see Plastaras, pp. 172–182), but they are theologically secondary (the degree to which the holy war is also mythic is left aside here). This is so because the effects are cosmic, not simply historical. The historical victory is real *because it participates in the cosmic victory.*

Hence, in interpreting "warrior," one must note that not a single instrument of human warfare is mentioned (or in chap. 14; see Ps. 20:7; Isa. 31:1–3). The sword that Pharaoh draws (v. 9) is not opposed by another sword; the chariot that he rides (v. 4) is not met by another chariot; the army that he leads (v. 4) clashes with no human fighting force. But the defeat of the Hitlerian horde is total. It is only at this point, and the strength it takes (of which "hand" and "arm" are metaphors—also used in mythological contexts, cf. Isa. 51:9), that the war analogy holds. Given the degree to which we associate war with armaments and bodily clashes, one wonders whether we can recover the warrior metaphor for today in any helpful way (see Terence E. Fretheim, *Deuteronomic History* [Nashville: Abingdon Press, 1983], pp. 68–75).

Yet God does not accomplish this defeat in an unmediated way. The divine instruments are *not* historical, however; they are entirely from the natural order: wind, sea, floods, waters, deep, earth (cf. Judg. 5:20–21; Josh. 10:11–13; I Sam. 7:10; Isa. 29:6; 30:30; to the degree that Moses acts in chap. 14, his hands carry no weapon). We have noted that the Egyptian enemy is metahistorical in that the chaotic forces of the world are concentrated there. To use Martin Luther King's language: "Egypt symbolized evil in the form of humiliating oppression, ungodly exploitation, and crushing domination" (*Strength to Love* [Philadelphia: Fortress Press, 1981], p. 73). Against such an enemy, traditional weapons will not do (cf. Isa. 59:17; Eph. 6:10–20). God fights the chaos monster with "weapons" appropriate to the enemy, as in the plague cycle, from within the sphere of nature. God's activity *in creation* overturns that which is chaos. God's control over the waters (see Job 41) is shown in the divine use of those very forces to undo the anticreation monster. The justice of God's created order exacts an appropriate judgment on the anticreational oppressors (see at plagues).

As a consequence, the morning light breaks through the

169

darkness, the people walk on dry land, God's just order is vindicated, and a new creation (v. 16) emerges into the brightness of a new day. It is called redemption (v. 13) because it is the *re*establishment of the created order of justice at a specific time and place (hence the importance of law for Exodus; cosmic order and social order are symbiotically related). God brings the broken creation back into alignment at one historical spot in the world. God's redemptive acts are for the purposes of a new creation, a creation that is already taking on flesh and blood. God reigns forever and ever, not just over Israel (or over the nations, historically speaking), but *in the midst of Israel over the entire cosmos.*

PART FIVE

The Wilderness Wanderings

EXODUS 15:22—18:27

Introduction: Life as an Adolescent

The wilderness wanderings, or at least their length and breadth, were a surprise to Israel. Instead of a land of milk and honey, they get a desert. The promise falls short. Deliverance at the sea leads into the godforsaken wilderness. Dancers and singers are stopped dead in their tracks. Salvation from one kind of death leads into the teeth of another. The sea crossing seems but a point of unreal exhilaration between one kind of trouble and another, only the last is certainly worse than the first. Bondage with security and resources seems preferable to freedom and living from one oasis to another. The wilderness is a place betwixt and between (see Cohn).

And the wilderness seems permanent. Forty years is a long time in the old sandbox. Even that grand mountaintop experience at Sinai looks like a one-time thing: it is out of the wilderness only to be led right back in. The wilderness is beginning to look a lot like home. What does it mean for God to create a people out of those who are no people, the grandest of all creative acts, only to leave the rest of their world in chaos? The experience of order leads immediately into disorder, freedom becomes anarchy. Into the jaws of the wilderness, where demons howl and messiahs are tempted, where familiar resources are taken away . . . . Lifelessness seems to be the only order on which one can depend. The journey from the Red Sea to the

171

promised land is littered with freshly dug graves, and not a single birth is recorded.

Wilderness is life beyond redemption but short of consummation; but the former seems ineffective and the latter only a mirage. The promise has been spoken, but who can live by words alone? The hope has been proclaimed, but the horizon keeps disappearing in the sandstorms. And so trust in God often turns to recalcitrance and resentment. Faith erodes with the dunes. Commandments collapse into the disorder that shapes daily life. And judgment is invited in to share one's tattered tent.

Yet even in the wilderness God is responsive to the needs of these complaining people. God provides what the context cannot. The protests are answered, the cries are heard, quite undeservedly. Deliverance comes, but not in being removed from the wilderness. A table is spread in the very presence of the enemy (cf. Ps. 23:5). There is a gift of food where the resources are only ephemeral. There is a gift of water where only rocks abound. There is a gift of healing where the pain never ends. The movement from death to life occurs *within* the very experience of godforsakenness. Death is transformed into life from *within* a death-filled context. A sanctuary is provided, but in the wilderness.

Deuteronomy 2:7 proclaims: "These forty years the LORD your God has been with you; you have lacked nothing." Surely this is a delusion, a late pious endeavor to cover up the realities of that meandering trek through the desert. The desert in such a view is not only painted, it is whitewashed. The disciples of such poppycock are legion. Or are they? Only if they neglect the fact that the complaints from the wilderness are genuine indeed. Only if they neglect the fact that true life must always be shaped by the wilderness, even for those who are living in the promised land. Only if they neglect the fact that God's own life has been decisively shaped by that same wilderness.

Hence, although the people are often ungrateful and disloyal, the divine blessing and graciousness pervade the narrative. Israel's time in the wilderness is finally shaped by God's incredible patience and mercy and the divine will to stay with Israel in this time of their adolescence as children of God. Coping with "teenagers" is no easy task, even if the parent is God (cf. Hos. 6:4). No divine flick of the wrist is capable of straighten-

172

ing them out without compromising their freedom. If God wants a mature child, the possibility of defiance must be risked. Parent and child even do a certain amount of "testing" of each other. God will not compromise in holding Israel to high standards—for the sake of the creation. And so God works through their feelings of abandonment and helplessness, their words of complaint and acts of rebelliousness, and their need for reassurance, protection, a new self-identity, and non-oppressive life structures. God sticks by them through it all. God has made promises to this people, and God is a promise-keeper. Only in Numbers will it become clear that the process of maturation takes longer than a single generation.

Tradition History. The Pentateuch preserves two blocks of literarily composite materials on the wilderness journeys, before Sinai (Exod. 15:22—18:27) and after (Num. 10:11—36: 13). It is common to claim that two different versions of the relationship between Yahweh and Israel in the wilderness are preserved, positive and negative, with the positive early and negative late (Noth). It is more likely that a corporate negative picture was present from the beginning, though it intensified in time (Childs). Yet one must stress that the wilderness traditions are used in various ways, depending on the interests and needs of the moment. Hence the emphasis could be placed on divine action (Ps. 136:16; Amos 2:10), or on the murmuring (Deut. 9:7–29; Ps. 78:14–54; 95:8–11; 106:13–23; Ezek. 20), or be quite balanced (Neh. 9:12–21) or positive (Deut. 32:10–14; Jer. 2:2–3; Hos. 2:14–15).

Childs (pp. 258–259) discerns two patterns in these texts, determined largely by the nature of the people's murmuring. Pattern 1 (e.g., 15:22–25; 17:1–7) focuses on a genuine need which calls forth complaint; pattern 2 (only after Sinai, e.g., Num. 11:1–3; 21:4–9) centers on murmuring "without a basis in genuine need," with divine judgment being present only in the latter. In time, these patterns influenced each other, with the differences being leveled to some degree.

This division, however, is not entirely a happy one, not least because certain texts follow neither pattern, for example, Exodus 16; Num. 16:1–35. Other factors better explain some of the differences, for example, Exodus 32—34 explains the new reality of forgiveness. It is best to speak of a single basic pattern that evolved as the stories were transmitted and as the Pentateuch

173

was developed, including the "splitting" of the wilderness narratives before and after the golden calf debacle. Hence the following structure is suggested, with items 3 and 4 present only in post-Sinai narratives.

1. Journey—Exod. 15:22; 16:1; 17:1; Num. 10:33a; 20:1; 21:4
2. Need/Murmuring—Exod. 15:23–24; 16:2–3; 17:2–3; Num. 11:1a, 4–6; 14:2–4; 16:3, 12–14; 16:41; 20:4–5; 21:4–5
3. Judgment—Num. 11:1, 19–20, 33–34; 14:11–12, 26–35; 16:20, 45–47; 21:6
4. Repentance—Num. 11:2; 14:40; 21:7; cf. 16:22
5. Intercession—Exod. 15:25; 17:4; Num. 11:2; 14:13–19; 16:48; 20:6; 21:7 Disputation—Exod. 16:6–8; Num. 14:6–9; 16:5–7
6. Deliverance—Exod. 15:25; 16:4, 12; 17:5–6; Num. 11:2; 14:20; 16:50; 20:10–11; 21:8–9

The effort to trace Israel's wilderness journey historically has complicated many scholarly discussions of these texts. No agreement has been reached in spite of much textual interest in the stopping places (see at 17:1; Num. 33). Hence the traditional site for Mt. Sinai at Jebel Musa in the southern part of the Sinai Peninsula is usually maintained. The special concern for specifying the stages along the way to and from Sinai may reflect a later dramatization of the wilderness trek in Israel's worship life.

Wilderness and Sinai. A number of texts in the wilderness narratives refer to Sinai or post-Sinai realities. A straightforward historical perspective can only term them anachronistic. Their frequency, however, suggests that they serve a particular narrative purpose. The major items besides references to Sinai itself (17:6, 9; 18:5; cf. 19:2) are (1) Keeping statutes and ordinances (15:25b–26; 16:28; 18:16, 20). (2) The glory of Yahweh (16:7, 10; cf. 24:16; 40:34–35). (3) The sabbath (16:23–29; cf. 20:8; 31:12–17). (4) The "testimony" and other references to a pre-Sinai sanctuary (16:33–34; 18:7, 12, 19; cf. 25:16). (5) Holy war (17:8–16; see Deut. 20:1–20). (6) The judiciary (18:21–26; see Deut. 16:18–20; 17:8–13).

174   What does it mean for these matters to be integral to the story of Israel's life prior to Sinai? They subvert any attempt to

read the narrative in a straightforward chronological or historical manner. It may be that this is no more than a foreshadowing of things to come; yet the explicitness suggests otherwise. Their presence may show that they are part of a larger liturgical use to which this material was put. Whatever may be the case, their pre-Sinai usage serves to show that there are significant continuities between Sinai and pre-Sinai Israelite life. *Sinai is not a radical departure in terms of God's ways of relating to Israel.* Even more, it may show that certain aspects of the ordered life of community are rooted, not in special revelation, but in creation.

Wilderness and Plagues. We have seen in the plague cycle how the created order was adversely affected by the anticreational policies of the Egyptians. In the wilderness stories, however, just the opposite happens; the natural order springs into new life. God's cosmic victory affects positively the very created order of things. These parallels are evident:

1. 15:22–27. The result of the first plague was that "they could not drink the water" (7:24). Now, when "they could not drink the water" (15:23), the bitter water is made sweet and potable. In fact, the wilderness is filled with springs of water (15:27; cf. 17:6). This too will be the cosmic effect of a later divine victory: "For waters shall break forth in the wilderness, and streams in the desert; the burning sand shall become a pool, and the thirsty ground springs of water" (Isa. 35:6–7; 41:17–18; 43:19–23; 48:21; 49:10).

2. 16:1–36. Whereas in the seventh plague God "rained" hail upon Egypt, which destroyed the food sources (9:18, 23), here God "rains" bread from the heavens (16:4). Rain and food become indistinguishable (see Deut. 11:11–17). In the eighth plague, locusts "came up" and "covered" the land (10:14–15), destroying plants and fruit trees. In 16:13, quails "came up" and "covered" the camp, providing food. In the Numbers (Num. 11:31) parallel to this story, the wind brings quail rather than locusts (Exod. 10:13).

3. 17:1–7. Here the "staff with which [Moses] struck the Nile" (v. 5) brings water for the people to drink rather than making all the water in the Nile unfit to drink.

4. 17:8–16. Here the "staff of God" is used against the Amalekites, whose destructive ways toward Israel were compa-

175

rable to that of the Egyptians (cf. Deut. 25:18). God will continue to judge all those who would cut off the blessings of God's
creative work.

In the wilderness stories God's cosmic victory is made evident in that the natural order provides for life and blessing
rather than deprivation and destruction. At the same time,
these signs of the new creation that God has wrought are related to the shape of Israel's life. Whether or not "the diseases
[=plagues] of Egypt" (see Deut. 28:27) happen to Israel will
depend on Israel's obeying the voice of God (15:26). Moral
order affects cosmic order universally. Moreover, while God's
cosmic victory is real, external threats still exist to the fledgling
new creation (e.g., the Amalekites); so God must exact Egypt-
like judgments to keep that creation intact.

This approach may help to explain why the stories of water,
manna, and quail are repeated in Numbers 11 and 20, especially when combined with the debacle of Exodus 32. The issue
after the "fall" of Exodus 32 is God's ongoing relationship, not
only to Israel, but to the larger created order. The continuing
natural provisions in Numbers testify to the continuing creational effects of God's cosmic victory.

Exodus 15:22–27
Obedience and Healing

This first story of the wanderings is brief, but its concerns
mirror many a story to follow: a problem arises; people complain; Moses intercedes; God responds with deliverance. But
added to this story is a (deuteronomic?) statement that lays out,
right at the beginning of Israel's post-exodus experience, God's
expectations for the shape of its daily life. It is not enough for
the people of God to sing; they must also listen to their God and
follow the divine leading. We consider especially the nature of
the deliverance, the understanding of obedience, and God as a
healer.

176

The transition from 15:21 to this section is very sharp. Israel's singing was still reverberating across the desert sands. But
within hours there is a major problem: no water to drink. Songs

of praise quickly turn to the complaining heard earlier (14:10–12). Forty years will prove to be a long time at this rate! God responds to Moses' prayer by directing him to a piece of wood (or branch), though the narrator reports no conversation. Moses throws the piece of wood into the bitter water. The wood sweetens the water. The crisis passes, at least for a while. And the people move on to a place with "twelve springs," one for each tribe.

The narrator's report of God's activity is remarkably minimal: God responds to Moses by showing him a piece of wood. But that speaks volumes. One observes a high level of *divine responsiveness,* both to Moses' prayer and to the people's need. God is immediately engaged in the situation, though not in independence of Moses' prayer, and provides a means *for Moses* to resolve the difficulty from the world of nature.

At the same time, the reader ought not heighten God's work beyond what the text says. To speak of miracle is to violate the passage. The implication is that God assumes that Moses knows what to do with the piece of wood and that the wood has certain properties that enable it to sweeten water (the bark and the leaves of some trees have such capacities). God is here working in and through human knowledge and the "healing" properties of certain elements of the natural order. God's providence is shown in leading Moses to *help that is already available in the world of creation.* It is noteworthy that one element of the natural order is used to put right another element from that order. The righting of a creational disorder accompanies the blessing for people. As we have seen in the introduction to this section, this is a positive parallel to the first plague. God's cosmic victory has creational effects.

A survey of the history of medicine and horticulture and the work of naturalists and other caretakers of nature would bring to the surface many similar incidents. The force of the biblical testimony is that God is the creator and has made the natural order in such a way that it has capacities such as this. Moreover, the text suggests that human beings need to be alert to the potential resources within creation itself for resolving many such problems. God is at work in the world in such a way that people are led to such discoveries. Most people today would ascribe them solely to scientific achievement. The biblical testimony, however, is that God is never absent from such endeav-

177

ors. But God does not do such work in independence from human questing, knowledge, imagination, and ingenuity. God's "healing" is not an unmediated divine activity. God makes use of what is available in the world to accomplish that which is right and good. Persons of faith should be more willing and open to speak of God's involvement in and through the use of human and natural capabilities. Even more, sensitivity to God's leading may lead to even more profound discoveries. God is always working for good in everything.

Ground Rules for the Journey

Verses 25b–26 seem to be related to the events of verses 22–25a, though this is never made explicit. It is not even intimated that Israel's lament constituted a failure to give heed to God's commandments. But, apparently, in view of this experience, it is anticipated that this could become a problem in the future (see 17:1–7). Thus, verse 26 is *a preventive measure;* it sets out guidelines for the shape of life beyond deliverance. Freedom from service to Pharaoh does not issue in an "anything goes" world for Israel. Israel is freed from Pharaoh for service to God. At the beginning of this new journey with God this is now made crystal clear. God's word to Israel is not casual advice, concerning which a take it or leave it attitude may be adopted. The giving of any word by God is assumed to be in the people's best interests, indeed, those of the entire creation; that word will always be on behalf of life and well-being. Hence obedience is in service of God's creational purposes. Even more, these purposes are at stake in Israel's obedience. This text amounts to *a sharing of the ground rules for the journey.* They are now known by all involved. Unlike some persons in authority, God does not keep these to himself.

The reference to testing or proving them "there" probably refers to the "statute and ordinance" (an instance of hendiadys) of the following verse. The "if you hearken . . . do . . . give heed . . . and keep" provides, not a specific law, but *a general guideline* by which Israel's relationship with God can be tested or shown to be true. Obedience is a way of exhibiting trust in the God who speaks the word. This is a perspective similar to that formulated in I John 2:3–4: "By this we may be sure that we know him, if we keep his commandments. He who says, 'I know

178

him' but disobeys his commandments is a liar, and the truth is not in him" (see John 10:6, 7, 10, 14; I John 3:19–24). Proving is an important matter for both God and Israel. Heeding God's commandments becomes a means whereby God "may be sure" that Israel will walk according to the word of God. It assumes, as 16:4 (see also at 20:18–21) will show, that God does not finally know until Israel actually responds to a given commandment. It also provides for a certain discipline for Israel, whereby walking in all of God's ways can in time become second nature, whereby obedience can become a way of life, naturally in tune with the created order of things.

It is not assumed here that there is already a body of commandments for Israel; it refers, rather, to any and all statutes that God may put forward as time goes on. It anticipates in particular God's later giving of the law in chapters 20—23 (see at 19:5). Both that law and the instance in the following story are described in proving terms (16:4; 20:20; cf. 17:2, 7). Also, this passage shows that *the giving of the law at Sinai is not something new* in the God-Israel relationship. God's law is given to Israel in at least two ways. There are those statutes which cut across life situations and are given as a body (chaps. 20—23); there are also those commandments which emerge in connection with very specific life situations. It is the latter that will be lifted up for Israel in the stories that follow. Hence, when the law is given at Sinai, Israel will know that that law does not exhaust what it means to do the will of God in its life. *Sinai fits into a God-Israel relationship in which obedience is already an integral component.* Consequently, Israel will need to be attentive to the will of God in every life situation, knowing that the body of law given at Sinai may not speak directly to the issue at hand. This is, of course, what the people of God in every age are called to do.

To speak of *God as healer* (physician) has reference both to the sweetening of the water—did the water cause illness?—(cf. II Kings 2:21–22; Ezek. 47:8) and to the immediately prior word about diseases. Ethical order and cosmic order are integrally related. God's not putting Egypt's diseases on Israel, if the people are obedient, sounds more like a threat than a promise: if you do not obey, I *will* put these diseases on you (this is stated in Deut. 28:27, 35, with the word that God will *not* heal, cf. v. 60). One almost expects the phrase "for I am your judge." But

179

the final clause, "for I am the LORD, your healer," takes the edge off the negative aspect and points the way to a more positive interpretation (see 23:25; Deut. 7:15).

The conditionality of the sentence is more matter-of-fact in nature: if you obey the speed laws, I will not give you a ticket. To use a more exact parallel in substance, if not in form: if you obey the speed laws, it is less likely that you will be injured in a car accident. The basic concern is for Israel's well-being. The negative possibility is, of course, explicit, but that is not what motivates the speaker. The God who speaks is most fundamentally a healing God, not a judging God.

Behind this kind of talk is Israel's understanding of the moral order. Being inattentive or in blatant disregard of the moral order, often embodied in commandments, will often (though not inevitably, given the loose causal weave) lead to negative consequences in life. To say that God will "put" diseases (or plagues; note the parallels in the introduction to this section) is to say, in effect, that God will function as judge. Given the connections between moral order and cosmic order, violations in the former will likely have effects in the latter, as the plagues have just shown. This is also sharply stated in 23:25, where bread, water, and healing are closely tied to Israel's loyalty to God. If the God who is healer becomes judge, that healing power will not be as available, and one is opened up to negative possibilities. To speak of God as healer is to speak of the work of God as creator, one who will heal but also one who will honor the moral order, and diseases/plagues may well be the effect, as was the case with Egypt. Israel is not exempt from what happened to Egypt.

Even should the people be visited with such disasters, God does not cease to be a healer. On the far side of judgment, God again and again enters into the pain-filled situation with healing power (see Num. 21:8–9; Ps. 41:4; 107:17–20; 147:3; Hos. 14:4; Isa. 53:5; 57:18–19), even—finally—for the Egypts of this world (Isa. 19:22). The divine will for the world is clear: God is one "who forgives all your iniquity, who heals all your diseases" (Ps. 103:3). The people of God can depend upon this.

Exodus 16:1–36
Food and Faith

Elim is a welcome oasis in the wilderness. There are springs of water and palm trees in abundance. But leaving time comes, and forty-five days beyond Egypt it is back into the wilderness, the wilderness of Sin (not the English word, but apt!). The continuing interest in an itinerary is evident, though scholars remain puzzled regarding the exact route (see at 17:1). The text is clearly composite, evident particularly in verses 4–12. Its focus has to do with a *food crisis,* which leads to a *faith crisis.* The lack of discernment of *God's presence in the ordinary* leads to a denial of *God's activity in the extraordinary.*

The complaints begin once again in earnest. This time it is food. Stress is laid upon the people as the "congregation" of Israel (rare elsewhere in Exodus), a recognition of the *new identity* they had received through God's creative act. But their perceptions do not correspond to this new reality; they have not yet become who they are. They wish they had stayed in Egypt. If it is finally a choice of places to die, satiety with oppression—an idealized and selective memory—is preferred to starvation with freedom. Complaining turns to accusation: Moses and Aaron intend to kill them (see Num. 11:4–9)! Faith is eroding with the sand dunes.

God responds to Moses with nary a word of anger: I will rain bread on you! (Ps. 78:24, 27 understood this to include both manna and quail; the anger of God in Ps. 78:21 may be related to the story in Numbers, cf. Num. 11:10.) As we have seen in the introduction to this section, in contrast to the raining of hail, this is *testimony to God's new creation.* Life and blessing abound in the natural order rather than destruction. (The stress on evening and morning recalls Gen. 1.) Food abounds even in the wilderness (see Isa. 49:9–10; 51:3).

For the various issues in this chapter, it is important to stress the naturalness of the manna and the quail (contra Durham, p. 224). It is precisely the "natural" that is seen as a gift from God. God's gifts to Israel are to be found not only in the unusual but

181

also in the everyday. If the provisions of God in the wilderness are all subsumed under the extraordinary or miraculous, then the people of God will tend to look for God's providential care only in that which falls outside the ordinary. The all too common effect of this is to absent God from the ordinary and everyday and to go searching for God only in the deep-sea and mountaintop experiences. Consequently, the people of God will not be able to see in the very ordinariness of things that God is the one who bestows blessings again and again. The result will often be that, when the miraculous can no longer be discerned in one's life, there will be a profound experience of the absence of God altogether.

There is an interest in a detailed description of the manna (also in Num. 11:7–9), which corresponds quite closely to a natural phenomenon in the Sinai Peninsula. A type of plant lice punctures the fruit of the tamarisk tree and excretes a substance from this juice, a yellowish-white flake or ball. During the warmth of the day it disintegrates, but it congeals when it is cold. It has a sweet taste. Rich in carbohydrates and sugar, it is still gathered by natives, who bake it into a kind of bread (and call it manna). The food decays quickly and attracts ants. Regarding the quails (see Num. 11:31–32), migratory birds flying in from Africa or blown in from the Mediterranean are often exhausted enough to be caught by hand. Such gifts of God's good creation are placed at Israel's disposal; but what they do with the gift is not an insignificant matter.

The naturalness of these gifts is not offset by certain unusual features of the story: the apparent (it is not entirely clear) leveling out of the amount according to need, regardless of how much was gathered (v. 18); its preservation for two days (v. 24; cf. v. 20); its nonavailability on the sabbath (vv. 25–27). Yet these extraordinary elements are worked in and through natural features, not in independence from them. The report of these developments is matter-of-fact; no effort is made to ascribe them to special actions of God, and the people give no sign of amazement. They are only curious (v. 15) and greedy (vv. 20, 27). At the least, the miraculous in this story has been downplayed sharply.

182

Verses 6–10 are the response of Moses/Aaron to the people's complaint of verse 3, to which God replies in verse 12. The issue is the relationship of *food and faith.* The people have expressed doubt to Moses/Aaron that they have had the people's best interests at heart in bringing them out from Egypt. God has disappeared as a subject of the deliverance; the people have reverted to the pre-exodus stance of 14:10–12. The food crisis has led to a faith crisis (see Burns, *Exodus,* pp. 124–126).

The resolution is not to ignore the need for food but to tie the gift of food to God's good intentions. The purpose of giving the people food is contained in the enclosing verses (vv. 6, 12): so *that they shall know* (1) that Yahweh is their God and (2) that it is *God* who is the subject of this event. God has heard their murmurings (repeated four times) and will provide food, even though the complaints are actually against God (three times). Even more, (the glory of) God will appear to them, so they can "see" that this provision of food is a gift from God himself. The very presence and activity of God can be discerned in connection with daily provisions. God's repeating (v. 12) of Moses' word of verse 8 reinforces the divine intention.

How common it is among the people of God that a crisis, whether of daily need or physical suffering, occasions a crisis of faith. Material and spiritual well-being are more closely linked than we often care to admit (see 6:9). The discernment of the people of God has often been so clouded by physical difficulties that they cannot see that God is much involved in providential ways in their everyday lives. Israel's situation is not unlike a community of faith whose understanding of "act of God" has been largely determined by their insurance policies. The connections of God with daily affairs has, for all practical purposes, disappeared. The resolution is not to stress the extraordinary acts of God one more time but to keep God linked with everyday blessings. And, as with Israel in this text, it will be in *discerning the presence of God in connection with daily needs* that they will be able to return once again to the confession: Yes, we now know, Yahweh is the one who brought us out of Egypt; Yahweh is God indeed. God's dramatic acts of creation are of one piece with daily blessings. The confession of the one is tied closely to the confession of the other. Moses' task is to instruct the people such that the divine factor in *every* blessing is made apparent.

The gifts of quail and manna appear (v. 13), though the subsequent narrative is exclusively concerned with the manna. The people do not recognize the manna—they see but do not

183

yet know (the question in Hebrew is *man hu'*, a popular etymology for manna). Moses instructs the people clearly: this is bread from God. The divine activity on behalf of the people is not focused simply on the dramatic moments in their lives. God is concerned about all the little things that go to make up their daily rounds. God is a factor to be reckoned with everywhere, in everything, even in the natural processes of the created order. God is one who cares for them in such a way as to respond to their prayers for daily bread. The people of God do not live by bread alone, but they cannot live without bread either. God's new creation is more than a spiritual matter; it is a comprehensive reality, effecting change in every nook and cranny of the world's life, including people's everyday needs.

The feeding miracles of Jesus also are a sign of the new creation that has dawned in the Christ event (see especially John 6). There, too, the close interconnections of the physical and the spiritual are emphasized, not least in the "divine feeding" that takes place in the Lord's Supper—cf. I Cor. 10:1–3. God's gifts come to people in and through that which is quite physical, natural, and ordinary—bread and wine.

But *with gifts come responsibilities.* And God has a stake in the way people carry out those responsibilities, for the use to which gifts are put affect the fabric of the new creation in positive or negative ways. Hence God's will for the new creation is not simply focused in a grand salvific design; it does not remain at the level of general principle. God also has a will for the daily particulars of life. God makes this clear to Moses (vv. 4–5), who passes it along to the people.

The prior word about *testing* (see at 15:25; 20:18–21) is put into play in this connection: only one day's supply at a time, except on the day before the sabbath. God will see whether the people will give heed to the divine will. Will they trust in the word of God or not? It is a time of uncertainty, even for God. This statement of God's will is not heteronomous, however, as if it were simply a matter of obedience for the sake of obedience. As will be noted below, the divine will is in the people's best interests, providing a time for rest and enabling a "discipline of dailyness" (Burns). In Deut. 8:2–3, 16, the divine motivation is more fully stated: that they might learn humility and remember that human beings do not live by bread alone but also by the word of God. All of this is informed by the most basic

184

of motivations: "to do you good in the end." The expression of God's will in the law is always to this end (cf. Matt. 4:4). The law, therefore, is not considered right just because it embodies God's will. It is right because it serves life and well-being, because it contributes to wisdom and understanding. (On the importance of this pre-Sinai situational law, see at 15:26.)

At the same time, both 16:4 and Deut. 8:2 (see Judg. 2:22; 3:4) are clear that the testing is not only for the sake of the people, it is also for the sake of God's knowledge of Israel. It enables God to know more completely the full nature of the Israelite response and to give the best possible shape to the future of the relationship with this people.

The particular expressions of the will of God for Israel in this story are threefold:

1. The people are to be mindful of a *time for rest.* They are not to gather manna on the sabbath. The sabbath rest is a recurrent theme in Exodus (see at 20:8–11 and 31:12–17; cf. 23:12; 34:21; 35:2–3). The noteworthy matter here is that it is understood to be an institution of the community quite apart from the giving of the law at Sinai. It is an aspect of God's created order. This connects with the sabbath rest that is built into the created order in Gen. 2:1–3; sabbath is part of the structures of the world as a whole, not a special day only for God's elect people. Israel's rest on this day is grounded in this creational reality (20:11; 31:17). It is presented to the people (v. 23), not as a day of worship, but as a day of solemn rest. As such, it is an integral part of their life in God's new creation. By so resting, they are in tune with God's creational design. This particularization of the divine will is obviously in the best interests of the creation, and hence its obedience is of utmost importance.

The implication of this creational understanding of sabbath is that the people of God are to be committed to a day of rest even for those who are not a part of their particular community, but quite apart from any concern for worship times and places. They will no doubt want to add the dimension of worship into their own practice; their argument for a broader participation, however, is to be pursued solely in creational terms, as God's concern for a proper rest for all people and animals.

2. A time for rest, *but not at the expense of daily needs.* A double provision is to be gathered on the day before sabbath, so that daily needs are given attention (v. 5). The sabbath is

185

made for people, not people for the sabbath (Mark 2:27). The sabbath is not to be made into a new oppressive system. In fact, it is a profound sign that the people's days of bondage are past. The contrast with the oppressive situation of nonrest is made explicit in the inclusion of slaves in the command (20:10; 23:12). Sabbath rest stands opposed to all oppressive systems, insisting on regularly timed days of rest for all, but providing for the needs of the day. Moses tells the people to enjoy a sabbath meal (v. 25). The sabbath is a day of rest from work, not from enjoyment of what God provides.

3. The gathering of provisions *for only one day at a time* (vv. 4, 19–20). The will of God for Israel is a "discipline of dailyness." One's prayers are to ask only for *daily* bread (Matt. 6:11). There is to be no hoarding of the gifts of God's creation, no building of larger and larger barns (Luke 12:18; cf. I Tim. 6:6–10), no anxieties about what they are to eat on the morrow (Luke 12:22–30). The coveting commandment may well be in view here (20:17), a matter of continuing concern for the prophets (cf. Isa. 5:8; Jer. 17:11; Amos 5:11; Micah 5:1–2). The issue becomes one of learning to rely on God for one's daily needs, "for where your treasure is, there will your heart be also" (Luke 12:34; cf. Deut. 8:17–18). The increasing gap between rich and poor in modern societies is certainly in part due to the hoarding of manna. It witnesses to a failure to recognize that all that we have is due to God's goodness, not our ability to gather manna better than anyone else. The world of God's creation, including the distribution of food resources, is to be so structured that those "who gather little have no lack" (v. 18; cf. II Cor. 8:15).

Israel's failure to adhere to these responsibilities earns the wrath of both Moses (v. 20) and God (v. 28). This is not an authoritarian reaction, as if the problem were the neglect of the command as command or divine pique at insubordination. If the commands are not heteronomous (see above), the reason for the anger is of the same order. The issue is the effect that disobedience has on God's new creation and the God-Israel relationship. Such behaviors are revealing of a disposition to disregard God's will for the best life possible, and hence they threaten to undo what God has just brought into being. In each case, this time around, the people respond positively to the expressed anger (vv. 21, 30). Even in the face of misuse, and the failure of the test, God's graciousness prevails. The manna

186

comes on a regular basis, right up to the border of the land filled with milk and honey (v. 35).

God then commands Moses to have about two quarts of manna kept for posterity, so that the people would be reminded how God had fed them in the wilderness. The idealized and unwarranted memories of Pharaoh's food (v. 3) are to be replaced with the genuine memories of the bread from God (vv. 32–34)—an inclusio for the chapter as a whole. As noted in the introduction to this section, the term "testimony" and other sanctuary references are historical anachronisms. But the narrative purpose of these references to a desert sanctuary not only anticipate the tabernacle, they link the experience of God's provision of daily bread with the community's worship. Worship has to do with all of life. The worship life of the people of God is not simply to focus on the dramatic acts of God but also to provide remembrances of how the seemingly little things in their daily lives are undergirded by the sustaining care of God. If this is not done, physical crises of one kind or another may lead into unbelief.

Exodus 17:1–7
On Testing God

Once again the people are on the move. This brief but composite story highlights the character of the *divine leading,* the continuing *human complaint,* and the unsurpassable *graciousness of God,* who opens up the sustaining *powers of creation* for Israel.

The regular notices of Israel's itinerary are neither simply literary devices providing transitions for stories nor historical anchors. They accomplish two things:

1. They set the people "on the way." This is a community on the move from a past act of redemption toward a promised goal. But promise is still promise, not fulfillment. And when the goal is no longer days or weeks away, but months and years, it is easy to lose one's moorings. These wilderness stories are increasingly about a people stuck between promise and fulfillment. Wilderness is no longer simply a place but a state of mind.

187

Even more, it is a typology for the life of faith. The direct allusion to Sinai in verse 6 points to the fact that Sinai too is in the middle of the wilderness. The law to be given at Sinai is also for life on the move. For the law to be given in the middle of a long journey says something both about people and law. The law too is on the move. There is no sedentary law for a nonsedentary people (see at chaps. 19—24).

2. They give shape to God's leading of the people. The wilderness is a place where it is often difficult to sort out perceptions and reality. It seems like a godforsaken place, but it is not. The people are being led by God himself (see at 13:17–22); in fact, through Moses, God has commanded what the route shall be (17:1). The notice that the people are being obedient to that command gives notice that their response to God (and Moses) is not simply one of complaint. It also, however, recognizes that disobedience is possible. God's leading may not always result in people going where God wants them to go. Leading does not entail coercion. Israel could have taken other paths through the wilderness.

God's leading does not always move directly toward oases. Here they are led to a place where, once again, there is no water to drink (see the parallel in Num. 20:2–13). God's interests do not always coincide with those of the people. As in 16:4, another proving ground comes into view. Obedience to one commandment sets up another opportunity for obedience. One instance of obedience does not bring the people of God to a plateau where obedience is no longer a consideration. Those on the way are always moving from one occasion for obedience to another. That's the way it is with personal relationships (see at 20:18–21). But the more one shows faithfulness to the relationship, the more natural that response becomes, and in most cases it ceases to be a test of any consequence.

The people complain to Moses again; this time they have no water to drink at all. Moses responds by noting that it is God whom they are putting to the test, though Moses connects the disputing (faultfinding) only with himself (cf. Num. 20:3, 13). But the people do not buy into what they must perceive as a deflection (they're thirsty!). They keep Moses' feet to the fire: Why did *you* bring us out of Egypt? For the third time in four complaints (14:11; 16:3) they wonder whether Moses intends to kill them, stressing the children and the cattle this time.

188

From verse 7 we learn that the double name given the place, Massah/Meribah (see NRSV footnotes), marks divine testing as the basic memory associated with this story. These memories haunt later Israel. The names became a type for testing God: "You shall not put Yahweh your God to the test, as you tested him at Massah" (cf. Deut. 6:16; Ps. 78:18, 41, 56; 81:7; 95:9). From Num. 14:22 we learn that the people had tested God ten times, severely testing the divine patience. In addition, it is at this place that "it went ill with Moses on their account" (see Ps. 106:32; Num. 20:2–13; Deut. 32:51).

Testing God. What does it mean? It is made especially problematic by the fact that it is appropriate for God to test Israel (15:25; 16:4) but not for Israel to test God. Verse 7 focuses the issue in the question, "Is the Lord among us or not?" The asking of this question in itself is not a testing of God. Testing has to do with "putting God to the proof," that is, seeking a way in which God can be coerced to act or show himself. It is to set God up, to try to force God's hand in order thereby to determine concretely whether God is really present or not. Israel's testing of God consisted in this: if we are to believe that God is really present, then God must show us in a concrete way by making water materialize. It is to make one's belief in God contingent upon such a demonstration. It is, in essence, an attempt to turn faith into sight.

An especially clear instance of this is in Jesus' temptation (Matt. 4:5–7). Jesus was asked by the devil to throw himself from the pinnacle of the temple. After all, if he jumped, God would jump and not allow him to fall to his death. Jesus quotes this wilderness tradition in response: that would be forcing God's hand, seeking to *make* God act in order to demonstrate the divine presence and power (see Luke 16:30–31).

This approach to God is often characteristic of believers. I will not take special precautions in the use of automobiles or guns or on dangerous ventures. God will take care of me. I will not take out insurance, God is my insurance policy. Such attitudes set God up for a test, holding God hostage, determining just how God is to show the divine power. It places God in the role of servant, at the beck and call of one in any difficulty. Besides violating the Godness of God, it endangers the understanding of faith. It leads to such attitudes as: God did not heal or protect you, because you did not have enough faith. If you

189

had, God would have acted. That is to put God to the test, demonstrating an inappropriate confidence that God will in fact intervene at the behest of one who has faith.

Moses leaves off disputing with the people and turns to God; his life may be in danger. He sounds like a parent in need of counseling (see Num. 11:11–13 for an extension of this parental metaphor). God responds, not with advice on how to deal with the people's complaining, but with directions on how to find water. With the elders as witnesses, Moses is to take his trusty staff and strike the rock at Horeb; water will come forth. But it is not simply Moses and the staff that will work wonders; God himself will stand before Moses while Moses does this. God works in and through Moses and his staff (and with the rock!) to provide water for the people.

The reference back to Moses' striking the Nile shows that this "striking" is its positive counterpart. Just as Moses' striking the Nile led to water being unfit to drink, so here his striking the rock leads to water fit to drink. This is a manifestation of God's creative activity, bringing water into a part of the world under the control of chaotic forces (see at 15:22–27). This theme will be picked up in the visions of the new creation in the later prophets (Isa. 35:6–7; 41:17–18; Ezek. 36:24–26; 47:7–12; cf. I Cor. 10:4).

God's standing "on the rock at Horeb" is another item anticipating events at Sinai (see the introduction to this section). *Water and law are linked.* The Sinai experience is enclosed by wilderness stories. The context in which the law is given to Israel is life in the midst of chaos and disorder. It is a place where lifelessness rules more than life, where the gifts of God's creation—such basic things as food and water—are scarce. The wilderness is not the creation as God intended it to be, but God's creative activity is having positive effects.

These anticipations of Sinai in the midst of chaos speak to a basic purpose of the law: *social order is a matter of creation.* Obedience in the midst of wilderness brings order into chaos. The reference to Sinai thus has a high symbolic value: *The gift of the water of life comes from the same source as the gift of the law,* a source of life for the community of faith. Even more, water from Sinai testifies to the fact that moral order and cosmic order are inextricably interconnected. Obedience to the law actually does affect the natural order of things. Anyone in the

190

modern era who has worked to conserve the lakes and streams of this country knows from experience what this means. Without obedience, modern travelers in this increasingly wilderness-shaped world may find themselves without water to drink. And God may not (be able to) come to the rescue this time (see Num. 14:22–23).

God's gifts of food and water in the wilderness are providential acts; they sustain the community of faith in the midst of hardship. But they are more than that; they are *acts of creation* or re-creation. They bring to realization God's original intentions for the creation in the midst of chaos. Yet the wilderness, for all of its discontinuity from creation as God intended it, is not without resources. Hence it is of high importance that any consideration of God's provision of food and water not be divorced from a recognition of nature's God-given potentialities. Similar to the provision of manna, there is water coursing through rock formations; God's actions enable their hidden creative potential to surface.

To cite modern parallels of finding water in rock formations in the Sinai region is not in the least irrelevant to the story. Such citations become problematic only if God's activity is not considered to be apposite. One has to move between "rationalization" on the one hand and supernaturalism on the other—it is no less a wonder thereby. God is here not creating out of nothing; water does not materialize out of thin air. God works in and through the natural to provide blessings for people. The rock plays an indispensable role. Moreover, God stands on the rock. It is God who "subdues" the earth (Gen. 1:28). Water in the wilderness is certainly for the benefit of the people; but it is also for the benefit of nature. The effects of God's creational activity are cosmic in scope.

Exodus 17:8–16
There's Power in Those Hands

The people of Israel had come out of Egypt "equipped for battle" (13:18). This brief, unified story reports their first and only use of that equipment in the book of Exodus. The some-

191

what passive, complaining stance of the people to this point is no longer in evidence. The occasion is a battle with the Amalekites, a desert region nomadic people, often hostile to Israel (see Judg. 6:3–4; I Sam. 27:8). After Amalek starts the battle, the initiative for the defense of Israel is taken entirely by Moses, demonstrating the leadership role he has assumed. God does not become the subject of a sentence until verse 14 but is not uninvolved in the prior verses.

This section concerns a *Pharaonic conflict revisited.* Once again God's new creation is threatened. Pharaoh may be dead, but Israel is not thereby forever free from such chaotic powers embodied in historical enemies. Deliverance, however, will not take the shape of a sea crossing. *Trustworthy human leadership* and *active community defense* will be needed to join with the divine will in the elimination of such an evil threat.

The two brief stories in chapter 17 are tied together in the attention given to Moses' hand/staff. As 17:5 gave notice of Moses' prior use of his hand/staff at the Nile, the present story invites a comparison with the use against the Egyptians (14:16, 21, 26–27). Continuities and discontinuities are to be noted. For one thing, Joshua (mentioned for the first time) picks a number of men and fights with them. Unlike the story at the sea, human participation is of obvious importance. At the same time, the course of the battle is not determined solely by Israel's warriors. The energies of Moses, as well as Hur and Aaron, who keep his hand/staff outstretched, are significant elements. (The plural "hands" in v. 12 is only a variant occasioned by the length of time.) The "staff of God" (cf. 4:20) is certainly the decisive factor, but it is clear that the staff is effective only in concert with the human participants. In fact, in the report of the results (v. 13), neither the staff nor God is mentioned. It is a combination of divine and human energies that is finally decisive.

Even more, the mere *presence* of the staff is insufficient. For it to be effective it has to be held aloft (see below), during daylight hours (v. 12), and over an extended period of time. Regarding the latter point, unlike at the sea, and in all other instances of its use, the outstretched staff/hand is not immediately fully effective. It takes some time, time for Moses to become weary and to receive help from Aaron and Hur, time for the human fighting force to do its work. The difference in the use of the staff on this occasion is probably determined by

192

the fact that the object of its use is a human endeavor rather than a natural occurrence. In the other cases, various effects in the natural order were immediately coordinate with the use of the staff; human beings are apparently viewed as less tractable (cf. Josh. 8:18). And so the staff functions differently here than elsewhere, and that has to be taken into account in one's interpretation of the passage.

The staff's effectiveness only when held aloft has sparked no little discussion. Three perspectives might be mentioned.

1. The outstretched hands are a prayer gesture. But no relationship to prayer is evident here, nor in other texts where the staff is used. Moreover, no speaking is associated with this activity (parallels with Balaam's curse are problematic). This would also entail a mechanical, even magical view of prayer, with effects depending on constancy.

2. The narrative has a folkloristic character, as in 4:1–9, and the staff is conceived as having certain magical properties. Parallels in the ancient Near East have been cited. This is a possibility, and God would be viewed as making use of such traditional understandings to further the divine purpose. At other times and places, God will work in and through other means.

3. A more likely view is that, while Moses is not said to be seen by the warriors, his being on a hilltop during daylight hours suggests that he was. The banner/signal language also suggests this; *to see the hand/staff of Moses was to see the hand of God* (see below). Hence the sight of Moses with his hand/staff outstretched gave encouragement to the Israelites and contributed to their effectiveness. Given the divine-human cooperation we have seen, it is not unimportant what the warriors think and feel about God's involvement in their (first-time) activity. The staff in and of itself does not radiate power like an electrical shock system, so that Moses turns it on and off by raising and lowering it. It is a realistic symbol of the power of God at work in the situation; yet God's power is not electrically conceived either. This suggests a symbiotic relationship between people and staff (whose value would be well established), such that the clearly significant human efforts are affected by the sight of the staff. It assures them, not only of God's active *hand* in the battle, but of *Moses' confidence* that God is so involved.

These factors speak to how one conceives of God's possibilities in the situation. God's activity is such that, though the

193

divine will in the matter is clear (v. 14), it will not be accomplished by a divine snap of a finger. Moreover, it will take generations for God's goals to be accomplished (v. 16). *Even for God, such things take time,* given the divine way of working in and through historical realities and not always dependable people. God's possibilities are thus circumscribed by the factors available in any given situation. Even more, the indispensable role of the human beings involved means that the outcome of the stages along the way is not predetermined. If one were to take the entire canon into account (cf. Jer. 18:7–8), even God's ultimate goal regarding the Amalekites (v. 14) would be subject to the divine repentance.

This last paragraph helps explain some of the elements of holy war present in this text (see at 15:3). Here the problem is less what Israel does than God's goal to blot out the memory of the Amalekites. This incident in the wilderness provoked strong memories for later Israel. According to Deut. 25:17–19, the Amalekites attacked "when you were faint and weary, and cut off at your rear all who lagged behind you." In other words, at a point of supreme vulnerability for the people of God, when their future was hanging in the balance, Amalek had sought to exterminate them. The Amalekites thus become an embodiment of evil, Pharaoh revisited, a veritable Hitlerian specter, threatening God's creational purposes. The divine goal is thus for the sake of God's creation.

This is such an irrevocable goal that it is to be written in a book (Num. 21:14?) and specifically impressed upon Joshua, the next leader of Israel. The Amalekites do finally meet their end (I Chron. 4:43; cf. I Sam. 15:8). Yet, finally, their story ends on a note of irony. Their memory is not blotted out; Israel itself sees to that memory by telling and retelling this story (not unlike the way the story of the holocaust is not forgotten). But as a people they cease to exist, and that is the force of the language of remembrance here.

Moses builds an altar and names it: The Lord is my banner or rallying signal. Isaiah 49:22, speaking of God's upraised hand as a signal for the nations, may help explain this (cf. Isa. 5:25–26; 13:2; 18:3; Jer. 4:21; 51:27). Inasmuch as a signal was normally put on a hill, where Moses was standing with his hand/staff outstretched, Yahweh *as* banner speaks of the activity/hand of God. Moses' hand upon the banner thus refers to the staff as a

194

realistic symbol of the hand of God. Moses' hand and God's hand are elided (cf. 14:26–27 with 14:31 and 15:12; 7:4–5; 3:20). So, finally, the memory of this place is associated with what God has done. When people recall this day, it will be God who is remembered.

Exodus 18:1–12
Faith and Family

Exodus 18, a unified story, witnesses to the two central aspects of what it means to be the people of God: *faith and law.* Verses 1–12 focus on the *declaration and confession* of what God has done for Israel. Verses 13–27 center on *community structures that give shape to the life of faith.*

First of all, verses 1–12. In contrast to the Amalekites, the Midianites give Israel a warm welcome. The family relationship is no doubt a factor (see 2:15–22; 4:18–26), but it is deeper than that. The narrator's emphasis on this relationship is shown by the repeated reference to Jethro as Moses' father-in-law (thirteen times; priest only once). The detail relating to Zipporah and Moses' two sons reinforces the interest in family. In particular, the attention given to the sons' names demonstrates an interest in family religious continuity. But there are now changes. This change is highlighted by the repeated reference to God's delivering Israel from Egypt (five times in vv. 1–12), virtually a refrain. To link these repetitions: the concern is *the integration of Moses' family into Israel's new identity as the exodus community of faith.* The basic elements in this integration are:

1. Jethro *hears what God has done* for Israel (v. 1). His hearing is an extension of the hearing reported in 15:14, only now the reception is positive. The bearer of the news is not known, but what God had done was of such magnitude that the word had spread like wildfire, from oasis to oasis, until it reached Moses' family.

2. Having heard the news, Jethro with Moses' family *visits the newly delivered community.* Expressing concern for each other's welfare, they begin to reestablish family ties (it is not

195

known when or why Moses' family had been separated). Moses' wife and children now drop into the background, being represented by Jethro.

3. They *go into the tent (sanctuary)*. This seemingly innocuous reference is important because of what happens in verse 12, apparently the same place. It may well be a reference to a traveling sanctuary (see 16:34; 33:7–11).

4. Moses *declares the good news* to Jethro concerning all that God has done on behalf of Israel—with no reference to his own considerable role. The word "declare" *(sapar)* was used in 9:16 to refer to the basic divine purposes in these events. This is the first reported instance of the carrying out of that purpose. It is to be noted that the hardships are also shared, not simply the blessings.

5. Jethro *rejoices* over all the good that God has brought to Israel, including the deliverance from the Egyptians. His use of much of Moses' own language testifies to the basic way in which the faith is transmitted from generation to generation (see Deut. 26:5–11; Josh. 24:2–13).

6. Jethro *gives public thanks* (=blesses) to God for the deliverance that has been wrought. This response to God's activity echoes other texts (e.g., I Kings 8:56–61; Ps. 135; I Chron. 29:10–13).

7. Jethro *publicly confesses* that Yahweh is God of gods and Lord of lords. He now "knows" (an important word in Exodus) that Yahweh is incomparable (see below). Whatever faith Jethro may have had before, there is now a new content to his confession in view of God's creation of a new people.

8. Jethro *presents an offering* to God and in the portable sanctuary ("before God") worships with the leaders of Israel (Moses is assumed to be present in the sanctuary from v. 7).

Jethro is the subject of all of this activity except for the crucial element of witness on Moses' part in verse 8. Jethro hears, visits the community of faith, rejoices, gives thanks, confesses, presents an offering, and worships. All of this activity is permeated with specific language regarding God's deliverance of Israel. Such activities give the appearance of the steps one might take to be integrated into the community of faith, and the conversion of Jethro is often claimed. Yet care must be used not to claim too much. Jethro's statement in verse 11 that he now knows that Yahweh is greater than other gods implies that

Yahweh was not unknown to him. But the exodus events have now changed whatever status Yahweh may have had in his community. Jethro identifies himself with *Moses'* understanding rather than the other way around. So, at the least, Jethro recognizes that this community, now constituted as an exodus community, is a new reality in the world, and he wishes to be associated with it.

The testimony of Moses to Jethro regarding all that God had done for Israel is central in the movement of this narrative. It issues in all of Jethro's subsequent words and actions. The verb *sapar* ("declare") is certainly intended to recall its use in 9:16 (cf. 10:2). Moses is the first of God's witnesses to another individual and another people. His witness serves to establish the exodus faith for the first time in a non-Israelite community. There is thus also an ancillary concern here for how an outsider becomes identified with this community. What Moses has done, Israel and all of God's people are also called upon to do (see Ps. 96:3–4, 10; 113:3; 57:9; 18:49; see 40:9–10; 67:4). Indeed, what Moses has done will be repeated "throughout all the earth" (9:16) in the years to come.

At the heart of all of this activity is the good news of what God has done. Thus, just before the law is given to Israel, the basic confessional identity of the community of faith is made clear. It is the gospel of God's deliverance which prompts Jethro's various responses. Issues of law and good order are immediately of concern to the community in the following verses, but those matters are considered *from within the context of an already existing community of faith in which God's redemptive acts are central.*

Exodus 18:13–27
Redemption and Good Order

God's redemptive activity does not respond to Israel's every need. Those who have experienced the salvation of God are not thereby given an answer to all the issues or problems faced by their community. They are indeed freed from bondage, but freedom brings with it new opportunities and responsibilities.

197

However much redemption may bring with it new perspectives and energies for such tasks, those who are redeemed are in need of other resources for life beyond the salvific experience. For example, a people freed from oppressive structures will need to develop societal structures of their own. While these must be in fundamental consonance with the meaning of redemption, resources from the wider sphere of creation will be needed in order to develop them in appropriate ways. In other words, the Creator has blessed the world with numerous gifts quite apart from God's redemptive activity. The *redeemed community should be anxious to discover what those gifts are and to make use of them with gratitude,* no matter their source within God's wide creation. Indeed, given the cosmic scope of God's activity, this becomes a matter of being in tune with that broader and deeper divine movement. This has to do with matters in both "secular" and religious spheres. The issue is justice permeating the entirety of God's creation.

Hence it should not be surprising that Moses is presented as a somewhat inept administrator. His experience of redemption did not immediately endow him or others in Israel with efficient and creative administrative skills. Nor should it be surprising that someone who is not an Israelite provides Israel with sound counsel regarding such matters. It is important to say that the appropriation of the exodus experience by Jethro noted in verses 1–12 is not irrelevant to what he now suggests. But his wise counsel has its origins essentially outside the chosen community of Israel. No special revelation has given him these administrative suggestions. They have been developed over time, drawing on a range of experience in God's creation quite untouched by the redeemed community.

Jethro has observed that Moses, in his capacity of deciding cases brought before him, is trying to do everything all by himself (see Judg. 4:4–5; II Sam. 15:1–6). Moses is not very good at delegating! Besides, people are having to stand in line all day long just to get an audience with him. He is not only wearing himself out, the people's patience is wearing thin as well. His own well-being as well as the good order of the community is threatened. Jethro is absolutely right: in this matter having to do with the order of things, what Moses is doing "is not good." One hears an echo of the divine ordering of creation in Genesis 1 in this statement. *The ordering of human affairs is integrally*

198

related to the cosmic order. The principles at work in the latter, the wisdom that God has built into the very structure of things, are important for the ordering of human life. Given the fact that issues of justice were central in God's deliverance from Egypt, this represents a concern that that justice be manifest in every aspect of the social order. In so doing, the social order in the community of faith would become more and more in tune with the justice of God's world order. Justice is not simply God's responsibility; it is also the task of the community which has been the special focus of God's making things right.

And so Jethro gives Moses some excellent "worldly" advice (note from v. 13 the ad hoc character of his counsel). He is alert to the needs of the community. Moses' energies are to be largely devoted elsewhere. Moses is to represent the community before God, bringing their concerns into the divine presence and discerning the will of God for their daily life (cf. 33:7–11). Moreover, he is to be the teacher of the community in the ways in which God would have the people to walk. But in deciding specific cases, he is to delegate this matter largely to trustworthy individuals who fear God. It is important to note that not just any persons of faith will do; they are to be people of integrity and incorruptible (on the fear of God, see at 1:15–22). They are to organize themselves in a decentralized structure, having authority at various levels in the community, bringing only the most difficult cases to Moses for decision (see Deut. 1:9–18). The responsibility for justice is thus dispersed throughout the community. Jethro concludes by noting how this will not only serve Moses well but bring peace to a people who no longer have to stand in queues all day long.

Jethro also says, in an almost offhand way: God so commands this. Yet there has been no verbal command from God, and one ought not be assumed. Jethro exudes the kind of confidence in his own plan that it will in fact be in tune with God's own will for the situation. *Wise discernment of what seems prudent in this situation is believed to be just as much the will of God as a specific divine verbal communication.* One should probably assume a "it seemed good to the Holy Spirit and to us" approach to the matter (see Acts 15:28). Moses does not hesitate for a moment and puts the plan into effect; the unqualified report of its operation indicates that it succeeds in its purpose. As is so often the case, the one who presents the suggestion for

199

improvement moves on to other things. Jethro returns to his home, never to be heard from again. But Israel tells and retells the story of the non-Israelite who was responsible for bringing "peace" (v. 23) and good order to the community of faith—a matter of creation. In most modern situations, in church and state alike, Moses would have gotten all the credit. At least in the community of faith such elitist practices ought to change.

In addition, the community of faith should give much greater recognition to this: much of what it does in its daily life has been informed by ideas and perspectives and methods concerning which there has been no special revelation from God. This does not mean that such matters are any less in tune with the will of God. Rather, the people of God, both as individuals and as community, should accept its common dependence upon general human experience in the world for much of what they do, recognizing that God the Creator has been powerfully at work in that sphere in the interests of the well-being of all. This God often makes use of the wisdom, insight, imagination, and common sense of the Jethros of this world to make the divine will known, to be of assistance to the religious community and in the furtherance of the divine purposes (cf. chaps. 1—2). The *specific revelation of God at Sinai,* now to be presented, is thus seen to stand in *fundamental continuity* with the discernment of the will of God in and through *common human experience.* The fact that chapter 18 takes place at the "mountain of God" (v. 5) affirms this. It is to be noted that this pertains not simply to Jethro's suggestions regarding administration but also to a variety of other "statutes and ordinances" (vv. 16, 20) already shown to be available to Moses in this judging work (see at 15:22–27; and see the introduction to Part Six).

Law and Covenant

EXODUS 19:1—24:18

Introduction: Law and Narrative

One of the most distinctive characteristics of Old Testament law is that it is enclosed by narrative (see chart). While law and narrative were no doubt passed down separately for years, the law has now been integrated into the story. The law does not stand in independence from that story. It is not even presented as a single chapter within that story but is woven into the narrative throughout. From present evidence, this integration of law and narrative is unique in the ancient Near East. Ancient Near Eastern law is drawn into civil or criminal codes, as were Greek and Roman laws.

What is the significance of this literary placement for both law and narrative? The following ten factors should be considered. (See especially Mann; Damrosch.)

1. *God is the subject* in both law and narrative. God is the giver of the law and the chief actor in the narrative. God is presented as one who speaks and acts in both law and narrative. The law fleshes out the word of God as speech; the narrative fills out the word of God as event. The narrative enables a fuller picture of the God who stands behind the law, while the law enhances the images of God available in the narrative.

2. Law is more clearly seen as a *gift of God's graciousness* when tied to story. Law becomes another part of the larger story of God's goodness and mercy. From the story it is clear that the law is grounded in a personal and gracious divine will. Narrative reinforces the divine intention in the law: never to leave the people without an indication of what it means to be

201

202

Structure of Exodus 19:1–40:38

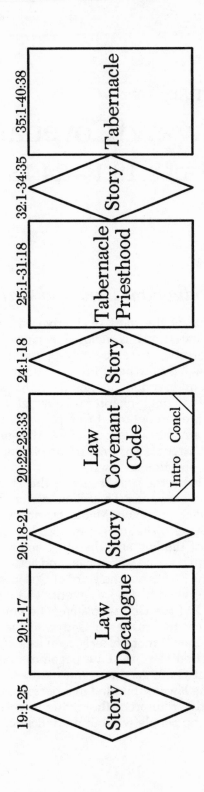

a community of faith, without a direction in which a person of faith could walk, without some instruction regarding the life of faith. Narrative enhances God's purpose that the law is "for our good always, that God might preserve us alive" (Deut. 6:24), that the law always has the best interests of the people at heart. The divine will in the law intends to extend into all aspects of life that already experienced salvific will described in the narrative. Narrative helps to show that law is fundamentally gift, not burden.

3. Narrative keeps the *personal character* of the law front and center. Experience has shown how easy it is for law to become an impersonal matter, manifested especially in a debilitating legalism. It can become, as it were, a "law unto itself," unrelated to any specific giver, dissociated from the dynamic will of the one who stands behind its formulations. In the narrative, one is confronted with the giver of the law as one who is living, personally interacting with people through every step of their journey. The narrative reveals a lively, pulsating relationship between God and people. It is this same God who gives the law and who gives it as part of an existing interpersonal relationship. The law must thus be understood in personal and interrelational terms.

4. This integration keeps *divine action and human response* closely related to each other. Law parallels liturgy (rituals, song, dance) in being so embedded in narrative. As such, law is understood as another way in which the people respond to what God has done on their behalf. At the same time, narrative keeps God's activity, especially in the exodus events, front and center for the law. This is seen, for example, in the opening sentence to the law, 20:2—I am the Lord your God, who brought you out of Egypt. Obedience to law is thus not seen as a response to the law as law; obedience is fundamentally a response to God and to all that God has done. Obedience is one way in which life can be set into a rhythm that is maximally responsive within a relationship. Obedience is a way of doing justice to this relationship in which Israel already stands.

More generally, the law points up the fact that God has chosen not to do everything in this world by himself. However much the story keeps God at the center as the agent of Israel's redemption, the law insists that there are important human initiatives and responsibilities to be undertaken. Human beings

203

are given important tasks in furthering the cause of justice and good order in Israel and the larger creation. Bringing order out of disorder, conforming the world to God's will for that world, is not fully accomplished in God's salvific acts. Israel too is given a role in promoting and enhancing the purposes of God for the creation, in building upon the foundations that God has established.

But such human activity would finally mean something quite different cut off from the prior divine redemption. To say that "the story exists for the sake of the law it frames" (Damrosch, p. 262) is not a helpful formulation. Story and law are now forever indissoluble, but the law exists for the sake of the story, as many of these considerations demonstrate. God's redemption does not simply launch the law, thereafter to slip into the past to become a matter subordinate to the law. God's exodus redemption remains the constitutive event for Israel and continues to be actualized as such in Israel's worship. There would be no Israel to keep the law without that ongoing, continually actualized story. The law remains forever grounded in those constitutive events.

5. This integration illustrates that *creation theology* is a prevailing theme of the book of Exodus. The law fills out that emphasis, thereby integrating cosmic order and social order. The activity of God as creator is often associated all too narrowly with the beginning of things. Or, such language is used to lift up the ongoing divine work of blessing manifest in, say, human fertility and the growth of flocks and fields. Not as often is the work of the Creator associated with societal matters. But it needs to be stressed that the bulk of the law belongs to the sphere of creation. In view of the symbiotic relationship between cosmic and social orders, the law is a means by which the divine ordering of chaos at the cosmic level is actualized in the social sphere, whereby God's will is done on earth as it is in heaven. The Egyptians have been an example par excellence of how the justice of God's world order has been subverted, creating injustice, oppression, and social chaos. The law is given to the people of God as a vehicle in and through which Egypt will not be repeated among them. The law is a means by which the cosmic and social orders can be harmoniously integrated, whereby God's cosmic victory can be realized in all spheres of human interaction.

204

6. The way in which God acts in the narrative serves as both the *norm and the particular content* for Israel's own action. The law is an exegesis of the divine action of the narrative. As God has shown love for the people while they were yet in bondage, so Israel is to comport itself toward people in comparable straits (see 23:9). Be merciful as your God is merciful. The shape that the law takes is always to be measured over against the basic shape of the narrative action of God.

Even more, the way in which God acts in the narrative serves to define the particular details of the law. God's will for Israel does not remain at the level of general principle. Because God has Israel's best interests at heart, God has a will for the ordering of life in its particulars (which may change over time in view of the contingencies of human life). The specific content of the life of faith is to be shaped by the report of what God has done. Thus, for example, God's involvement in sociopolitical realities means that Israel as the people of God must also be so involved.

7. The *motivation* given for obedience to law is contained in the narrative: you were slaves in the land of Egypt, therefore you are to shape your lives toward the disadvantaged in ways both compassionate and just (22:21–27; 23:9). The basic motivation for obeying Torah is drawn from historical experience, not from abstract ethical argument (see 12:26; 13:8, 14; Deut. 6:20). Negatively, the law is not understood as something to be obeyed just because God says so. The law is not an imposition from God that is unrelated to Israel's particular history or to common experience regarding what is in the best interests of true life. The law is to be obeyed because it can be seen to serve life and well-being. It is to be obeyed because it contributes to wisdom and understanding and can be recognized as such by those who are not a part of the community of faith (cf. Deut. 4:6). This leads into the next point.

8. For law to be a part of story means that it is not abstracted or isolated from life. Law is *integrated with life,* in at least two ways:

a. Law *emerges from within* the matrix of life itself. This has two points of significance. On the one hand, the law is not simply a matter of special revelation. The wilderness narratives (18:13–27 especially) have spoken of statutes and ordinances emergent from the wisdom of common human experience.

205

There is thereby shown to be a significant continuity between the word of God speaking in and through such experience and the word of God given in more direct ways. On the other hand, laws are not simply given as a legal corpus, such as they are at Sinai. In the wilderness (see at 15:22–27) God gives Israel particular ordinances related to specific narrative situations. Obedience was already a part of the God-Israel relationship before Sinai. This testifies to the fact that there is a will of God relating to specific matters quite apart from the Sinai revelation. The people of God will thus need to be attentive to a will of God for life situations not articulated in that body of law.

b. The law is *woven back into* the very fabric of life. This also has two points of significance. On the one hand, for the law to be placed so specifically in a context filled with divine promises and divine redemptive activity means that the law is kept from being understood in legalistic terms. It is thereby made clear that the law is not a means by which one is made a member of the community of faith. The law is given to those already redeemed. On the other hand, for the ordinances to be placed at a number of points in the ongoing story (from Exodus 12 to Deuteronomy) means that the law is not viewed as eternally given in a certain form; it is not immutable, never to be changed in its form or content. The laws are time-bound. The law is always intersecting with life as it is, filled with contingency and change, with complexity and ambiguity. It moves with the times, taking human experience and insight into account, while remaining constant in its objective: the best life for as many as possible. This constantly changing life of the people of God means that ever new laws are needed: New occasions teach new duties.

To state this in somewhat different terms: this combination maintains an important tension between the tendency toward absoluteness and certainty in the law, on the one hand, and the contingency and uncertainty of historical existence on the other hand. Law in and of itself tends to promote a myth of certainty, that one knows exactly what the will of God is for every aspect of life. Historical existence, especially when seen from the perspective of the wilderness narratives, is filled with contingencies, in which nothing on the ship of life seems to be tied down. The law provides a compass for wandering in the wilderness;

the contingencies of wilderness life keep the law from becoming absolutized in a once-for-all form and content.

9. The integration of law and narrative means that obedience to law becomes another form of *witness* to God and to what God has done. By means of obedience to law as much as by singing songs of thanksgiving, the people show forth their God and their God's wonderful deeds. The people in conforming their lives to that of God's ways thereby exhibit before others the nature of their God (see Deut. 4:6). Hence retelling the story and obeying the law constitute two different but related ways of witnessing to God and God's activity.

10. Tradition has given the word Torah to both law and narrative genres. The force of this is that the Pentateuch is *instruction* (see 24:12) in both its laws and its stories. On the one hand, the stories have a certain imperative character to them; they serve to instruct, to provide guidance, to impel toward certain kinds of conduct in life. One cannot hear the story without recognizing that it issues in norms for the shape of one's life. On the other hand, the laws are given a certain narrative force. By being reflective of God's own activity, they retell the story in a somewhat different form.

Instruction in both of these forms thus says something very basic about the shape of the life of faith. On the one hand, the life of faith is a matter of responding to some quite particular matters. Life in relationship with God means that certain words and acts do justice to that relationship in a way that other acts and words do not. Yet life is not to be shaped simply in terms of particular commandments; the life of faith is also narrative, it is story. And so narrative also functions as life-shaping. Stories shape lives in at least three ways: *(a)* A constitutive function— they shape a people's identity. They become the people of God in and through the retelling of the story. *(b)* A descriptive function—they become a mirror for self-identity. By looking at the story, one can come to recognize what being a person of faith in this God is like. You are like Israel. *(c)* A paradigmatic function—they provide a pattern for the life of faith, giving one an indication of what shape the life of faith should take in the various particulars of daily life. Be like Israel.

Exodus 19:1-8
On Eagle's Wings

The rest of the book of Exodus (plus Leviticus and Num. 1:1—10:11) takes place at Mt. Sinai (cf. 3:12). The people of God spend eleven months at the foot of this mountain. It is a time of no little consequence for Israel's future. This brief section constitutes the basis for all that follows.

Exodus 19 is a highly complex chapter, almost certainly a composite, to which all the major pentateuchal sources have made a contribution. At the same time, the final redaction presents a reasonably coherent perspective. The people's response in 19:8 and 24:3-7 frames this Sinai account. Yet the pledge in verse 8 is of a different order from 24:3-7; it is a pledge of commitment to God's larger purposes in the world, articulated in verses 5-6. In view of this response, the particularization of the law can proceed forthwith.

Verses 4-6 are central in interpreting what follows. The difficulty of these verses is found in the meaning of individual words as well as in the relationship of the clauses to one another and to 24:3-8. Scholarly opinion regarding source and dating is sharply divided (though Deuteronomic influence is likely). Contrary to some scholars, it is unlikely that this text has been influenced by a treaty form (see McCarthy, *Old Testament Covenant;* Nicholson, *God and His People*).

It is important to interpret these words in the larger context of chapters 1—18. It has been claimed that Israel's election as the people of God took place at Sinai. There are, however, a number of passages that make such an interpretation unacceptable. Israel has been identified by God as "my (firstborn) son" (4:22-23) or "my people" (3:7, 10; 5:1; 7:4, 16; 8:1, 20-22; 9:1, 13, 17; 10:3-4; cf. also 5:23; 15:16) throughout the narrative, its usage cutting across various sources. In fact, the expression "my people" occurs only in Exodus in the Pentateuch (except Lev. 26:12). This suggests a special emphasis on Israel's status as God's people during the Egyptian sojourn. There is no "election" of Israel in the book of Exodus; election is assumed. The

208

covenant at Sinai does *not* establish the relationship between Israel and God.

Moreover, the recurring references to the God of Abraham, Isaac, and Jacob, and the promises sworn to them, simply assume that this people is already God's people, the inheritor of the promises given to their ancestors (3:15–17; 6:4, 8). God remembers the covenant with the fathers (2:24; 6:4–5), which was made not only with Abraham but also *"with your descendants after you"* (Gen. 17:7). Israel in Egypt is understood already to be a part of that covenant relationship, and this before Sinai (see at 6:7). God made a promise or assumed an obligation that applied not simply to Abraham but also to Israel in Egypt. There is thus no good reason to suggest that the "my covenant" of 19:5 is any different from that of 6:4–5, the last Exodus reference to covenant (cf. 2:24). This suggests that for Exodus *the covenant at Sinai is a specific covenant within the context of the Abrahamic covenant.* Other Old Testament texts also suggest that the covenant at Sinai, whatever its tradition history, has here been drawn into the same orbit as the covenant with Abraham, and hence it too has a fundamentally promissory character (32:13; Lev. 26:42–45; Deut. 4:31; 9:27; Judg. 2:1; cf. I Sam. 12:22; Ps. 105:8–11; 106:45).

Already in 4:31 these people believe the gospel word of God spoken by Moses and bow down and worship Yahweh. The passover materials continue this worshiping theme (12:27), and it comes to a climax in the worship activity of 15:1–21. The people who are delivered from Egypt are the elect people of God, a community of faith already worshiping Yahweh. It is as such a people of God that they "fear the LORD" and "believe in the LORD" (14:31). God's saving actions, undertaken at the divine initiative, have drawn the community into a new orbit of life and blessing, to which the people have responded in faith/worship. Before there is any talk about obeying the law, what God has done fills their lives. To repeat: the covenant at Sinai is a specific covenant within an already existing covenant with an elected, redeemed, believing, worshiping community.

We return to verses 4–6. God briefly recapitulates what has been done on Israel's behalf, delivering them from Egypt and bearing them on eagle's wings to Sinai, where God dwells in an especially intensified way. The image of *God as a mother eagle* is most fully described in Deut. 32:10–12: God found Israel "in

209

a desert land, and in the howling waste of the wilderness; he encircled him, he cared for him, he kept him as the apple of his eye. Like an eagle that stirs up its nest, that flutters over its young, spreading out its wings, catching them, bearing them on its pinions."

This is a wonderfully gracious image of God as a mother who cares for her young during that time when they are especially vulnerable. They can find refuge from the threats of life under the shadow of her wings. In addition, it is an image of growth and maturation, a time of testing, as the mother eagle seeks to help her young learn to fly for themselves. She pushes them out of the nest so that they can try their wings, and if they flounder, she swoops down under them and bears them up on her own strong wings. This is an image of God which is common in the psalms (Ps. 17:8; 36:7; 57:1; 61:4; 63:7; 91:4) and is applied there not simply for the time of youth. God is one whose wings are always available for refuge in time of attack, for shelter from the destructive elements of the environment, and for loving concern at all times. This God, then, has been fully involved in Israel's life from Egypt through the wilderness to this point in their lives.

Given all that God has accomplished on Israel's behalf, a "therefore" is stated. The priority of God's gracious action toward the elect people of God has been made clear; it stands as the foundation of all that follows. It is only because of what God has done that these words can now come into play. This order of things is made especially prominent in Deuteronomy. For example, after a rehearsal of God's saving activity, Deut. 4:40 states: "Therefore you shall keep his statutes and commandments" (see also 11:7–8). When the children ask their parents why they are to keep the commandments (6:20–24), the reason is stated in terms of what God has done. Obedience to the commandments is thus a concern that grows out of a relationship already established by God. Hence, when the people respond as they do in 19:8 and 24:3–7, it is a pledge to the God with whom they are already closely related.

"Obey my voice and keep my covenant." First to be noted is that the matter is presented in personalistic terms: I did; I bore you; brought you to myself, giving heed to my voice, keeping my covenant, being my own possession, being to me a kingdom of priests and a holy nation. That which is called for on

210

Israel's part is couched in language that speaks more of personal commitment to God himself than to particular commandments. There is as yet no specified content to the voice to be obeyed.

Second, obeying the voice of God is a concern already expressed in Exodus (see at 15:26). We have seen that issues of obedience are not simply associated with the law revealed at Sinai but also emerge in connection with various situations in Israel's life. Hence, when combined with the lack of specificity, there is an openness here regarding the shape of Israel's obedience, a recognition that *to obey the voice of God entails more than obeying the laws given at Sinai.*

Third, much the same point can be made regarding the phrase "keeping my covenant." This is not new language either, being an integral part of the covenant with Abraham (Gen. 17:9–10). In that context it refers to circumcision, but later passages make clear that it finally entails obedience to other divine commands that emerge along the way. Abraham's "obeying my voice" (Gen. 22:18; 26:5) and "keeping my charge, my commandments, my statutes, and my laws" (26:5; see 18:19), tied as they are to the divine promise, are testimony to Abraham's keeping covenant. Also to be noted are the references to "keeping" statutes and laws in Exod. 15:26 and 16:28 (cf. 18:16, 20; 13:10). In 19:5, then, keeping covenant is essentially equivalent to obeying God's voice, but with the specific reference back to Abraham. Israel as a *community* for the first time responds as Abraham did. Keeping covenant has as broad a reference as obeying the voice of God. In the widest sense, it is doing justice to, being faithful to, the relationship with God in which the people stand, *a responsibility that is more extensive than obedience to Sinai law.*

This point is confirmed by the redaction of chapters 19—24. It can be agreed that 19:3–8 anticipates and interprets the covenant ceremony of chapter 24 (Childs, pp. 367, 502). Yet the redactional placement of the people's response in 19:8 shows that it ought not simply be collapsed into the response in 24:3–7, so that both end up being responses to the law given in chapters 20—23. Verse 8 must be related to what God has said in verses 4–6, without the Sinai commandments in view. If obeying God's voice and keeping covenant is a *wider and deeper matter* than obeying the Sinai commandments, then 19:8 is a commitment to obey *whatever words God may command over the course of*

211

Israel's history, and 24:3, 7 is a *particularization* of this with the commandments given at Sinai specifically in view.

Exodus 19:8 is then an *open-ended* commitment to God, to whatever God may have to say at any point in its history. This would include, for example, the Deuteronomic law. (If so, this is a forceful way to build in an early commitment to that later law!) This is in concert with the personalism of God's language. The people's commitment in 19:8 entails a high level of confidence in God himself, that what God may have to say in any future is in their best interests, that they are under the care of a mother eagle in all of their undertakings.

Three new elements in 19:5–6 are (1) special possession from among all peoples, (2) a kingdom of priests, and (3) a holy nation. The meanings of the phrases are related but distinct. One of the keys to their proper meaning is the phrase "All the earth is mine." This creational theme is too important in Exodus to be considered a disturbing parenthesis (Childs, p. 367) or simply the grounds for God being able to choose Israel rather than some other nation. This theme is prominent in the plague cycle, associated with the recurring passages on knowing Yahweh (9:29; 9:14; 8:22), and related to 9:16, "that my name may be declared throughout all the earth." In view of these texts, the best sense may be captured in this translation: *Because* all the earth is mine, so you, you shall be to me a kingdom of priests and a holy nation. This suggests that the phrases relate to a mission that encompasses God's purposes for the entire world. *Israel is commissioned to be God's people on behalf of the earth which is God's.*

Israel is called to be (1) God's *own possession,* a special group of people from among all the nations belonging to God, and hence people whom God can call on to be the bearer of this purpose (for different formulations, see Deut. 7:6; 14:2; 26:18). (2) *A kingdom of priests,* that is, "a servant nation instead of a ruling nation" (Durham, p. 263). It is to be devoted as a nation to *a mediatorial role* between God and other kingdoms, to function among the nations as a priest functions in a religious community (see Isa. 61:6). As such, all the people of God, not just the clergy, are to be "committed to the extension throughout the world" of the knowledge of Yahweh. Here is a strike against all forms of clericalism that would claim a special status in the divine economy. (3) A *holy nation,* that is, a people set

212

apart, not simply *from* other peoples/nations, but *for* a specific purpose. Israel is to embody God's own purposes in the world. The language of nation rather than congregation draws in all aspects of the life of Israel as pertinent to the fulfillment of this purpose, not just the specifically religious.

The force of the "if" and the conditionality of the covenant have to be carefully stated (see also at 20:5–6; 23:21–22). The issue is not how they might become God's people; Israel is the elect people already. There is no interest in warning Israel that its status as God's people will be taken away if it is disobedient. The issue is what the relationship to God entails: *what does it mean to be God's redeemed people in the world?* It is an invitation to be a people that carries forth God's purposes in the world (see Patrick, "The Covenant Code Source"). *The way to be this kind of people is to keep the covenant; to keep the covenant is to be this kind of people.* The condition would be that a disobedient Israel would not be able to be the kind of people God has called them to be, and hence God would not be able to use them for this purpose as God would like. It is noteworthy that Abraham's *obedience* is also linked with the relationship to the nations (22:18; 26:4–5) and does not take away from the unconditionality of God's promise to him.

This text does not signal a change from being "the sons of Israel" to a relationship "transcending biological descendancy" (contra Durham, p. 262). The reference is to Israel as a *"people"* among "all peoples" (see 33:16). What is stressed is Israel's purpose as a people among the nations. Israel responds by giving itself over to this divine purpose (19:8). This is a commitment to take on the responsibility of being a kingdom of priests. This, essentially, is the task of mediation, of obeying the law, not for its own sake, but for the sake of the world. It is a means by which the will of God can move toward realization in the entire earth.

The laws that ensue, and that the people agree to follow in 24:3–7, are instruction into some of the most basic ways in which Israel can be the kind of people God has invited or called them to be. The rite of 24:3–8 is a formalization of this commitment to the divine commission in view of the specific instruction given in chapters 20—23. Deuteronomy 4:6 may well state how the effect of obedience to the law is related to the other peoples: "Keep them and do them; for that will be your wisdom and your understanding in the sight of the peoples, who, when

213

they hear all these statutes, will say: 'Surely this great nation is a wise and understanding people' " (see Deut. 26:18–19; Exod. 34:10; Ezek. 36:23). Israel then will have to get its own act together. It has no little difficulty doing so, as we shall see. But standing before all that follows is this invitation to be God's people among the nations, carrying the knowledge of God "throughout all the earth."

I Peter 2:9 captures this sense of these verses: "But you are a chosen race, a royal priesthood, a holy nation, a people for his possession, that you may declare the wonderful deeds of him who called you out of darkness into his marvelous light." The church, in continuity with Israel, is to take up the mission to which the people of God have long been called. It is to be noted that many of the central mission texts in the New Testament are specifically grounded in the Old Testament (Luke 24:45–47; Acts 13:47; 15:14–18; Rom. 15:8–12; Gal. 3:8–9).

Exodus 19:9—20:21
Theophany and Law

Scholars have often noted that many different traditions feed into this complex narrative. Yet, in spite of continuing difficulties, a certain coherence is evident. It has been suggested that this passage is reflective of later reenactments of the Sinai event (cf. Deut. 31:9–13). While this may be so, there is no stipulation that these preparations are to be repeated (unlike Exodus 12—13). Whatever later cultic celebrations of Sinai may have been, they do not have the immediacy of this theophany. This is the only instance in the Old Testament where the gathered community is confronted with such a direct experience of God, hearing God speak without an intermediary. It is *a unique divine appearance.*

The purposes for this direct experience bracket the section (19:9; 20:20—*ba'*, "come"; *ba'abur*, "in order that"). The first relates to the people's response to Moses, the second to their response to God. In the midst of the unit are the ten commandments. *The unique character of this divine appearance is for the sake of a right hearing and understanding of these words of*

214

God, not an experience of the presence of God as such (contra Durham, pp. 264, 269).

In *19:9,* God will speak *in such a public way* to Moses for this purpose: to convince the people—now and forever—that Moses is *a mediator of the word of God* and not his own opinion. The enclosure of this statement by the repetition of Moses' report (19:8c, 9c) highlights this purpose as well as Moses' mediatorial role (sometimes too narrowly called "covenant mediator"). The various trips of Moses up and down the mountain reinforce this. The importance of "believing Moses" has been underlined in prior narratives (4:1–9, 31; 14:31).

It is to be noted that this kind of appearance would not be necessary to convey the word to Moses. Moses normally receives words from God in less spectacular ways (cf. 33:7–11); for Moses, most clouds are not storms. In 24:9–11, seventy-four leaders "saw the God of Israel" amid surroundings devoid of nature's activity. In fact, these persons show no fear; nor are special precautions taken, warnings issued, or matters of nearness closely specified (24:1–2). Yet they experience the presence of God in an even more direct way than did the people in chapter 19. All the earth-shaking phenomena are for a special purpose: the people's believing that what Moses says comes from God.

This divine determination to accentuate the credibility of Moses lifts up the importance of leadership. If people of faith do not have confidence in those who speak the word of God, that word and its effectiveness in the lives of people will suffer. God has chosen to be dependent upon such individuals in conveying God's word rather than speaking directly. This action sets in place a divine economy relative to the revelation of the divine word and will. Audible words from God to people will no longer be the way God "gets through" to them. God will work in and through specially chosen leaders, endowed with gifts for this purpose. It is thus not surprising that God, having called such persons to their tasks, works to enhance their standing within communities of faith.

The people respond to God's direct speaking of the ten commandments with fear and trembling; they cannot take this divine directness any longer (20:18; so also Deut. 5:23–28). Let Moses do the hearing, and they will listen to him. Thus the people themselves, *on the basis of their experience of need,* call

215

on Moses to mediate; it is not imposed on them. The divine administrative skills are exemplary! Because Moses exercised this role already in 18:26 and 19:3–8 (see 18:19–20), this is a *confirmation* of Moses' role in view of the importance of these divine words. Moses alone then draws close to God and receives the remaining words of God (20:21).

The purpose articulated in *20:20* for the uniqueness of the theophany is *to center the reverence and attention of the people on the God who gives the law.* It is often thought that 19:18–21 originally followed 19:19a. Yet good sense can be made of the present placement, if 19:20–25 is an interlude and 20:1 picks up where 19:19 left off. It is in fact the direct hearing of God's speaking to Moses that convinces the people of Moses' mediatorial role. Verses 18–21 may interrupt the divine speaking, but it is precisely the interruption God hoped for. Literarily, these verses also enclose the decalogue within the more direct aspects of the theophany and set it off as distinctive from the laws that follow.

Moses' language, "Do not fear, . . . that there may be fear of God," plays on the word "fear." The people were deathly afraid of all that was happening; Moses assures them that they need not be afraid. The people are not to obey this word because God stands before them as a threat. The proper response to what God has said and done is not fright but reverence, which is not the same as obedience; it is a deeply engaged centering of the self upon God as Lord. It is just such a focus on God and the divine purpose that will keep them from sin, that is, from violating the established relationship. The phrase "that you may not sin" does not mean sinlessness, or that the law would never be broken, but that in the fear of the Lord it is possible to live lives that are in fundamental accord with the relationship that God intends (cf. Deut. 30:11–20).

The fear of God, which provides the relational grounding for obedience, keeps obedience personally oriented (see at 19:1–8). It is not obedience vis-à-vis an objective law code, obeying the law for the sake of the law. *It is obedience to the one who gives the law.* It is to keep God himself, and loyalty and allegiance to this God, as the focus of their attention in these matters. That is why the law initially comes as direct divine address to the people: to keep the law oriented in terms of personal relationship. God has appeared personally before them to speak

216

these words in order that they might revere and hold fast to God (the giver of the law). If they so focus their eyes on God, it is that which will enable obedience more than attention to the details of the law. Truly then they will see that God comes with this word "for our good always, that he might preserve us alive" (Deut. 6:24).

All the *preparations for the meeting* with God are designed in terms of the two above-noted purposes. For the people, such an event is extraordinary, not least in view of the general knowledge that human beings do not see God and live. But the preparations and the precautions would not only make them ready, it would also impress upon them that this was the real thing, an actual divine appearance. As a part of these preparations, Moses is to consecrate the people, that is, formally set them apart from their ordinary affairs. They are now holy. On their part, for reasons of purification when coming into contact with the presence of God, the people are to wash their clothing (see Gen. 35:2) and abstain from sexual behavior (see I Sam. 21:4–5). Moses is also to instruct the people regarding boundaries for their presence and behavior. The entire mountain area will be consecrated ground (19:23), the violating of which is considered so heinous that it carries the death penalty. The mountain is thus treated like the Holy of Holies.

It is often suggested that this reflects an ancient view of *holiness* as a mysterious, threatening power, as if the mountain were charged with electrical power. Such a perspective, however, cannot be sustained, at least in this form. It is important to note that touching in and of itself would not cause death. The person who touched was to be put to death by the community (see Num. 1:51; 4:15). Thus II Sam. 6:6–8 is not a direct parallel, even though the verb *paraṣ* ("break forth") is used (as in 19:22, 24). Moreover, it is not suggested that the person who touched such a one (19:13) would thereby die. Nor is such a person "infected" with holiness; the text does not state this, and there is no parallel elsewhere. Perhaps it should be explained in terms of Num. 16:26, where the command not to touch anything associated with the wicked is spoken lest those who touch also be swept away to their death.

This question needs to be related to 19:20–25, "lest they break through [or, come up] to the LORD to gaze and many of them perish," because the Lord would "break out upon them." **217**

In this context, the latter phrase must be explained by 19:12–13; God's "breaking out" would be effected by a community death penalty (for comparable human activity in conjunction with God's "breaking out," see II Sam. 5:20). The issue is seeing God. To "gaze" is the same verb used in the formulation, "You shall not see God and live" (33:20). This does *not* mean that God cannot be seen. Rather, it assumes that God can be seen, but that one cannot live if this happens. Yet in 24:10 God does allow some to "see" and no harm comes to them; hence it is not a matter of approaching the holiness of God as such.

Why, then, is the penalty so severe for the people as a whole? The issue is not a concern for God, as if the divine transcendence or sovereignty would be compromised or violated. The concern is explicitly for the sake of the people, to preserve them alive. Not seeing God has reference to a structure of creation for the purpose of preserving human freedom and life. For God to be fully present would be coercive; too direct a divine presence would annul human existence, as a flame kills a butterfly. God must set people at a certain distance from himself. The vision of God must be of such a nature that disbelief remains possible. Leaders such as Moses are made partial exceptions to this (though ambiguity is not fully removed) because of their mediatorial capacity, for the sake of communicating the word of God to the people (for details, see Fretheim, *The Suffering of God*, pp. 90–92).

Right on schedule, God appears on Mt. Sinai. Natural phenomena, from both thunderstorm and volcano, accompany the divine presence. All of nature seems to be caught up in the event, for the purposes noted. Then Moses brings the people out to the mountain "to meet God" (19:17; cf. 19:13). Unlike Moses, the people react with fear and trembling. As they stand there at the foot of the mountain, with everything in nature filling the air with extraordinary sounds and sights, God speaks to Moses (19:19, not in thunder as the NRSV suggests, but in a "voice," perhaps not fully articulate to the people's ears). The purposes for all of this are brought to an initial stage of completion: the people *hear* God and Moses speaking with each other (note that Moses is still standing with the people!) and their attention is centered on God.

218

The theme of *testing* has occurred before (15:25 and 16:4), referring to means by which God could see whether the people would do justice to this relationship or not, how they would respond to the responsibilities of relationship put before them. The primary focus of the testing in this context is the first commandment: undivided loyalty to Yahweh. The following section is enclosed by this very concern (20:23; 23:24-25, 32-33).

As we have noted, testing must be relationally rather than legalistically understood. The initial stages (especially) of *any* relationship are times of testing, as the parties to the relationship find themselves in various situations where their loyalty to one another is tested. What constitutes testing will be determined by the nature of the relationship and the expectations the partners have for it. Testing in a marriage will have components different from testing in a business partnership. As the relationship matures, and trust levels are built up, faithful responses to the testing of the relational bond will tend to become second nature and hence less of a test (though finally will never become automatic).

In order for these developments to occur, it is important that the expectations be clear, that the parties know what it means to be faithful to the relationship (otherwise, one will never know whether disloyalty has occurred). The law given by God to Israel is, in effect, a laying down of the expectations for the relationship (God does not keep the people in the dark about this!). The law is a means for Israel to know what being faithful to God entails in the living out of life within the relationship. For God to have expectations for the relationship with Israel at all is, willy-nilly, to acknowledge that these constitute a test. God does not want to put Israel in a situation where its loyalty will be sorely tested (see 23:33; 34:12; cases like Gen. 22:1 are not envisaged), but God knows that life in relationship will bring tests again and again.

It has long been considered that 19:20–25 disturb the flow of the narrative. It is possible, however, to understand those verses as an interlude between 19:19 and 20:1. God calls Moses up into the mountain and asks him to warn the people. Moses resists God at this point, suggesting that God is repeating himself. But God insists, thereby making clear that *Moses' authority is subservient to God's.* There are no new acts of preparation for the people in view (only for the priests, here mentioned for the first time, showing that even the priesthood to be estab-

219

lished [28:1] is subordinate to Moses in approaching the special nearness of God).

The new reality that prompts this conversation is that God has appeared and has begun to speak with Moses. The situation has now changed for everybody. The possibilities for disorder and chaos have been heightened. A new word is deemed necessary for this new moment. In view of what has developed, the people must remain obedient. The fundamental consideration, however, remains the same: to preserve the people alive. Moses, then, returns to the people and tells them of God's concern (19:25), with the words of God following immediately.

These verses are thus in the service of the twofold purpose of this section as a whole: to center the people on the reality of the divine presence and to clarify the role of Moses as intermediary (he crosses the consecrated boundary!) Literarily, these verses retard the flow of activity to lift up what is yet to come. It is not simply being in the divine presence or hearing God speak to Moses that is finally central; it is what God actually says. All is for the sake of the word of God to be spoken and its proper interpretation.

Exodus 20:1–17
The Ten Commandments

Considerable scholarly effort has been expended in the study of these ten words over the last generation (see Harrelson). Only introductory notes can be offered here (see also at chaps. 19 and 21—23).

The Old Testament has a number of decalogues or decalogue-like formulations (e.g., 34:17–26; Deut. 27:15–26; Lev. 19), but only Deut. 5:6–21 is strictly parallel. The number ten first appears in 34:28, and the division into two tables—at an unknown point—is first stated in 34:1. The second person singular addressee is consistent (note the shift from divine first person in v. 7). The differences from Deuteronomy 5, in both commands and expansions (cf. 20:9–11; Deut. 5:13–15), demonstrate that they were not transmitted in a never-to-be-changed form. Scholarly opinion differs regarding their age, collection,

220

and original setting; it is probable that they were all originally brief and negative in formulation. Over time they were
expanded or adjusted in view of particular needs in the
community.

The parenetic form of the expansions suggests that Israel's
worship was the primary life setting for the commandments.
Their collection in this simple, direct, easy-to-remember form,
however, no doubt fostered their use beyond the sanctuary and
kept them alive in the community. Their citation by prophets
(e.g., Jer. 7:9; Hos. 4:2) demonstrates their general familiarity
and importance. While their catechetical use is post-biblical,
the redactional placement in the Sinai narrative (see above)
suggests something approximating catechesis (see 24:12), as
does the address to individuals. But, while the address is individual, the concern is not some private welfare. The focus is on
protecting *the health of the community,* to which end the individual plays such an important role.

That eight commandments are negatively formulated is
pertinent at this point. As such, they open up life rather than
close it down; that is, they focus on the outer limits of conduct
rather than specific behaviors (though chaps. 21—23 draw out
such specific implications). At the same time, the negative formulation indicates that the primary concern is not to create the
human community but *to protect* it from behaviors that have
the potential of destroying it. Yet the commands implicitly com-
mend their positive side (cf. 20:3 and Deut. 6:5). The two positive commands suggest the appropriateness of this for all ten
words. For example, not bearing false witness invites speaking
well of one's neighbor, not killing suggests efforts to preserve
life, and not wrongfully using the name of God commends the
praise of God. It is not enough for a community's life and health
simply to avoid crimes.

There is a certain comprehensiveness in their ties to a considerable range of life experience, encompassing relationships
to God, neighbor, and nature. Yet the latter in particular is less
than what we would insist on today, the absence of self-related
commands is noteworthy (e.g., care of one's body), and one
cannot help wishing that the passionate concern of 22:21–27
had found its way into the expansions. Changing social attitudes
and perspectives have also blunted this comprehensiveness.
For example, changed perspectives on the place of women in

221

society have introduced a level of severity concerning certain behaviors (e.g., rape) simply not dealt with in the laws. Or, the complexities of modern society raise many issues that they address in indirect ways at best (e.g., corporate ethics). A multitude of sins are sometimes drawn into the interpretation of one or another commandment, but the fact is that many modern evils are simply not covered or anticipated.

Hence it is of considerable importance that these commandments not be understood as eternally limited in scope or as ethical principles more important than any others that might be formulated. The various canonical expansions of some commandments (see 20:9–11) witness to an ongoing effort by Israel to address changing life situations. This *gives the people of God in every age an innerbiblical warrant to expand on them.* If the decalogue is understood as Israel's bill of rights, the way for amendment is open. While we probably would not withdraw any one of the ten today, we almost certainly would add a few and expand on others. The canon of the ten commandments is an open canon, and our instruction should recognize this. But the ten words we do have are an indispensable starting point for our ongoing ethical task.

Also to be noted is that the commandments are apodictic in form (relatively uncommon elsewhere in that world), straightforward declarations expressing core concerns of the community applicable to all situations. No juridical consequences for disobedience are specified (in 20:5–7 the subject is God, not the courts). As such, they are not generally motivated by negative reinforcement, a common way in which we tend to use them. Their being obligatory is not conditional on their being enforceable. The appeal is to a deeper motivation for obedience: these are commands of "the LORD *your* God." The address to the individual "you," and not to Israel generally, lifts up the importance of internal motivation rather than corporate pressure or external coercion.

The degree to which one can universalize the applicability of the commandments is not addressed directly, though their creational import demands exactly this. That is, they serve to keep order in the world, restraining the forces of disorder so that creation does not revert to chaos. The explicitness of the connection between sabbath and creation points the way to such an understanding. Obedience of these commands by all

222

would mean that God's intention that creatures be one thing and not another would be more closely realized. The tie to creation—which is also Torah—shows that the commands are not the heteronomous imposition of a set of rules; to obey them is to be what one was created to be (on the place of command- ment in the creation narratives, see Gen. 1:28; 2:16–17).

From a New Testament perspective, Christians have not been made exempt from these provisions. In fact, Matt. 5:17–29 (see 19:18–22) states that the commandments are not to be relaxed at all but pushed to their deepest level in the human spirit (see on coveting). The commandment to love (22:37–40; see Rom. 13:9) does not set the commandments aside but incor- porates them and extends them without limit, as part of what it means to do what love requires. The will of God does not lose its particularity in the command to love; it simply opens up those particularities to limitless possibilities. Love always means going beyond whatever laws may be articulated, but it needs their particularity for instructional purposes, charting some- thing of what love may entail in specific life situations.

Because human beings always fall short in loving, the law can function to point up that that has occurred, driving one to God in Christ, in whom the law has been fulfilled. The one who is in Christ is liberated to do the works of the law, not as a vehicle for remaining a Christian, but as instruction for shaping a life of faith active in love. The New Testament polemic against the law as a means of salvation is directed, not against the Old Testament, but against mistaken interpretations of the law in the first century, also prevalent today.

(For further discussion of the continuing applicability of the law, see the discussion of social justice at 20:22—23:33.)

I Am the Lord Your God (20:1–2)

Unlike other laws, the decalogue was God's direct address to Israel. This demonstrates the high position in which it was held by the community; there could be no question of its having been God-given. This introduction is of extraordinary impor- tance (recognized in Judaism by being made the first word). On the one hand, it keeps the law personally oriented; obedience is a matter of relationship to Yahweh—not God-in-general, not adherence to law for its own sake (see above). I am the Lord

223

your God. This is in effect a promise that Yahweh will be their God. Obedience is relationally conceived.

On the other hand, this God identifies *himself* in relation to a particular history. This ties the law back into the prior narrative (see 19:1). The activity of God in redeeming Israel *from bondage* means that the law and the service to God and world it entails is not understood to be another form of bondage. The law is a gift of a redeeming God, and a particular redemptive act is seen as undergirding and informing the law, not the other way around. Those who are given the law are already God's people. Hence the law is not understood as a means of salvation but as instruction regarding the shape such a redeemed life is to take in one's everyday affairs.

Yet these are not commands among which the people of God can pick and choose; they do lay a claim on life in very particular ways. At the same time, being grounded in redemptive reality means that the law must be viewed as open-ended (see above), continually responsive to changing situations in life. New occasions teach new duties. In fact, God's surprising and unconditional move on Israel's behalf is a standing invitation for Israel to go beyond the law. To be gracious as Yahweh has been gracious means that the people of God must always be on the lookout for ever new ways to conform their lives to that of God himself. And God's ongoing gracious activity will continue to point the way to such new vistas for life.

You Shall Have No Other Gods Before Me (20:3)

However one might translate the phrase usually rendered "before me," the command is to be absolutely loyal to Yahweh, rejecting all other gods (cf. 22:20; 23:13; 34:14). The formulation of Deut. 6:5 is a positive variant of this commandment: You shall love the Lord your God with all your heart. To use the language of Luther's *Small Catechism,* it means to fear, love, and trust in God above all things. This commandment is thus the basis for all the others, which draw out what loyalty to God entails in various aspects of the relationship. In this sense the first commandment is the most important of all.

Sometimes it is suggested that this commandment with its reference to "other gods" exhibits a henotheism or monolatry, essentially identical words that denote belief in or worship of one God without denying the existence of others. Whether this

224

commandment entails a theoretical monotheism—there is only one God—is an important historical question but is largely beside the point of the commandment. Its force is decisively informed by the historical fact that many Israelites did turn to the worship of other gods. Those who formulated and used the commandment saw the power of such idolatry, whether or not they recognized the reality of such gods. Those who make claims about gods they serve, even though those gods are a figment of their imagination, can draw and have drawn the people of God away into disloyalty to Yahweh. Hence it has been possible for persons in any age who maintain a high monotheism—from final redactor to modern theologian—to continue to use this commandment, indeed to see it as a central issue even in cultures where all the gods are dead. The upshot is that the commandment's language is theologically compatible with a high monotheism, whatever one's historical judgments.

You Shall Not Make for Yourself an Idol (20:4–6)

The prohibition against images sets Israel off from religious practices common to the surrounding cultures. But its exact meaning is not very clear. For one thing, is it a separate commandment or only an elaboration of verse 3? This question is deeply rooted in precritical religious traditions, with many groups designating verses 3–6 as a single commandment (Roman Catholics, Lutherans, Jews; the former divide v. 17 into two commandments; Jews consider v. 2 to be the first). There are difficulties with both interpretations.

Those who view verse 4 as a separate commandment tend to regard it as a prohibition of images of *Yahweh*, stressing the "for yourself" (i.e., Israel's worship), other divine images having been dealt with in verse 3. However, the language of verse 3 and verses 4–6 is interwoven in the rest of Exodus, seen especially in the frame of the Book of the Covenant (see 20:23; 23:32–33) and in the golden calf apostasy and its aftermath (34:13–17). The repetition of "bow down" and "serve" in verse 5 ("them") and 23:24 in particular demonstrates a broader reference to verse 4 than images of Yahweh, as does the reference to Yahweh's jealousy. Yet those who view verses 4–6 as an elaboration of verse 3 encounter difficulty with its inclusion of images of Yahweh, an apparent move beyond verse 3. This can be overcome if worshiping images of Yahweh is in fact understood

225

to be idolatry. This could be descriptive of what happens in Exodus 32. Keeping verses 3–6 as a single multifaceted commandment on idolatry seems to do less violence to the final redaction.

This interweaving of other gods and idols may also be seen in other parts of the Old Testament. The Deuteronomic History may be cited as illustrative (cf. II Kings 17:7–18). The heart of the matter is that they "did not believe in the LORD their God." Instead, they "had feared other gods and walked in the customs of the nations" (II Kings 17:7–8); they "went after false idols . . . and followed the nations" (II Kings 17:15). To "forsake *all* the commandments of the LORD" (II Kings 17:16) finds its definition in terms of idolatry, the serving of gods other than Yahweh. This again shows the priority of the first commandment.

A further matter of unclarity is, Why were images forbidden? Insofar as this has reference to other gods or their images (no matter how god and image were thought to be related), the issue of disloyalty to Yahweh is at the heart of the prohibition. The ubiquity of images in the surrounding religions, especially among the Canaanites, impressed the importance of this on the tradition. The drawing power of these religions was considerable, and images were part of the picture.

But why were images of *Yahweh* forbidden? Wherein does the idolatry lie? The usual answer is that this compromises Yahweh's transcendence. Yahweh is above and beyond everything in all creation. But it seems more likely that this prohibition arises more out of a concern to protect God's relatedness than transcendence. Texts such as Ps. 115:5–7 and Jer. 10:4–5 make this point directly (see I Kings 18:27–29 on the gods not being affected). Unlike plastic images, which are static and immobile, deaf and dumb, unfeeling and unthinking, and fix God at a point in time, Israel's God is one who can speak and feel and act in both nature and history (and in this sense is free). This is, of course, a problem with other gods and their images, quite apart from what their adherents or detractors might believe about them. Hence other gods (with whatever reality or nonreality they were thought to have) and images of Yahweh are exactly parallel in these respects. The worshipers of the golden calf were engaged fundamentally in a false theology, which led to false worship, believing that an image, even of Yahweh, could have accomplished their redemption from Egypt.

The link sometimes made between images and divine self-

226

revelation is pertinent at this point. There is an intimate continuity between God *an sich* (God in himself) and God as revealed; God entirely corresponds to himself in revelation and activity. Images imply that not only does God not think or feel or act in relationship to the world but that this is the very character of God. To worship images is to deny some basic things about God's very nature as well as the divine relationship to the world. Thus, in the aftermath of the golden calf, God in Exod. 34:6–7 interweaves statements about the divine character and the divine activity.

Hence Israel turns to verbal images, for they have the capacity to convey God's relatedness in a way that plastic images cannot. This is continuous with talk about human beings, with all of their capacities for interrelationships, having been created in the image of God. It is also consonant with the New Testament claim that Jesus Christ is the image of the invisible God (Col. 1:15); the one who revealed God most decisively was a living, active human being.

"I the LORD your God am a jealous God." This metaphor from the sphere of marriage is linked with the worship of other gods and serves to stress allegiance to Yahweh alone (see at 34:14; Deut. 6:14–15). The judgment for disloyalty—and "iniquity" is focused on such unfaithfulness—is sharply noted, and the showing of steadfast love is stated in conditional terms. However, because in 34:6–7 God himself revises this formulation in view of the golden calf apostasy, this passage is finally provisional. Hence it cannot stand alone in any theological statement or contemporary appropriation. God is here strikingly revealed as an experimental theologian! Moreover, God is shown to be one who does not insist that specific theological formulations are set in stone; the tablets can always be broken and new ones carved out. This is an especially sharp illustration of the importance of contextuality in using the text for exegetical or theological purposes.

You Shall Not Make Wrongful Use of the Name of the Lord (20:7)

This prohibition is basically concerned with the divine reputation. That is, it is designed to protect the divine name from being used in any way that brings God or God's purposes for the world into disrepute. It assumes the close relationship between

227

name and renown (Ps. 135:13; see 30:4; 97:12). God's good name is as important to God as any human being's name is to the person who bears it. A name is a precious thing; the way in which people talk about others—such as gossip or other vain and hurtful talk—will affect their standing in the community (in many ways the eighth commandment does for people what this one does for God).

A central concern of God in Exodus to this point has been "that my name may be declared throughout all the earth" (9:16). That name is most fully defined in Exodus in the proclamation of the name in 34:6–7. A central issue at stake for God is the declaration of this name to the world and the effect the hearing of that name will have on people. Will they be drawn to it or repelled by it or remain indifferent to it? If that name has been besmirched in some way by the manner in which it has been used by the people of God or by the practices with which it has been associated, then the divine intentions may fall short of their realization. Or, if in the very declaration of the name itself it is used in misleading or false ways (e.g., false prophecy; see Deut. 18:20), God will not treat this hindrance to the divine intentions lightly.

Discussions of this commandment have all too often limited its applicability. It has been especially associated with the use of the name in magic or divination, or false swearing (Lev. 19:12; cf. Ps. 24:4; Matt. 5:34–37) or profanity (cf. Lev. 24:16). This may be the case, but more is at stake. The name of God is so commonly associated with empty phrases or easy religion or the latest ideology of a social or political sort. The name thereby gets dragged down to the level of the contexts in which it is used. As people hear it so used, they may come to associate the name of God fundamentally with a cause they wish to avoid or reject. Consequently, they will not be drawn to this God and the name will not receive its due honor and respect. At the deepest level, use of God's name is a matter of mission.

Positively, God's name is to be used in prayer and praise, one important dimension of which is witness. Many psalms do so: "I will praise the name of God with a song; I will magnify him with thanksgiving" (Ps. 69:30; 34:3); "I will tell of your name to my brethren; in the midst of the congregation I will praise you" (Ps. 22:22; 45:17). God's name is to be declared even more widely: "For this I will extol you, O LORD, among the

228

nations, and sing praises to your name" (Ps. 18:49; 96:2–3). Indeed, "we boast of the name of the LORD our God" (Ps. 20:7) with a worldwide goal in focus: "As your name, O God, so your praise reaches to the ends of the earth" (Ps. 48:10; 86:9). God's mission for the world is linked to the use of the divine name.

Remember the Sabbath Day, and Keep It Holy (20:8–11)

To keep the sabbath day holy is to keep it separate from the other six days as "a sanctuary of time" (Patrick). People are not to live as if all time were their own, to do with as they please. The God of all time retains the right to determine how one day shall or shall not be used. This weekly separation (emphasized by the inclusio in vv. 8 and 11) is to be publicly demonstrated by a time of rest for all engaged in work, including the servants and the animals. "Remembering" is more than a mental act, it is an active observance (see God's remembering in 2:24). There is no mention of it as a time for worship, but the fact that it is a "sabbath to the LORD" leaves room for worship as a way of developing that commitment.

It is probable that the sabbath is an ancient institution (the ancient Near Eastern connections are uncertain), but it's understanding and use developed considerably over the years. This is reflected in the various rationales given in 20:10–11; 31:12–17; Deut. 5:13–15. Such developments expanded in post-biblical times, even into the modern era, with the sabbath subject to detailed legislation (e.g., blue laws). In the face of this, every discussion of the sabbath should be decisively informed by the fact that this day is a divine gift to the world, not a burden. "The sabbath was made for human beings, not human beings for the sabbath" (Mark 2:27).

The rationale given is God's resting on the seventh day of creation (Gen. 2:2), thereby hallowing it. Keeping sabbath is therefore a matter within the sphere of creation rather than redemption or specifically Israelite law (see its pre-Sinai use in 16:22–30). It is not simply something for Israel to keep; even animals and strangers are to honor it. Yet the divine rest is more than a humanitarian gesture or a paradigm for creaturely resting—because God did so, the creatures should. It is a religious act with cosmic implications.

229

INTERPRETATION

The divine rest in creation is not a picturesque way of speaking of the end of God's creating; rather, the divine rest "finished" the creation. God's resting is a divine act that builds into the very created order of things a working/resting rhythm. Only when that rhythm is honored by all is the creation what God intended it to be. The sabbath is thus a divinely given means for all creatures to be in tune with the created order of things. Even more, *sabbath-keeping is an act of creation-keeping.* To keep the sabbath is to participate in God's intention for the rhythm of creation. Not keeping the sabbath is a violation of the created order; it returns one aspect of that order to chaos. What the creatures do with the sabbath has cosmic effects. Such lines of thought may help explain the death penalty which Israel attaches to sabbath-keeping (31:12–17; 35:2); the order of creation is at stake.

It may seem incoherent to suggest that not doing work helps keep chaotic forces at bay. Yet one needs only to participate for a moment in the rat race which is the modern world to realize how the neglect of the sabbath contributes to the spread of chaos. This points to something fundamental about the relationship between human endeavor and cosmic order. There is a place for human dominion within the created order (Gen. 1:28). But sabbath-keeping puts all human striving aside, recognizes the decisive role of God in creation, and provides for a weekly oasis to rest back in the arms of this reality.

The humanitarian concerns associated with the sabbath deserve special mention; they are picked up again in 23:12 and 34:21, and especially in Deut. 5:14–15 (which roots the sabbath in God's exodus deliverance). The sabbath is a fundamentally egalitarian institution. The sabbath rest is for all, rich and poor, master and servant, human beings and animals. One must certainly do more than keep the sabbath to address these divisions (see 22:21–27). Yet the sabbath brings this matter to the regular attention of the community. Thereby one moment in creation is recaptured when the world's creatures were at peace with one another. And it calls for, indeed anticipates, a new world order when once again it will be so and everything will be very good.

230   This humanitarian concern of the sabbath is a bridge to the commandments concerned with interhuman relationships.

Honor Your Father and Mother (20:12)

No interhuman relationship is so basic as that between children and parents. It is a fundamental order of creation. At no age do people cease to be children of parents. The importance of this command is measured not simply by its foundational relationship to society but also by its nurturing role for those who will inevitably function in that context.

If this commandment were written today, it would no doubt take into account the grave problem of child abuse and lift up parental responsibility toward children (see Eph. 6:2–4). At one point the commandment does have a contemporary ring; it places father and mother together as equally to be honored (see Lev. 19:3). This is striking, given the evident patriarchal character of Israelite society. If the command reflects the divine concern and authority exercised through the parent, the female as divine representative is even more noteworthy. This is consonant with the use of both mother and father as metaphors for God (see Isa. 64:8; 66:13).

The positive formulation, along with the use of the wide-ranging verb "honor," means that there is no one specific behavior that is commanded. It is an open-ended commandment, inviting children to respond in any way that honors parents. In all dealings with parents, respect, esteem, having regard and concern for, and showing affection, considerateness, and appreciation are the order of the day (see 21:15, 17).

It has been shown (see Harrelson, pp. 92–95) that the commandment is directed more toward adults than children. Perhaps especially in mind are cases where elderly parents are misused or abused when their working and/or mental powers have significantly receded. This dimension also shows that obedience is not at the center of what it means to honor. These aspects of the command should be clearly evident in the teaching of children, so as not to imply that they are the special objects of its concern or that there will come a day when this obligation has been removed.

This command has become exceedingly complex in a day of increased longevity, when social security income, nursing homes, and extended medical care for the elderly are so much a part of life. Governmental authority at various levels has often been given responsibility for this commandment; adult children in particular will need to examine carefully how well they or their governmental surrogates are handling the above-noted characteristics of "honor." While there is no commandment relating to other authorities such as state or judiciary (see 22:28), this one has been so extended by the Reformers on the basis of such texts as Prov. 24:21 and I Peter 2:13–17. While a host of issues is raised thereby, it is a legitimate extension, not least because such authorities have been granted a "parental" role in many situations.

The unique extension of the commandment, "that your days may be long," is neither strictly promise (cf. Eph. 6:2) nor implied warning (though severe judgments for some acts against parents are noted in 21:15, 17). This is matter-of-fact moral order talk, more typical of Deuteronomy (Deut. 4:40; 5:33; 22:7; 25:15). That is, the effect of such conduct is *intrinsic to* the deed; forensic judgments will be rare. If the commandment is obeyed, life will go better for one, generally speaking. But this is not inevitably the case, nor is there some point in life at which one can say that such a word has been fulfilled. For both these reasons, the language of promise or reward is misleading, unless one uses the word "promise" in a very general sense (life holds more promise). On the other hand, if the commandment is not obeyed, then the effects on life are apt to be negative. Again, not inevitably so; characteristic of such moral order talk is a loose causal weave, a highly important factor in Old Testament theology.

You Shall Not Kill (20:13)

The last six (five) commandments have to do with relationships among social equals. This commandment has come in for more than its share of consideration over the years, not least in more recent times. Those concerned about war, capital punishment, suicide, euthanasia, self-defense, and abortion have all appealed to it in one way or another. Though the command does not make these distinctions, one is faced not only with its meaning but with its possible legitimate extensions.

232   The meaning of the verb "to kill" *(raṣah)* has been much debated. In view of certain passages (e.g., I Kings 21:19) it has been suggested that the verb means murder (so NEB; NRSV). It

can also, however, refer to unintentional killing (Deut. 4:41–42) or to the execution of a convicted killer (Num 35:30); it is never used of killing in war. Scholars have sought more refined meanings, from blood feuds to illegal violence against an Israelite to taking the law into one's own hands. Probably its meaning changed over the years in view of shifting historical circumstances, but that is difficult to demonstrate.

Perhaps the command is best seen to function in 21:12 and Num. 35:20–21: any act of violence against an individual out of hatred, anger, malice, deceit, or for personal gain, in whatever circumstances and by whatever method, that might result in death (even if killing was not the intention). "Murder" does not sufficiently capture this sense for the word. The more general word "kill" serves the community of faith best, forcing continual reflection on the meaning of the commandment and reminding all that in the taking of human life for any reason *one acts in God's stead,* in the face of which there should be a lengthy pause filled with careful soul-searching and the absence of vengefulness and arrogance. As a result, taking a human life should be very rare indeed.

The basis of the command is that all life belongs to God (Lev. 17:11; Gen. 9:6). The divine intention in creation is that no life be taken. Life is thus not for human beings to do with as they will; they are not God. It is up to God to determine what shall be done with life. The issue thus becomes one of discernment regarding that divine determination. Human beings are never to kill on their own authority; they are only agents of God. Israel's limited use of capital punishment, as specified in certain God-given laws (see 21:12–17; 22:18–20), had to do with violations of God's created order. The issue thus became a matter of world restoration under God.

Similar arguments were used in ancient Israel for divine support in some wars. But has not this all changed today, not least with the development of nuclear arms? They constitute a threat to God's world order unparalleled in human history. This should prompt new reflections on war and peace and hence give a new meaning to the word "kill."

The issue of discernment regarding the divine will remains the central issue, not least in recognition of the principle, New occasions teach new duties. Who would claim, for example, that 21:15–17 is applicable today? But the criteria to be applied in

233

many other cases are much more complex. An openness to both the limit and the extent of the meaning of the commandment beyond its original formulation for new life situations is needed, but always with God's creational intentions in view. This corresponds to Jesus' own usage in Matt. 5:21–26; he extends the commandment beyond physical violence to include verbal abuse and other manifestations of anger. Above all, he expresses the concern that reconciliation among those estranged from one another be given a high priority, even above religious practice.

You Shall Not Commit Adultery (20:14)

This is another commandment designed to be protective of the family. Israel's attitude toward adultery is not unique in the ancient Near East. The phrase "the great sin" is used in Israel and elsewhere (see Gen. 20:9). The use of this phrase for idolatry (32:21, 30, 31) links up with the use of adultery language for Israel's disloyalty to Yahweh (Isa. 57:1–13; Ezek. 23:36–49; Hosea). This demonstrates the seriousness with which adulterous relationships at the human level are taken. Issues of disloyalty strike against the very integrity of the marriage. The seriousness of such a violation of relationship is seen in the prescription of the death penalty (see Deut. 22:22), even for a king (II Sam. 12:13). It is sometimes linked with sins of oppression and violence (see Job 24:13–17). Adultery is a crime against persons, but it is also a sin against God himself (Gen. 39:9; II Sam. 12:9). It violates God's creational intention, which links a positive role for sexuality with commitment and loyalty (Gen. 2:24–25).

The verb is used with both men and women as the subject and concerns those who are married *and* those who are betrothed (see Lev. 18:6–20; 20:10–21; Deut. 22:23–29). There is a double standard in the law's treatment of men and women in this regard, however. Men commit adultery only with other married women, women with any other man. This reflects the patriarchal character of Israel's society. Any contemporary use of the commandment would be compelled to treat men and women in the same terms, if it were to remain true to the inner-biblical warrant to update laws in view of changing perspectives and social circumstances.

The commandment had to do with adultery and the un-

234

faithfulness which that entailed, not with fornication. At the same time, at least some forms of the latter were considered a moral offense (see 22:16–17; cf. Matt. 15:19; I Cor. 6:18) and may have been considered an extension of the commandment along with other sexual offenses (22:19; see Lev. 18:1–30). Any contemporary usage of the commandment should draw into its orbit of consideration other sexual activities in view of changed attitudes. The resolution of such issues is not often a clear-cut matter, however. Sexual harassment, rape, and pornography are certainly violence against the personhood of another; they must not be considered of second-level importance just because they are not explicit in Israel's laws. Jesus' own extension of the command strikes at precisely this point (Matt. 5:27–28). Other matters, such as homosexuality or sex prior to marriage, are more complex. Once again such an assessment should occur fundamentally within a theology of creation, drawing on both biblical and nonbiblical resources.

This commandment insists that *issues of sexuality are not a casual matter* for the good order of God's world. From a positive perspective, this means a lively concern for healthy male/female relationships in all aspects of daily life. Respect, honor, and integrity should inform both attitude and behavior toward members of the opposite sex.

You Shall Not Steal (20:15)

While some commentators have suggested that this commandment focuses on kidnapping (see 21:16), it is likely that stealing of any sort is in view. Yet Israel understands property to be an extension of the "self" of its owner, so that theft of property is a violation of person, not just a person's wealth (as anyone who has been the victim of burglary knows). Stealth may be a particular nuance of the verb, but stealing of any kind is no doubt included. Except for kidnapping, where the penalty is death, a fine or restitution is the punishment. Theft of property in Israel is considered a tort, that is, the injured party is restored so far as possible to the pre-theft position. As an apparent deterrent, "overcompensation" was called for in certain cases (22:1, 7, 9), though this would hardly have deterred the rich. This command is extended to include any form of dishonesty in Deut. 25:16.

Theft is an attack on the dignity of human beings and their

235

work. God dignifies human beings by giving them work to do, from which they can expect to receive some of the fruits of their labor. This is central to God's creational intentions for humankind (Gen. 2:15–16). Theft is a refusal to accept this, and hence the humanity of both the thief and the victim is diminished. Moreover, human beings make use of God-given gifts in and through their work. For the thief not to consider these gifts and the blessings they bring is to treat with disdain what God has given.

Within the larger context (e.g., 23:4–5), the positive side of this commandment is stressed in that each person (and by extension other societal structures, e.g., government) is responsible for the preservation and well-being of the property of the neighbor, *even if that neighbor is an enemy.* This commandment is not a basis, however, for the sanctity of private property as such or of particular economic systems. It does not forbid, say, structures that may stress communal ownership (see Acts 2:44–45). Basic to this understanding is that the people of God do not possess property because they have some natural right to do so but only by the grace of God (see Deut. 8:18).

These considerations raise profound issues regarding the affluence of modern society. The attachment to things, the extravagance in life-styles, and the mountains of waste generated, all in the face of incredibly widespread hunger and want, raise the question of theft to new levels. The prophets rail against Israel at precisely this point (see Isa. 3:16–26; Amos 8:4–6; Micah 3:1–3; James 5:1–6). At whose expense is this wealth gained? Does it not often constitute theft, for example, inadequate wages or benefits? But at such remove that we will seldom know the victims' names or have to look them in the eyes. New definitions of theft need to be considered in view of the complexities of modern society, not least its corporate and governmental structures.

You Shall Not Bear False Witness (20:16)

The original focus of this commandment was on the giving of false testimony in legal proceedings (see 23:2). The penalties for such deception are severe (see Deut. 19:15–19), understandable in view of its insidious effects (see I Kings 21; Ps. 27:12). The concern would not simply be an attack on another individual,

236

and the danger therein posed to a person's reputation (see at 20:7), but an undermining of the corporate structures of justice which so depend on truthfulness. At stake is justice for anyone who uses the judicial system.

The extension of the commandment to lying more generally (see Deut. 5:20; Lev. 19:16; Josh. 7:11; Hos. 4:2) takes place early and includes any deceptive, slanderous, idle, or empty talk about other persons (neighbor=anybody) that would undermine their reputation or otherwise cast them in a bad light. This would entail not only deliberate efforts to deceive but the more casual gossip and rumor that often damage the regard or esteem in which one is held. This recognizes a concern beyond that of individuals to the well-being of community so dependent on trustworthiness among its members. Jesus' extension of the meaning of this command in Matt. 5:33–37 is consonant with these developments internal to the Old Testament.

Positively, this commandment calls for a commitment to the truth in all of one's dealings. Even more, it calls everyone to use speech constructively, to so speak of others that their well-being is furthered and enhanced. The Epistle of James is particularly pointed regarding the importance of these matters for the public peace (3:1–18; 4:11–12). What is at stake here is the good order of God's creation.

You Shall Not Covet (20:17)

Exodus and Deuteronomy interchange "house" and "wife," for unknown reasons. It may be that Deuteronomy separated out "wife" into a separate commandment because it pertains only to men. The word "house" in Exodus may be inclusive of all that belonged to one's neighbor, but inasmuch as the listed items are all living, it could have reference to material goods. The listing of people and animals could be considered a special commandment specifying that which is most valuable.

The basic interpretive problem is determining what *hamad* ("covet, lust after") entails. It has been troublesome to many that this is the only commandment seemingly concerned with an offense of the heart/mind. Because possession is occasionally implicit in the verb itself (34:24; Ps. 68:17), it is not uncommon to conclude that coveting referred originally not simply to an impulse of the will but also to actions leading toward the posses-

237

sion of that which is coveted. Eventually it came to be used for subjective impulses (see Prov. 6:25). But no simple development in meaning seems likely. At best, it can be said that coveting often leads to action. The more explicitly subjective verb for desire, *'awah,* is used in Deut. 5:21 (cf. Amos 5:18; Jer. 17:16), but this may be nothing more than the choice of a synonym (the two verbs are used interchangeably for God's desire of Zion in Ps. 68:17; 132:13–14).

Hence the commandment is probably solely concerned with attitudes of the heart/mind that subtly or not so subtly lead to the misuse of that which is not one's own. It relates to the spirit of the individual that forms the interior ground of the violation of the other commandments. Without covetousness, disobedience of them would probably not occur (see examples in Durham, p. 298). This command reveals how demanding these words of God are. True obedience involves avoiding not only certain actions but also intentions or attitudes toward others in relationship, perhaps best captured in such words as envy or greed or lust. Covetousness has a way of breeding discontent and easily leads to abuse and crime; it is a basic source of social disorder and trouble in interpersonal relationships. It betrays a deep dissatisfaction with that which one has been given. This understanding approximates that of Jesus in Matt. 5:21–22, 27–28. Jesus' "But I say unto you" is thus not a radical reinterpretation of the commandments at all but a drawing out their (perhaps neglected) meaning in terms of the coveting roots of all disobedience.

The force of this commandment for an affluent society has been stated well by Harrelson (p. 153): "Ours is an age in which the appetite for more and more seems almost impossible to assuage. We find it increasingly difficult to maintain any sense of balance regarding our use of food; gadgets for home, office, or auto; clothing; entertainments done in our behalf as we look on; or recreational goods and equipment." We must learn how to make distinctions between desiring that which is wholesome and good and beneficial for both people and nature and that which only feeds a hunger for more than we need.

This commandment shows that the language of rule or regulation or even law for the commandments is not entirely appropriate. Coveting cannot be regulated or policed, let alone clearly observed. The language of instruction is more appropri-

238

ate (see 24:12), the inculcation of an attitude of the mind/heart. It may also demonstrate the fundamentally Godward orientation of these materials. Only God can look upon the heart, can observe the presence or absence of obedience within the human spirit. In the commandments one has to do most basically with one's relationship with God. Or, to put it in other terms, sin against one's neighbor is not simply an interhuman matter. It involves God, and the passion with which God can respond is soon to be noted (22:21–27).

Exodus 20:22—23:33
The Book of the Covenant

This collection of laws commonly called the Book of the Covenant (24:7) consists of a diversity of forms and content. The forms range from case law (21:26–27) to apodictic declaration (22:28) to divine exhortations (22:21–27) and promises (23:27–28). The content exhibits a concern for ordering a wide range of daily life, from sexual ethics (22:19) to care of the disadvantaged (22:21–27) to worship calendars (23:14–17) to loyalty to Yahweh (20:23). (For further discussion, see Patrick, *Old Testament Law;* Hanson.)

The Book of the Covenant ought not be considered a list of laws in force at a particular period in Israel's history. It represents, rather, a refinement of specific issues thought to need attention at some early time. These cases are representative of a larger body of materials, in connection with which some *fundamental principles of law are articulated,* which are to inform the judicial task. Hence it may be said that these texts "do not have the force of binding codified law" but are "designed to inculcate the concepts and principles of Israelite law for judges and the community at large" (Patrick, *Old Testament Law,* pp. 190, 198). As a whole, its function is to draw out the implications of the ten commandments, its introductory foundation.

While there is a unity to be discerned in this "book," it has grown over an extensive period of time and experienced various redactions. The sharp differences between the two major sections suggest an original independence. The relationship to

239

the various pentateuchal sources is disputed, but an early association with the E tradition with a northern provenance is commonly claimed. The bulk of the material was likely in place before the monarchy.

The larger structure of this "book" is relatively straightforward. It is framed by an introduction (20:22–26) and a conclusion (23:20–33). This framework provides the basic hermeneutic for interpreting what it encloses (see below). The "body" of the book consists of two major sections: (1) case laws in impersonal style with legal sanctions (21:1—22:20); (2) apodictic formulations that address the people personally, with many accompanying motivations, and are nonjuridical (22:21—23:19). Within this structure, the details are ordered according to patterns difficult to discern (perhaps chiastic).

How are these two sections of the book related? Generally speaking, whatever diverse traditions may be represented, this twofold structure affects the interpretation of each law and section. But the two sections do this in different ways. The last half provides a hermeneutic for the whole through the personal and intense level of the divine concern, the linkage of obedience to loyalty to God himself, and the ties to specific elements in Israel's history and worship.

At the same time, the first half has an integrity of its own and provides a hermeneutic for the second half. In many ways it corresponds to those chapters in Exodus (e.g., chaps. 1—2; 5; 18:13–27) where the unobtrusive work of God the creator undergirds the narrative. These seemingly "secular" laws are informed by a lively concern for certain rights and duties for the sake of the good order of the community. This represents the work of God the creator in the shaping of communal life. This section is also important in that the formulation of these laws corresponds more closely to the laws of human societies through the ages. The temptation for such societies will be to separate off their legal structures and procedures from the presence and activity of God. This section in Exodus insists that even such details are part and parcel of God's creative work for the sake of good order in every nook and cranny of the world. In this respect, *these laws are an extension of the work of God as creator in Genesis 1.* God through the law fosters and establishes creational rightness and justice in all relationships. Life in Israelite society is intended to be a *microcosm of life in creation*

240

as God originally intended it. The redemptive deeds of God are not an end in themselves. They propel people out into the various creational spheres of life. Redemption is for the purpose of new life within the larger created order. The law points the way to the will of God for every aspect of life in that order.

Fundamental to this creative work of God is the recognition of the equality of all persons under the law. There is to be no regard for differences in socioeconomic standing in the community, whatever the situation. The laws regarding murder, for example, apply to all persons. Respect for the rights of the weakest members of Israel's society is strongly upheld, even to the point of direct divine involvement on their behalf (22:24). Another basic creational principle at work is the valuing of human life over property (even for a thief, 22:3). No monetary value could be placed on a human life, and any desire to harm another was considered morally reprehensible (21:26–27). Finally, the admixture of the sacred and the secular in both sections is implicit testimony that all of life is a seamless web and that the God of this life will not be split off to care simply for the religious realm.

Regarding specific life settings, the section 21:1—22:20 may be reflective of village court practice. This material is often similar to other ancient Near Eastern laws. This bears testimony to Israel's conviction that the Creator God is at work in the surrounding cultures; those societies are understood to be ordered in some ways congruent with God's intentions for the world apart from specific divine revelation. The community of faith is thus not well served by overinterpreting any "improvements" that Israel may have made on ancient laws. In many instances, those ethical sensitivities are just as sharp as Israel's. As to 22:21—23:19, the presence of parenetic material suggests a proclamatory or cultic context. In terms of the final redaction, the whole is presented within a proclamatory setting (20:22; 21:1). Yet the village court setting remains very much in view, for it is there where these laws will inform practice. This is important, for it links Israel's actual judicial practice with modern legal realities and gives attention to the work of God as creator.

Our discussion will tend to deal with larger patterns rather than specific laws as well as with issues of continued application for subsequent generations (see also at 19:1 and 20:1).

241

Loyalty and Worship (20:22–26)

The starting point for the word to the people is not simply what they have heard but also what they have seen (see 19:4). The people should now know that what is to be spoken to them has a basis outside Moses' own mind; God is the source of this word. Moreover, the word to be spoken is a personal word, from a God who has actually appeared to them and *tied this word directly to himself.* Obedience is thus not to some abstract theory of justice or impersonal code; it is a response to a personal God who has entered into a genuine relationship with them. In addition, the seeing element sharpens the idea that the divine address is for the entire person, not just their minds. This means that the human response that this divine word invites can never simply be to believe or to speak. It must also mean to do, to embody the word in the world.

There are two emphases in these verses: loyalty to God on Israel's part (command) and loyalty to Israel on God's part (promise). This same combination is to be found interwoven in the concluding frame (see at 23:20–33) and in the renewal of the covenant in 34:11–16. The law thereby is shown not to be inimical to promise. The issue of loyalty is comprehended in both. God does not expect loyalty *from* Israel apart from declaring the divine loyalty *to* Israel. In fact, *it is only from within the context of divine faithfulness that human faithfulness is possible.* Those who are called to obedience know that the God who so speaks is a God who is *for them,* and for their best interests, not against them or standing over them as a threat. The God who gives the law is the God who makes promises.

1. *Israel's loyalty to God.* The first word (v. 23) is of great importance. This is shown in that it repeats the essence of 20:3–6, and with 23:32–33 provides an inclusio for the Book of the Covenant. The entire law, defining the essence of Israel's expression of faithfulness to God in daily life, finds its focus in this matter: Yahweh is the only God for Israel. The issue for Israel is loyalty to Yahweh. The matter of obedience to the various commandments within this frame is thus shown to be encompassed within the consideration of faithfulness to Yahweh as their God.

242

The heart of the matter for Israel, therefore, is not subscription to an external code of conduct. It is a matter of faithfulness to a relationship with a personal God. The specific commandments have to do with how Israel's loyalty to God is to be expressed in the ins and outs of daily life in specific times and places. The peril for Israel ("snare," 23:33) is not that this or that commandment will be disobeyed but that it will be disloyal to Yahweh and serve other gods. The golden calf debacle demonstrates this. Israel's future as the people of God is centered on this matter. If Israel is loyal to Yahweh, then that faithfulness will be manifested in obedience to the commandments; faithlessness to Yahweh will be manifested in a life of disobedience. The central placement of the loyalty commandment thus shows that issues of obedience and disobedience of all other commandments proceed from issues of loyalty and disloyalty. In other words, faithfulness to God himself takes priority over obedience. That does not make obedience of the detailed commandments somehow unimportant, but obedience follows from faithfulness, not the other way around.

The transition from idols to altars (vv. 24–26) shows that *the concern for the proper worship of Yahweh is understood to be a natural extension of the issue of idolatry.* Loyalty to God will find its most explicit expression in the nature of Israel's worship (cf. chap. 32). The reasons for the (originally independent) specific instructions regarding the altar, however, are not always clear. The reference to nakedness, associated with idolatrous worship, suggests that these are matters in which Israel is to be distinctive from religions round about. The simple construction and natural materials contrast with later lavish Israelite temple workmanship (Hos. 10:1–2); it may suggest a concern for focus on the God who is worshiped rather than the setting. In contrast to Deut. 12:5–14, many altars are allowed; this probably reflects an earlier decentralized practice in Israel. (In the larger pentateuchal redaction, the Deuteronomic law is a revision of this law in view of Israel's continued faithlessness.) Nevertheless, there are limits on the number of altars. Altars are to be built only upon the divine initiative, at those places where God has appeared and given the divine name (see Gen. 26:24–25), and they belong to God ("for me"). They are thus not places that Israel can do with as it pleases; practices associated with them are to be "meet, right and salutary" according to the will of God. Israel's worship of Yahweh must thus not be careless of

243

times and places; they will have a profound impact on issues of continued loyalty to God (see at 25:1).

2. *God's loyalty to Israel.* At these places God promises to come and to bless the gathered worshipers (20:24). The focus is on the divine promise: God will come to Israel; God will bless Israel. These altars and their associated worship are thus different from any other place of worship, indeed any other place on earth. It is not that God will never come and bless elsewhere; it is that God *promises* that God will do so at these places. This provision is thus a gift wherein God graciously wills to be present *with* the people and *for* the people and has provided vehicles in the life of worship in and through which that is accomplished.

The people in their worship can thus be confident that God will do what has been promised; they need never be in doubt about this. Indeed, that confidence can be boldly expressed at times: "Today the LORD will appear to you" (Lev. 9:4). This may sound like a limitation of the divine freedom, and indeed it is. God has freely made this promise, but having made it, God will stick to God's promises. God will be faithful. The promise is an everlasting one. At the same time, the people can remove themselves from the sphere of promise, as they later do in the apostasy of the golden calf. But the promise of God will always be there for the believing to cling to and for the apostate to return to (which is the force of the reiteration of the worship provisions in chap. 34).

It is important to emphasize that this promise of divine coming does not stand in contradiction to the later promise of divine dwelling (29:45). In fact, in that later context, meeting and dwelling are easily combined (29:42–45; Lev. 9:4–6). God can appear in places where God dwells (see at 25:1).

God in the Book of the Covenant (21:1—23:19)

A somewhat different lens through which to read these texts is to note the specific reference to God/Yahweh (21:6, 13–14; 22:8–9, 11, 20, 23–25, 27–31; 23:7, 13–15, 17–19). Except for 21:13–14, God is mentioned only in the third person up through 22:20; thereafter reference is more often in the first person (except 22:28; 23:17, 19). This division corresponds to impersonal and personal references for the people of God.

Generally speaking, these references show clearly that the

244

issue is not simply that God has given the law but that God *the Creator is intimately involved in the ongoing functioning of the law* in the community. The law for Israel does not become an independent entity, with only its own inherent authority or status. Nor is it something that is placed in the hands of a judiciary to do with as it will, important as that may be; there are only two specific references to such persons (21:22; 23:8; cf. 21:13–14, 23). The law remains finally in God's hands. God's own continuing presence and activity are integral to the law's use, even to the point of God himself hearing the case (22:23, 27) and exercising judgment (22:9, 23–24; 23:7).

It is therefore clear that general good sense or moral sensitivities or family structures do not provide sufficient explanation for the concerns lifted up in these laws, however much in the background they might be. Caring for the poor, respecting property, and helping one's enemy are not understood fundamentally as matters of sociology or even morality; at the heart, they are theological matters. Israel must be concerned about these things because God *the Creator* has chosen to be concerned, not simply in giving the laws in the first place, but in attending to them in a personal way. They are a part of the divine agenda for the world. Hence they are integral to the relationship that Israel has with God. It is not fortuitous that the laws are punctuated by specific commands relating to Israel's loyalty to God (22:20, 28; 23:14), as is the framing material (20:23; 23:24–25). One is invited to draw the conclusion that loyalty to God goes hand in hand with close attentiveness to the various issues the laws raise.

The third person references to God often have to do with God's presence in the sanctuary (21:6; 22:8–9, 11), where certain formal judicial processes occurred. Two other such references (23:17, 19) refer to God's presence in worship. These link the judiciary closely to the religious sphere. The judicial judgment is a *divine* judgment (see the first person reference in 21:14); the worship of God cannot be separated from issues of justice (see below). Two references relate specifically to actions toward God himself: 22:20 reiterates the first commandment in connection with sacrifices; 22:28 prohibits disrespect of God. One passage (21:13) has to do with an accident (no divine causality is intended; only that God is responsible for a world in which such is possible).

The first person references to God move these laws to a

245

different level of intensity. As one moves past 22:20, God is shown to relate more and more personally to the issues involved. Moreover, there is *exclusive* use of the second person for those to whom the law is addressed (as in the decalogue, the framing material, and 34:10–26). The "I" of God addresses the "you" of the people. The language used is more parenetic in form and tone (see 22:27, 31; 23:13; cf. Deuteronomy). These laws are usually (contrast 23:4–5) apodictic and unconditional in form, with no punishments or procedures specified (save from God himself). Moreover, this section has a number of references to the Egyptian experience (22:21, 29; 23:9, 15), thus tying this section into the prior narrative in explicit ways. These references demonstrate the importance of keeping law and narrative integrated (see at 19:1).

We will take a look at some details, beginning with the first person passages and moving back into the prior texts. The former have to do primarily with two matters, those of justice for the poor and loyalty to God/worship.

The Divine Concern for Social Justice

God's personal involvement in matters relating to any of "my people . . . who is poor" is pointed and intense (see Deut. 15:1–11). If they are oppressed, God will hear their cry, for "I am compassionate/gracious." The other use of this word in Exodus is in the more abstract confession regarding God in 34:6. Here we see one way in which this divine attribute functions, on behalf of the poor and disadvantaged. The enclosure of this intense section by two direct words on Israel's loyalty to God (22:20, 28) reinforces the intensity—such loyalty has direct implications for the treatment of the poor.

The reverse side of such compassion is severe judgment for those who are the victimizers. God's gracious hearing will lead to strong action indeed: "My wrath will burn, and I will kill you with the sword." Oppression of the poor is believed to be so heinous a crime that it carries with it the death penalty; it is a capital offense. The oppressors' families shall themselves join the ranks of the disadvantaged as widows and orphans. God himself does not wield the sword, of course; while the human beings who do wield it are not specified, they would know that they are the agents of the wrath of God. While one has to use

246

great care in thinking through how, when, and where human beings can be such agents for God, the intensely personal response of God here lifts up the high importance of the way in which a society treats the poor. Can persons from any age who walk in God's ways be any less intense about this matter? Those who follow this God ought to be using language of comparable intensity more often than they do.

Such a question regarding the imitation of God on the part of the people of God is invited by the sentence, "You shall be persons holy (consecrated) to me" (22:31). This continues the theme struck in 19:5, "a holy nation," and is extended by the strong emphasis on holiness in Leviticus (cf. 19:2; 20:26). Here the reader can see an expansion of the connections being made between holiness and a concern for social justice (Lev. 19:9–18). The issue for Israel is not how it can *become* a holy people but how it can *be* in daily life the holy people it has already become by God's action on their behalf. The pattern for a life of holiness has been provided by the holy God, and that includes a life lived on behalf of the less fortunate. Israel has been set apart by God, not to a life apart from the world, but to life of service within the world. To serve God is to serve the world.

This motivation for such a life is stated clearly in the repeated reference to the exodus (22:21; 23:9; see Deut. 10:19; 15:15). This repetition echoes 20:2, the statement about divine deliverance that introduces the law and is understood to inform all that follows. Israel was the disadvantaged one in Egypt, enslaved in an alien land. God delivered Israel and gave the people of God their freedom from human masters. Israel was now in a position where it could in turn become master. As such, it was not to follow the example of Egypt but that of the God who delivered it from bondage. This command carries a straightforward implication. When the people of God mistreat the poor, they violate their own history. It is not simply a violation of the laws of God; more fundamentally, it is a disavowal of their own past, of those salvific acts which made them what they were. The people of God are thus given the task of extending the sphere of God's salvation to include other less fortunate ones.

This sphere of salvation is not some spiritual realm, removed from the mundane aspects of daily life. The specific points of concern for the poor cited in 22:25–27 (see Deut. 24:6,

247

10–18) focus on the economic sphere, particularly the lending of money. Interest is not to be exacted, and great care is to be used in financial dealings so as not to deprive the poor of the basic necessities of life. Matters relating to property in the last half of the first section could well be drawn into this orbit, even though the entire community's interests would be at stake, those of rich and poor alike.

The question as to *the continuing applicability of such matters* for the people of God is often raised. The language of this section of the text points the way. The general reference to affliction (22:22–23) extends the concern in this text beyond this particular matter—within or without the economic sphere—to include any injustice that might occasion the cries of the disadvantaged. Concerns about the lending of money thus become *only illustrative* of what is at stake for God's people here. This means that there is an open-endedness to the application of the law. The text invites the hearer/reader to extend this passage out into every sphere of life where injustice might be encountered. In other words, *one is invited by the law to go beyond the law.* The law here provides only a general direction for life, and one is invited (using the illustration as a pattern) to so act in all areas of life. At the same time, the discussion is not left at the level of generality. The people of God cannot escape with a response such as, "I care about the poor." Caring for the poor means caring for such people in very particular ways.

Moreover, this general reference recognizes that new occasions teach new duties, so that the law itself may need to be revised. Changing social and historical circumstances as well as sharpened ethical sensitivities would raise up new contexts wherein consideration of new applicabilities of this general principle would be called for (as Jesus himself does in Matt. 5). The redactors of later legal collections as well as the Pentateuch as a whole would have understood this, shown in the expansion of these matters into other spheres in view of changing life situations (e.g., Deut. 23:24–25). So important is this principle understood to be that God himself will become involved in its ongoing application. If they cry out to God—wherever, whenever, however—God will hear. Knowing the stake that God has in these matters, the community is called to the task of discerning what the will of God might be for ever new occasions.

248

While the people of God today may not be able to follow literally these specific laws (or their later revisions), for our complex society is often unlike Israel's, they are *invited to extrapolate from these specifics along the grain of the original formulations.* Thus, for example, financial possibilities and arrangements for the less advantaged in our society are a matter about which the people of God should be concerned with an intensity that matches God's. Their scrutiny should range widely across the financial spectrum from regressive taxes to loan sharks to addictive lotteries to housing payments to debt reduction to food stamps.

The courts also come in for some attention in this regard (23:1–3, 6–8; cf. Deut. 16:18–20), which prompts one to think of how the "secular" (though not thereby less God-ordained) orders of society serve as instruments for the judgment of God. The most fundamental concern here is that everybody get fair treatment, that justice not be perverted through false reports/charges or bribery or in order to please the majority. Special care is to be given to the poor, so that one is not partial for or against them (23:3, 6; see Lev. 19:15). No matter what the courts do, it is to be remembered that God himself has a stake in the judgment: *"I* will not acquit the wicked." The illustrative character of these concerns is shown once again by the insertion of 23:4–5. Such impartiality is to extend beyond the specifically judicial sphere into everyday life, even to one's enemy (cf. Deut. 22:1–4). This inclusion of the enemy within the sphere of Israel's action provides important ties to certain New Testament emphases regarding the love of the enemy (see Matt. 5:43–48; Jer. 29:7).

Much of the segment of 21:1–32 is also concerned with social justice. The slavery materials (21:1–11, 20–21, 26–27) provide some protection for slaves from long-term servitude and inhumane treatment. At the same time, they stand in no little tension with 22:21–27. The female slave does not have rights equal to her male counterpart, and the statement "The slave is his money" (21:21) is strikingly inadequate. Yet this is a start in the concern for slave rights, implicitly inviting the reader to interpret it in such a way that the tensions are removed. This would be consonant with the reinterpretation in Deut. 15: 12–18.

The remaining verses in this segment are concerned about

249

other interhuman relationships and are basically designed to protect human beings from physical harm by other human beings (animals in vv. 28–32) in order to promote the well-being of all. Some of the penalties may seem unusually severe to us today (e.g., 21:15–17), but these need to be assessed in view of the perceived importance of certain human interrelationships for the well-being of Israelite society. The question for the contemporary reader becomes: How can such concerns be manifest in particular ways in our own culture?

The phrase "an eye for an eye" (21:24) has prompted unfortunate popular understandings, giving it a barbaric sense. Ancient Near Eastern parallels, however, have shown that its purpose is to provide equality before the law (e.g., the rich could not get by with fines in cases of physical violence). To be applied by the courts (not by individuals), it marks "an important advance in the history of law" (Childs, p. 472). Jesus rejects the general applicability of this principle (Matt. 5:38–42); this probably corresponds to a conviction of early Christians that, even if they have been wronged, they ought to settle their differences amicably outside the courtroom (I Cor. 6:1–8; Rom. 12:14–21). This is not a rejection of a judicial system or the penalties it must impose.

The laws concerning damage to property in 21:33—22:17 range widely over instances of carelessness, stealing, neglect, and trusteeship. A common theme throughout is proper restitution to persons who have been wronged. Words of sorrow or regret are not sufficient in righting these matters; it is a matter of payment in money or kind (and in some cases doubly so). Such issues are considered to be of such consequence to the well-being of the community that God himself enters into judgments (see 22:9). This is a remarkable testimony to the work of God as creator, seeking to bring order into all of life. If God is so concerned about property, the people of God can be no less caring. This entails an expectation that the people of God in any age will seek to promote fairness and justice in comparable "nonreligious" issues.

Worship and Ritual

250

Texts regarding worship are interwoven with social justice matters in a way that suggests a deliberate linkage of concerns.

For one thing, structurally, the two sections on worship/ritual are each preceded by sections on social justice. For another, concern for the poor is integrated into the ritual calendar. For example, every seventh year the land was to lie fallow (23:10–11). While in Leviticus 25 this practice centers on the steward-ship of the land in view of the divine ownership thereof, here the focus is on the benefits for the poor in making the "volun-teer crop" available to them (see Lev. 25:6–7, 12). The same is true for the observance of the sabbath, where rest for those who work is the predominant interest (23:12–13; see at 20:8–11; 34:21). Ritual here has not become ritual for its own sake but in the service of wider human concerns. This same prioritiza-tion is enunciated by Jesus: The sabbath was made for people, not people for the sabbath (Mark 2:27).

Also to be noted in both 23:11 and 23:12 (cf. also 20:10; 23:4–5) is the explicit provision for the care of the animals, both domestic and wild. This is one of the more neglected themes in the law (see Deut. 5:14; 22:1–4, 6–7; 25:4; Lev. 25:7; Prov. 12:10). Such concerns are rooted in Israel's general understanding that God provided for the animals in the ordering of the world (see Gen. 1:30; Ps. 104:21–28; 145:15–16); even God's salvific activity includes them (see Gen. 6:19–20; Ps. 36:6; Isa. 11:6–9). Human care for the animals is thus a way of being in tune with God's own creational concerns (see also Matt. 6:26; 10:29; Luke 12:24).

Once again this humanitarian concern is coupled with Is-rael's loyalty to Yahweh (23:14; cf. 22:20, 28). Faithfulness to God cannot be separated from the practice of justice in every-day life. This integration brings to mind a comparable linkage on the part of the prophets; they insist that Israel's life of wor-ship cannot be separated from the practice of social justice (see Jer. 7:1–11; Isa 1:10–17; Amos 5:21–24). The life of the people of God is of one piece, and the worship of God is to manifest itself in everyday life by the way in which people and animals are treated. The character of worship and the quality of life are inseparably interwoven. The people of God must be closely attentive to the ethical implications of its worship language and forms.

The consecration of the firstborn and the gift of firstfruits **251** are basically statements about God's claim on all (22:29–30; 23:14–19; see at chap. 13). The specification of the three festivals specifies the nature of Israel's "church year" (see 34:18–23; Deut. 16:1–17; Lev. 23:1–44). What were originally only agricultural festivals have been drawn into the orbit of the worship of Yahweh. Once again various aspects of everyday life in God's creation are linked directly to the relationship with God. The "secular" is not separated from the sacred; indeed, such festivals provide an occasion for acknowledging the presence and activity of God in every sphere. In time, all the festivals are linked to particular historical events, as unleavened bread is here (v. 15). But it is important to note that such festivals have an importance for Israel's faith quite apart from God's redemptive activity. They celebrate the work of God the Creator.

Law and Promise (23:20–33)

With 20:22–26 this section encloses the intervening laws and provides the basic hermeneutic for their interpretation, underlining the nature of the relationship to Yahweh. As noted, two emphases are interwoven: loyalty to God by Israel and loyalty to Israel by God. God's expectations of loyalty from Israel are inextricably linked to the loyalty that Israel can depend upon from its God. The latter motivates, informs, and undergirds the former, making human loyalty possible (though not inevitable) and keeping obedience relationally oriented.

1. *God's loyalty to Israel.* Divine promises permeate 23:20–33. Some of this language harks back to previously articulated historical promises (see 3:8, 17): God will guard Israel and bring them to the land (v. 20), driving out its inhabitants (vv. 23, 27–31). But also strongly represented are creational promises: God will bless them with food, drink, healing, fertility, and long life (vv. 25–26, 30). This ties back into the creational themes struck in 1:7, 12, 20, and in the wilderness stories. Once again God's larger purposes in the created order are being served by this historical activity.

A good dose of historical reality is introduced into this narrative. No doubt in view of what actually happened (see Judg. 1), it is anticipated that driving out the land's inhabitants would take time and their potential religious influence will need attention. Interestingly, the rationale for the delay is stated in creational terms (v. 29). Nonetheless, divine activity is stated more in terms of process ("little by little") than event. Even apart from the delay, it is noted that God's activity is conceived in terms of one year (v. 29). The driving out of the inhabitants will not happen with a simple divine move.

This temporal reality and other factors point to the recognition of nondivine agency in these events. It is not known for certain what the "terror" (pestilence?) and the "hornets" (actual insects?) are, but God's use of entities from the natural order may be in view (as often in Exodus). Moreover, the people themselves have a definite role to play (v. 31). While God will deliver the inhabitants into Israel's hands, Israel's "driving them out" is not simply an usher's job. It is a virtual refrain in Judges 1 that, for all of Israel's use of power, it did not drive out the inhabitants of the land.

The messenger of God is still another divine agent, but the referent is not entirely clear. It appeared to Moses in the burning bush (3:2), was active in the sea crossing (14:19), and is used in 32:34; 33:2 as in this text. We have suggested that the messenger was none other than God himself, but in human form. Here too, only God ("in" the messenger) could be one who guards, brings, and forgives or retains sins. The combination of third and first person language shows that that which is other than God is present, namely, the human form. Moreover, the hortatory language shows that it will not be transparently obvious that it is God who is present in and through this figure. Most likely it is a figure who is *"in* the pillar of fire and cloud" (14:19, 24) and speaks to the people in and through Moses (see 33:7–11).

2. *Israel's loyalty to God.* The exhortations to Israel focus almost exclusively on the first/second commandments, thus making loyalty to Yahweh the touchstone of the relationship. Israel is not to worship the gods of the peoples of the land nor follow their ways nor make covenant with them or their gods; indeed, Israel is to break down the places of worship of these peoples (vv. 23–24). Hence it is best if these peoples do not remain in the land, for Israel may fall prey to the enticements of the religion they practice. All the other ordinances are to be viewed from within the context of this central reality of loyalty to Yahweh.

253

While the voice that Israel is to heed has primary reference to the ordinances just articulated, there is a wider sphere of obedience that is in view. Such obedience would also encompass those matters which might be voiced relative to specific situations on the continuing journey (not unlike those which emerged along the way in 15:22—18:27). To this wider sphere of obedience the people had agreed in 19:8.

The above-noted divine promises and activities are not only made conditional on the people's obedience, no hope for forgiveness is given in case of sin. This divine lack of openness to pardon the people's transgression seems unduly harsh (see 32:32–33). In later passages God's pardon is said to be available to the people (34:7, 9; Num. 14:19–20). This is to be explained in the same terms as 20:5–6 (and possibly 20:20). The uncompromising language regarding Israel's loyalty is cast in different terms by God after the golden calf debacle. In that context, these promises will be reiterated without any conditions whatsoever and forgiveness made available to a sinful people (see 33:2; 34:6–16).

But this text's way of stating the matter is very important. It shows the seriousness with which God takes the relationship. Undivided loyalty is a matter concerning which God will not compromise; if one is unfaithful, one then stands outside the sphere in which the promise functions—no ifs, ands, or buts. Only with such a sharp statement of the nature of the relationship—to which the people agree—will it be possible later to see what divine graciousness really means (chaps. 33—34). Only if one is *genuinely* faced with death can one grasp what grace is all about. Only then can one see that it is a gift, pure and simple, an incredible gift. Any halfway house regarding the issue of loyalty would mean that grace would never be seen for what it really is; at best, it would be a kind of divine indulgence. Grace means that the promise still stands and sin is forgiven though one deserves only death.

Even on the far side of the demonstration of God's graciousness in chapters 33—34, this text stands as a reminder that God will not automatically forgive sins or bear them forever (see Num. 14:13–25; Isa. 1:14; Jer. 44:22). Nor does grace mean that one ought to live close to the margin of God's patience and mercy in order to experience more grace (Rom. 6:1). The one who lives in the shadow of grace will "hearken attentively" to the voice of God (see I John 2:3–6).

254

Exodus 24:1–18
Covenant and Vocation

Chapter 24 functions as a "swing" chapter, responding to the ordinances of God while at the same time preparing for the chapters that follow. This is part of what makes the chapter so complex. How does one follow all the references to Moses going up and down the mountain, and with whom at what stage? Or, verses 3–8 appear to interrupt the flow from verses 1–2 to verses 9–11, just as verses 1–2 seem interruptive of the connection between 23:33 and 24:3. While this lack of smoothness no doubt reflects different traditions, a certain coherence is available in the final form of the text.

In verses 1–11, one is struck by the fact that, after all the words from God in chapters 20—23, God speaks only in verses 1–2, 12. Yet this provides the beginning point for the two major movements in the chapter. In verses 1–2, God calls Moses and other leaders up the mountain *in order to worship*. Worship has occurred at key junctures in the story to this point (4:31; 12:27; 15:1–21; 18:12). Both verses 3–8 and 9–11 are another such response, not least in view of the concern about the worship of other gods (20:5; 23:24; cf. 32:8). The focus is on *the response to God himself and not to the laws in and of themselves*. The laws are important because they are the words of the God with whom they are in relationship.

The reason for the placement of verses 1–2 and 9–11 is to enclose verses 3–8, which have to do with the people as a whole. The role of the leader in Israel, especially Moses, is thereby given a special place vis-à-vis the people. They are the ones who will interpret the meaning of these words to the people, and what their obedience entails (see 18:18–23), which Moses proceeds to do (24:3). The effect of the combination of these segments (whatever their origins) is to divide the act of covenant-making into two stages. Both stages—the blood sprinkling and the meal fellowship—have the common themes of 255 *communion, real divine presence, and the sharing of life in and through concrete earthly realities*. Distinctive themes are *the proclamation of the word, the commissioning to service, atonement, and the vision of God.*

Some general comments on *law and covenant* are in order. It is noteworthy that there are only three references to covenant in these chapters; this suggests that covenant language should be less prominent in any consideration. We have noted that the reference to covenant in 19:5 is Abrahamic. What of 24:7–8?

Over the last generation it has been common to suggest that Israel's understanding of the Sinai covenant was based on analogy with international political treaties of the suzerainty type, formal alliances between a ruler and his subjects. But the application of this analogy, especially to the texts in Exodus, has been seriously challenged, and it plays little role in many recent discussions. These factors are most prominent: (1) Formally, the various constituent elements of such treaties are not found in comparable form in Exodus. (2) Substantively, the political, interstate-oriented treaties do not correspond well with the content of these texts. (3) Theologically, the relationship between God and people is too personally oriented for contractual language to do it justice. Their responses to one another are neither legalistically defined nor schematically determined.

According to verse 8, *God* "makes a covenant" with Israel at Sinai (the same language used in 34:10, 27). This is a performative speech-act which creates a certain state of affairs in and through a particular ritual, the people's response, and the word of God, which is written in a book (24:7; see 34:28). What is it that has been "created"? One common understanding is that the covenant "formally established a relationship in which Yahweh was Israel's God and Israel was Yahweh's people" (Patrick, *Old Testament Law,* p. 225; Nicholson, *God and His People,* p. 210). We have shown, however (see at 19:1–8; 6:7), that this cannot be the case. Such a relationship between God and people has been in place throughout Exodus. A less comprehensive creative act has occurred, within an already existing relationship. This relationship is, as we have seen, a reality for the people of Israel within the context of the Abrahamic covenant. Sinai may be said to provide *a closer specification* of what is entailed in that relationship in view of what Israel has become as *a people* and in the light of their recent experience. *The Sinai covenant is a matter, not of the people's status, but of their*

256

vocation (see below). Sinai is a covenant within the context of an existing covenant, to which the community as a whole responds.

It can be agreed that the covenant is "a formal act of promising between two parties" which "created the situation of mutual obligation the covenant described" (Patrick, *Old Testament Law*, p. 224). Perhaps it would be more exact to say, however, that God made the covenant, that is, set its terms (23:22) and invited Israel to become a participant. While one might speak of a certain democratization evident in the opportunity given the people to respond, they are given no options to choose from. Yet the absence of coercion is important (see Levenson, *Creation*, p. 147).

In this case, God makes certain promises to the people and commissions them to a task; the people respond by making certain promises to God (24:3, 7). Both agree to accept the obligation inherent in the promise, to order their activity in such a way as to be true to promises made. That God's promises are in view is shown in the sixfold use of the word "all" for what God has said (vv. 3–8; 23:22). Moses wrote down *all* the words of God; hence this would include *both laws and promises.* The people respond by agreeing to do all that God has said and to hearken to the divine voice (v. 7; the same words used in the conditional sentence in 23:22). The people thus agree to do what God has spoken, but what they have agreed to do is enfolded within the divine promises. Thus *the people's commitment to God does not stand isolated from God's own commitment to them.* Their commitment entails a high level of confidence in God himself, that God will see to what God has promised. Their obedience will always be undergirded by the constancy of the divine will and word on their behalf.

At the same time, the conditioning of the divine promises has been sharply stated in 23:21–22. Such conditions have not been so explicitly characteristic of the Abrahamic covenant, though the importance of keeping covenant has been evident (Gen. 22:18; 26:4–5; see at 19:1–8). The conditions are not stated in such a way that Israel would cease to be the people of God upon disobedience. Yet, if God were to follow through on what is said in 23:21–22, it would mean a major dislocation in the nature of the relationship (cf. 33:16). In fact, the golden calf apostasy issues in an *initial* divine word that threatens the

257

community to such an extent that it would mean God starting over with Moses as a new Abraham (32:10).

It is noteworthy that, when God makes the covenant in chapter 34, there is no response from the people. Moreover, there is no conditional language used, as in 23:21 (and the language of 20:5–6 is significantly revised). This suggests that the failure associated with the way in which the covenant is stated in this section leads to a restatement of the covenant in view of the golden calf apostasy. This move from conditionality to unconditionality with the people of Israel parallels the later divine move from Saul to David (see I Sam. 15:28–29).

The *rite in verses 3–8* puts this covenant into effect and reveals its precise nature. The initial response to the hearing of God's words (v. 3) indicates that the people are prepared to proceed with the formal rite. The writing of the words probably serves a purpose not unlike a written (rather than simply oral) agreement in modern society. There can be no question as to what God has said on this occasion (see Josh. 24:25–26; Deut. 28:61; 29:20; Josh. 1:8). The altar and the pillars concretely represent the presence of God and the twelve tribes.

The use of the blood was probably a customary feature of such rites. In the final redaction, it is to be explained primarily by its use in the consecration and ordination rite of Aaron to the priesthood, also followed by a meal (29:19–21, 32–33; Lev. 8:22–31). There too, the blood is thrown against the altar and Aaron and his sons are touched and sprinkled with it. So too, Israel is consecrated for a particular purpose, a people ordained to God's service (note that both people and priests are consecrated for other purposes in 19:14, 22). The theme of a holy people has been struck in 19:6, 14; 22:31, and the people as priests commissioned for God's service is also evident in 19:6. This act thus formalizes the purposes of God for Israel already in view in 19:5–6.

This covenant is for a specific purpose: *the vocation of the people of God.* It also picks up on that aspect of the Abrahamic covenant concerned with God's purposes among the nations (Gen. 26:4–5). Moreover, atonement or peace-making is implied, given the significance of the offerings and the parallels with Aaron (29:35–37; Lev. 8:34). Blood is the vehicle of life and belongs to God, recognized in its being sprinkled on the altar. Its being sprinkled over the people also signifies that atonement

258

has been made for the people, a sharing with the people of that life which belongs to God.

This rite thus has a twofold result: (1) atonement for the people and (2) the people's being commissioned for a task. The force of the covenant, therefore, is not that it *establishes* the God-Israel relationship (any more than with Aaron and his sons). Rather, it is a specific covenant, in which God sets Israel apart for a task, which entails the people's faithfulness and obedience. This loyalty is necessary if God's purposes for the creation would be fulfilled through Israel. To this the people agree. This rite may also signal that this is a matter of life and death for both God (see Gen. 15:7–17) and the people (see 32:10). This is a "written in blood" kind of occasion. Moses' statement in verse 8 is a formal word putting the covenant in effect. Both concrete act and proclaimed word make the covenant an effective reality for the participants.

This ceremony is often identified with a regularly celebrated service of commitment to the covenant ("covenant renewal ceremony"). While the ritual pattern of sacrifice, reading, response, and blood rite may suggest this, future observances are not called for as in Exodus 12—13, nor does the Old Testament elsewhere so designate such a ceremony. Moses is also often referred to as "covenant mediator" between God and people, though his actions seem not to entail more than that of a faithful priest.

While verses 9–11 were probably originally a tradition unrelated to covenant, they now function as an aspect of the rite (see 29:32–33; Gen. 26:28–30). It climaxes in a meal—a communal occasion of friendship and joy, life-giving in function—in which the leaders of Israel participate (cf. 18:12), in connection with which they are granted an "audience" with God. Their mediatorial role within the community would certainly be enhanced thereby (see Num. 11:16–17, 24–25).

The special import of this visit is *the special presence of God* that is vouchsafed to these individuals as representatives of the people. This divine presence has no fearful aspects; nor did any harm come to them—as one might have expected (see 19:21). It is not a theophany in the strictest sense; God invites them up. God stands on something like a clear slab of sapphire (see Ezek. 1:26). This may have a royal significance, a kind of red carpet, indicating the status of the one who has deigned to be so close.

259

The lordship of God is comfortably combined with the familiarity of the scene. *Divine sovereignty is not compromised by intimacy and closeness.* This experience anticipates, not another theophany, but the more intimate presence of God with the people in the tabernacle (40:34–38).

The exact nature of the divine participation in this meal is ambiguous, but God was certainly fully present in the midst of the people during the eating and drinking. It is a communal activity, in which both God and people participate. The seeing of God is an actual, if impressionistic, seeing (it is stated twice), not an inner perception or a perception without analogy in human experience. This serves to make an important point: *God is committed to a real presence with this people* in all of their journeyings, a deeply personal level of involvement. The God who has made promises will personally see to those promises. This anticipates the discussion between Moses and God in chapters 32—34, where the continuing divine presence with Israel is at issue.

The blood and the meal are brought together in the Lord's Supper in the Christian tradition (see Matt. 26:28; Mark 14:24; I Cor. 11:25), in view of the atonement wrought through the death of Jesus, the mediator of a new covenant (Heb. 9:15–22). The themes of the proclamation of the word of God, communion, atonement, real presence, setting apart for a task, and the sharing of life in and through concrete earthly realities are common to both covenant rite and Eucharist.

Verses 12–18 are parallel to the two parts of verses 1–11, with emphases on (1) the divine authority that lies behind the "instruction" given to the people and (2) the theophanic context for the tabernacle instructions, which provide a worship complex in which the presence of God is the central reality. This *ties law closely together with worship.* Worship grounds the ins and outs of daily life in God. Obedience to the task set for the people is in need of the sustenance provided by the ongoing experience of the promised presence of God in worship. Without the presence of God, there would be no point in Israel's continuing journey (so chaps. 33—34). *Worship must inform and undergird obedience.*

260

In verse 12 God picks up on verse 2 and asks Moses to come closer to receive two (see 32:15) tables of stone on which *God* has written the ordinances. Tradition has it that God wrote the decalogue, but it is likely no different from what Moses wrote. This stresses the divine authority behind the law and provides for a heavenly/earthly patterning, not unlike the tabernacle. For the first time, God explicitly states the purpose of the law, "for their instruction" (the word is from the same root as Torah). Moses proceeds, taking Joshua with him. The elders are asked to wait for them; Aaron and Hur can deal with issues that might arise (a variation of the arrangement in chap. 18). This is a portentous provision, for it sets the stage for the events of chapter 32.

Moses ascends by himself ever higher into the mountain (vv. 15, 18 must now mean stages in the ascent). The glory of the Lord enveloped by the cloud appears on the mountain. Verse 17 describes the appearance from the perspective of the people below; it must have been something like a lightning storm or a volcanic eruption. This continues the theme struck in 19:9; the people are able to see what is happening between God and Moses. Moses enters into the cloud itself and stays there forty days and nights (returning in 32:15).

PART SEVEN

The Plan for the Tabernacle

EXODUS 25:1—31:18

Introductory Issues

Nearly one-third of the book of Exodus is devoted to considerations regarding the tabernacle, Israel's wilderness sanctuary. Detailed descriptions occur twice: when God commands Moses how to build it and when that command is *being* executed. God specifies the materials and the height, width, and length of each section, including details about curtains, clasps, beams, and pegs. All objects to be placed within the structure are described—ark, mercy-seat, altar, lampstand, table, and other ritual paraphernalia, as are certain ritual procedures and matters pertaining to the priests associated with its ministry. There are even precise recipes for anointing oil and incense. Thirteen chapters having to do with the tabernacle is a long stretch of non-story that can become wearisome reading. One wonders whether the ancient reader would find the account any more compelling. Haran (p. 150) says it well: "We are faced with a unique combination of long-winded description on the one hand and total omission of various particulars on the other."

At the least, the volume of material demonstrates *the importance of worship* to the narrator. Moreover, the movement in the book of Exodus as a whole is one from slavery to worship, from service to Pharaoh to service of God. More particularly, it is a movement from Israel's enforced construction of Pharaoh's

263

buildings to the glad and obedient offering of themselves for a building for the worship of God (see at 35:1).

Chapters 25—31 constitute the message that God gave to Moses on the mountain. It centers on the forms of worship that are to provide the vehicle for the close divine presence with Israel on its journey. Fundamentally, it signals a change in the way God is present with Israel: (1) The *occasional* appearance of God on the mountain or at the traveling tent (33:7–11) will become the *ongoing* presence of God with Israel. (2) The *distance* of the divine presence from the people will no longer be associated with the remote top of a mountain but with a dwelling place in the center of the camp. God comes down to be with the people at close, even intimate, range; they no longer need to ascend to God. (3) The divine dwelling will no longer be a *fixed place.* God's dwelling place will be portable, on the move with the people of God. Overall, these chapters represent a climax not only in Israel's journey but in God's journey.

If the sociohistorical setting for the basic form of the tabernacle texts is the exile, as seems likely, then they were written at a time when Israel had no central sanctuary. Israel in exile found itself in a situation similar to its forebears in the aftermath of the golden calf apostasy, standing in need of forgiveness. If that ancient apostasy is in many ways parallel to the idolatry that led to the fall of Jerusalem, then exilic Israel too was left wondering about the shape of the future. Would Yahweh dwell among them again? Does the divine purpose still hold (25:8)? Are the divine promises still valid (29:45)? Or, have they been set aside in view of Israel's apostasy? If a sanctuary is to be rebuilt, how can this be done in such a way as to minimize the potential for idolatry?

This setting may help explain *the extensive detail* of these chapters. (1) The material is programmatic, related to specific plans for a sanctuary to be built beyond exile. As it once was with Israel and Moses, so shall it be again. (2) The language creates a tabernacle in the minds of those who have none. A sanctuary begins to take shape within, where it can be considered in all of its grandeur and beauty, living once again in the memory (see Ps. 48; 74; 137). (3) In view of the apostasy, it is made clear that the worship of God is not a matter in which details can be neglected. Inattention to detail may well have been a major factor in the syncretism and idolatry that developed in temple worship (see below). A change or a compromise here and there, and it does not take long for worship patterns to become diverted from their original purpose and for something quite inappropriate or foreign to emerge. (4) In view of apostasy, it is clear that only God can provide the detail appropriate for the worship of God and the presence of the God who would dwell among the people. The forms of divine worship are not to be fundamentally a matter of human innovation or effort. And so God is not only the architect but the giver of the specifications for construction and the bestower of the right spirit or inspiration for the artisans and builders. In every conceivable way the tabernacle and its associated worship must be built according to the will of God.

Yet this is not enough to explain the extensiveness of the repetition in chapters 35—40. This additional material may have been used to make basically two points: (1) The importance of obedience to the divine command. Stress is placed on the fulfillment of the command down to the last detail. When it comes to obedience, attention to particularities is important. It is not enough to be obedient in a general sort of way. (2) As a form of assurance to Israel that, just as God once before went forward with such plans after their apostasy, so God would once again. The detail would indicate the extent of the continuity in God's dwelling place before and after the debacle. Moreover, the actual description of the tabernacle in the process of being built would create an active sense of hope that this would be the shape of the future for them: God would dwell among his people once again. Hence these chapters are a highly concrete way in which the hopes of Israel are brought to focus. Their future sanctuary virtually materializes before their eyes through such detailed description. (Ezek. 40—48, perhaps a rival program to the one presented here, may be said to function in a comparable way.)

Over the centuries, there have been a variety of approaches to the study of the tabernacle. They have varying values.

1. *Allegorical/symbolical.* This has been the predominant hermeneutic for both Christians and Jews from early times. Generally, this approach claims that in all the detail, all the colors and specifications and patterns, a hidden, spiritual meaning is to be discerned. Thus, for example, an interpretation of long standing is to see the tabernacle as the symbol of the cosmos: "Every one of these objects is intended to recall and

265

represent the universe" (Josephus, *Antiquities*, 3.7.7). Christians, too, have often seen hidden references to Christ and the church. The lack of exegetical control, however, with the text subject largely to the imaginations of interpreters, has not commended this approach to many in recent times. Yet certain insights, particularly relating to creation (see below), do have a textual basis. Symbolic values are also evident in connection with the priestly garments (see 28:12, 29–30).

2. *Historical.* This is to see the text as an actual blueprint, probably utopian to some degree, for the (re)construction of an ancient tent structure. The interpretive task is essentially that of historical architecture. One seeks to reconstruct an actual edifice from off the biblical pages and other known sanctuaries and to determine its historical function and setting. Thus, the more one knows about the actual appearance of the tabernacle and its setting in life, the more one will discern the text's intentions. It has been frustrating for such interests, however, that some details are missing, so that any reconstruction involves considerable guesswork.

3. *History of Tradition.* This is to study the tabernacle in terms of the development of ideas and institutions associated with God's dwelling place, including Israel's theological reflections about sanctuaries and God's relation to them. Interpreters have often concluded that the tabernacle actually does not belong to the time of Moses but is a retrojection into ancient times from the exilic or postexilic period, dependent for many of its details on the temple of Solomon. This conviction has been qualified to some extent by more recent scholarship. The account is now more often seen to be more dependent upon an evolving tent tradition, rooted in the ancient tent of meeting, the tent at Shiloh, and the tent that David built for the ark (and perhaps other tent shrines from the ancient world). In fact, this account may even be anti-temple, in spite of some commonality with temple details, seeking to be truer to an understanding of God who is not localized in a high place but on the move with Israel.

4. *Literary.* Literary studies of these and related passages are uncommon. A comparative study of the narratives that describe building projects is one helpful approach; it has the virtue of seeing this text in the light of formally comparable material (see Josipovici, pp. 93–107).

266

First of all, *the golden calf.* God asks Israel to build a tabernacle, and before they even get the instructions in their hands, they have built a golden calf. In fact, the building of the calf takes place between the two tabernacle sections. The narrator thus invites the reader to compare and contrast the two building stories.

Tabernacle	*Golden Calf*
God's initiative	People's initiative
A willing offering requested	Aaron commands gold
Painstaking preparations	No planning
Lengthy building process	Made quickly
Safeguarding of divine holiness	Immediate accessibility
Invisible God	Visible god
Personal, active God	Impersonal object

It is evident that the construction of the golden calf contrasts at every important point with that of the tabernacle. The tabernacle is thus seen to stand over against all forms of idolatry. In fact, the tabernacle may be said to be a divinely instituted way for the community to exclude idolatrous practices from its worship life.

This may help explain the extent of the detail. Israel's worship practice before the exile—most supremely the temple—had not protected the community very well from the intrusion of idolatry. To lay out this program in such detail to an exilic audience would constitute a major effort to prevent this from occurring again. Israel must return to its fundamental roots in the Mosaic period to preserve its identity. Whatever detail may have been borrowed from historically post-Mosaic institutions, this is claimed to be in continuity with the Sinai revelation (the law was conceived in much the same way). If this detail is followed, idolatry should prove to be a less compelling alternative; indeed, there is hardly room for idolatry to make inroads into such a carefully controlled worship environment. Hence the redactional placement of chapters 32—34 provides a clue to interpretation.

A comparable contrast can be made with the *temple of Solomon.* The tabernacle plan is at least in part dependent on temple features; not everything about them was in need of

267

reform. Especially to be noted is the common way in which both temple and tabernacle are related to creation themes (see below; Levenson, *Creation,* pp. 78–99). Yet, significant differences stand out. The temple is built on human initiative rather than divine, and the directions for building come from human imagination, not God (though see I Chron. 28:19). The builders of the tabernacle are not architects; they are only craftsmen, carrying out God's plan. Non-Israelite architects and builders are used for the temple; spirit-filled Israelites are used to build the tabernacle. Forced labor gangs build the temple, slaves rather than willing servants. This sounds suspiciously like Pharaoh's using Israelites as slaves for his projects. God accepts the temple for his dwelling, but questions about it remain. It finally redounds more to the glory of Solomon than to the glory of God and becomes the precinct for numerous idolatrous practices through the years. The tabernacle stands over against the temple in important respects and in some ways parallels the construction of the golden calf.

Creation and the Tabernacle

The important place given to creation themes throughout Exodus makes these parallels highly significant. In contrast to the above, the comparison with the "constructions" of Noah's ark and the creation is a favorable one.

1. *The Ark of Noah.* Both ark and tabernacle are commanded by God, whose precise directions are communicated to the human leader, who proceeds to carry out the directions in obedient detail. Both Noah and Moses found favor in God's sight (33:12–17; Gen. 6:8). At the end of the building of each (39:42–43; Gen. 6:22) it is said that they did just as God had commanded. The same Hebrew word is used for the ark and for the basket in which Moses, like Noah, was set afloat on the chaotic waters (see at 2:1–10). It has even been suggested that the ark of Noah is a temple structure, similar in construction to those found in Mesopotamia. This is in tune with Christian symbolism of the ark through the ages, which commonly sees it in terms of a church afloat amid the waters of chaos. Floodwa-

ters and wilderness are the two most prominent symbols for chaos in the Old Testament. Both "sanctuaries" are portable, one on sea, one on land; they are used to carry the people through the waters/sands of chaos. Both are viewed as a means by which the people of God can move in a secure and ordered way through a world of disorder on their way to a new creation. It is on the first day of the new year that the floodwaters abate and the covering of the ark is taken off (Gen. 8:13), the same day that the tabernacle is set up and dedicated (40:2). One is thereby invited to see the building of the tabernacle in chapters 35—40 in terms of re-creation, God's beginning again with world/Israel on the far side of apostasy.

2. *The Creation of the World.* Verbal and thematic ties between tabernacle and creation have long been noted (see Kearney; Blenkinsopp). It seems clear that these detailed parallels are quite intentional. Levenson (*Creation,* p. 86) puts it well: "The function of these correspondences is to underscore the depiction of the sanctuary as a world, that is, an ordered, supportive, and obedient environment, and the depiction of the world as a sanctuary, that is, a place in which the reign of God is visible and unchallenged, and his holiness is palpable, unthreatened, and pervasive" (cf. Ps. 78:69; Isa. 66:1–2). These common themes might be noted:

a. *The spirit of God* (31:1–11; Gen. 1:2). Bezalel executes in miniature the divine creative role of Genesis 1 in the building of the tabernacle. The spirit of God with which the craftsmen are filled is a sign of the living, breathing force that lies behind the completing of the project just as it lies behind the creation. Their intricate craftsmanship mirrors God's own work. The precious metals with which they work take up the very products of God's beautiful creation and give new shape to that beauty within the creation. Just as God created such a world in which God himself would dwell (not explicit in Genesis, but see Ps. 104:1–4; Isa. 40:22), so now these craftsmen re-create a world in the midst of chaos wherein God may dwell once again in a world suitable for the divine presence.

b. The dedication of the tabernacle occurs on new year's day (40:2, 17), which corresponds in *liturgical celebration* to the first day of creation. The worship of God at the tabernacle is a way for the community of faith to participate in the divine creational work. God's continuing work in and through the

269

worship of Israel is creative of a new world for Israel; it is a means whereby the community itself can take on the characteristics of that new creation in every aspect of its life. If, as seems likely, Genesis 1 is a hymn to the Creator, the tabernacle becomes the liturgical context for that hymnic activity, which shows forth before the world the effects of God's re-creating deed.

c. There are *seven divine speeches* in chapters 25—31 to correspond to the seven days of creation. Some of the speeches have parallels with creation days, and both accounts conclude with a concern for keeping *the sabbath* (31:17; Gen. 2:1–3). The reference to Genesis 1 makes the creation connection explicit. Just as the first tabernacle account ends with a sabbath notice, the next account begins with it (35:2–3). The enclosure of chapters 32—34 with these references suggests that God's decision to renew the covenant with Israel makes for the possibility of picking up the narrative at the point where it was interrupted. God's gracious response to Israel means that work on the tabernacle can proceed forthwith; God's promise to dwell among the people (29:45) still stands. The keeping of a time that is in tune with the created order is once more a reality in Israel, and this prepares the way for the hallowing of a particular place for God's dwelling in Israel. Chapter 31 ends on a note of harmony, rest, and preparedness. It is a paradise scene, Genesis 2 revisited, but decisively marked by the temporal order (see below).

d. The importance given to *shape, order, design, intricacy*—for example, the embroidery (36:37; 38:18)—and *the visual aspect,* including color (36:8, 35; 38:18–23), in both structure and furnishings, corresponds with the orderly, colorful, artful, and intricate creation of Genesis 1. It is especially to be noted that God's creative activity is sometimes mediate, working in and through that which is already created (Gen. 1:11–12, 20). The end product of the "construction" in both instances is a material reality that is precisely designed, externally beautiful, and functionally "literate." There is careful attention to the relationship between form and function. God is present and active in both creation and tabernacle, not simply in the verbal, but also in and through that which is tangible. In both instances, the creative work of God ranges widely across the physical order of things, integrating the world of nature and that which is built with human hands. The prominent use of the general word for making, *'asah,* in Genesis 1 shows that God's creative work is not without analogy in the human sphere. The tabernacle is one such instance. Israel's use of these interrelated spheres in its imaging of God (e.g., God as rock; God as shield) demonstrates the theological import of this confluence of the various physical orders of the world. Both heavens and earth (Ps. 19:1) and tabernacle show forth the glory of God.

e. God looks at the finished world and *sees that it is very good* (Gen. 1:31); this corresponds to Moses "seeing" and evaluating the finished product to be exactly as God had commanded (eighteen references in chaps. 39—40!). An act of blessing also occurs in both (39:43; Gen. 2:3). The end result in the "building" of both creation and tabernacle is that they are the products of the divine command. Just as the creation through the word of God meant that the creation was completed precisely according to the will of God, so also the completion of the tabernacle according to a heavenly "pattern" (25:9, 40) meant that it corresponded exactly to the divine will. This is one spot in the midst of a world of disorder where God's creative, ordering work is completed according to the divine intention just as it was in the beginning.

At this small, lonely place in the midst of the chaos of the wilderness, a new creation comes into being. In the midst of disorder, there is order. The tabernacle is the world order as God intended writ small in Israel. The priests of the sanctuary going about their appointed courses is like everything in creation performing its liturgical service—the sun, the trees, human beings. The people of Israel carefully encamped around the tabernacle in their midst constitutes the beginnings of God's bringing creation back to what it was originally intended to be. The tabernacle is a realization of God's created order in history; both reflect the glory of God in their midst.

Moreover, this microcosm of creation is the beginning of a macrocosmic effort on God's part. *In and through this people, God is on the move to a new creation for all* (see Introduction). God's presence in the tabernacle is a statement about God's intended presence in the entire world. The glory manifest there is to stream out into the larger world. The shining of Moses' face in the wake of the experience of the divine glory (see at 34:29–35) is to become characteristic of Israel as a whole, a radiating out into the larger world of those glorious effects of

271

God's dwelling among Israel. As a kingdom of priests (see at 19:5–6), they have a role of mediating this glory to the entire cosmos.

Further Theological Reflection

While creation, fall, re-creation may be the pattern of chapters 25—40, the re-creation is not a static matter. The creation is not a matter that is all said and done; creation is in the making. Chapters 35—40 present us with "a dramatization of making, not the description of a finished object" (Josipovici, p. 103). The emphasis is always on making, weaving, joining (see 36:8–38), not on picturing the completed whole (see 39:32–42). The text is not encouraging the reader "to stand back and contemplate the finished object." The tabernacle is not something that can be contemplated like the golden calf. God only allows his back to be seen!

This emphasis on the process of making and portability is a sign of the nature of the divine-human interaction. It stresses process, not end. It is God who has given the design, the pattern for the moving and the joining and the threading and the weaving. But the God who gives the pattern chooses to dwell in the very pattern created; the exact continuity between the heavenly pattern and the earthly reality collapses the divine dwelling places into one another. The God who commands the building of the tabernacle dwells within the obedient result, taking up life in the world among the newly created people, all for the sake of Israel and the world. At the same time, it is the obedience of the people that provides just such a sanctuary for God. Yet the obedience of the people is not finished with the tabernacle's completion; their entire life and worship are to be conformed to this obedience.

Complementary to this activity-oriented picture are various other emphases.

1. The shift in the divine abode *from mountain as dwelling place to tabernacle* in the midst of Israel is not only a spatial move, it is an important theological move. The language used for God's presence on Mt. Sinai (24:15–18) becomes the lan-

guage for God's tabernacle dwelling (40:34–38), enclosing the entire tabernacle account. God leaves the mountain, the typical abode for gods in the ancient Near East, and comes to dwell among the people of God. God is not like the gods who remain at some remove from a messy world, enjoying their own life, often uncaring and oblivious to the troubles of the creatures. God leaves the mountain of remoteness and ineffable majesty and tabernacles right in the center of a human community. No longer are the people—or their mediator—asked to "come up" to God; God "comes down" to them. No more trips up the mountain for Moses!

2. *The importance of places,* the hallowing of space and not simply time, is given prominence. God chooses a place because God has entered into history with a people for whom place is important. If places are important for people, they are important for God. To speak of divine presence at a place also helps preserve the personal character of that presence, for persons are always associated with places. Because the human is so shaped by place as well as time, worship for Israel could never be careless of times or places. Because the human is not simply a spiritual creature but physical through and through, there had to be a tangible place, as well as sights and sounds, touch and movement, in Israel's worship. The tabernacle provides for this.

The use of a sanctuary, a specific place for worshiping, for Israel and for any religious community, is thus not unimportant, as if "under any green tree" would do. To summarize its import: *(a)* A sanctuary brings *order* to the worship of God. An undifferentiated proliferation of worship sites leads to a lack of discipline and focus, which may issue in an "anything goes" attitude, a sure recipe for idolatry. *(b)* A sanctuary provides a *tangible* aspect for the divine presence. In their humanity, God's people have a need for concreteness in their relationship with God; a purely spiritual worship is incomplete and left unrelated to body and life. God's condescension interrelates with people in the entirety of their lives. *(c)* A sanctuary provides a point of *assurance* of the divine presence and a point of *stability* in the midst of the unstable wilderness. God *promises* to be present in a given place (29:45); the people thereby may have confidence that they can experience the presence of God there. God can be relied upon to be a stabilizing and beneficent presence.

273

Other tabernacling traditions will speak also of God's "desire" to be so present (cf. Ps. 132:13–14; 78:68; 87:2; cf. Hos. 6:6). This suggests that tabernacle makes a difference to God as well as people. Such a presence will enhance the closeness of the relationship with the people whom God loves.

At the same time, such understandings of tabernacle would need to guard against a "house of God" syndrome, as if God had taken up residence in a given place and could thereby be localized, that the divine presence was fixed. This could lead to notions that God could be controlled, at the beck and call of the worshipers. God's presence in the world is not coextensive with the divine dwelling in the tabernacle; God is both near and far (see Jer. 23:23). This leads to the importance of the next consideration.

3. While a specific place for worship is important, a specific geographical locale is not. *The tabernacle is portable,* not a permanent structure (see II Sam. 7:4–7). The tabernacle is a kind of "portable Sinai," a mobile home for God. With its carrying poles, never to be removed (25:15), it is constantly being put up and taken down, carried with the people as they are on the move. As such, it stands over against attempts to find a mountain or an immovable temple to which the God of Israel can be confined, a view that also radiates strongly monarchial images of God. The tabernacle will be forever on the move. Each time it is taken down and then erected again, the process of making and joining is renewed. It is in the ongoing dismantling and reassembling of the tabernacle, day in and day out, that the new creation is being formed and shaped. Even though the tabernacle does find a "resting place" in Jerusalem (I Kings 8:4), its carrying poles remain in place (I Kings 8:7–8) and tabernacle language is used for the temple itself (Ps. 26:8; 43:3; 46:4; 74:7; 84:1). This suggests continuing concern for this issue even in temple theology.

To have such a portable sanctuary more accurately reflects the way it is with the people of God in the world. This people has left the safety of servitude and headed into the unknown, guided only by promises and clouds. No wonder they grumble and fret, begging to be led by that which they can see and touch. The way of the sojourner, forever wandering, is not an easy way. But that will always be the way of the people of God, and God chooses to accompany them all along that way.

274

God and the Tabernacle

To have such a portable sanctuary is also more accurately to reflect *the God who dwells there*. This is the way not only for the people, it is also the way chosen by the God of this people. This is a God who is on the move, who cannot be localized, who cannot be pinned down to one time and place. It is less comfort, perhaps, not to have a visible god whom one can see with one's own eyes leading through the wilderness. It would be much easier to have a sanctuary that is tied down and a god who is fixed. Israel's God, however, is a God who dwells in a traveling tent, as do the people (II Sam. 7:6–7).

Moreover, this is a God who does not stand above them, enjoying the precincts of the palace while the people plod through desert sands, with never a secure, fixed place they can call home. This God takes up residence with the people, tabernacles with them. This God dwells, not at the edges of Israel's life, but right at the center of things. This God is committed to the journey. This is a God who is with and for his people for the long haul, not just for the laser beam-like moments on mountaintops. It is a commitment to intimacy rather than remoteness. In their own times and places this God will be with them always (see Lev. 26:11–12). This language is also used by prophets after the fall of Jerusalem to speak of God's dwelling once again with the people in the time of restoration (Ezek. 37:26–28; 43:7; Zech. 2:10–11). It is no wonder that the New Testament utilizes this tabernacling language to speak of the Word becoming flesh in Jesus (John 1:14) and of God in eschatological vision (Rev. 21:3).

But this God is also one who moves with the people in unseen, ambiguous ways, who shows the back but not the face. This is complementary to the concern for the divine holiness, evident in the care the priests are to use in approaching the holy place (30:20–21) and the consecration language used throughout (e.g., 28:36–38; 30:22–38). The divine presence is not to be presumed upon. Israel's God is indeed dwelling among them, but, to use language from other traditions, this

God is the "Holy One in your midst" (see Isa. 12:6; Hos. 11:9).

God dwells in the midst of Israel entirely at the divine initiative. God's presence in the tabernacle is not evoked by Moses or made possible by some liturgical ritual. The divine glory fills the tabernacle in God's own time and Moses is not able to enter the area (40:34–38). This twice-spoken divine "filling" of the tabernacle parallels God's "filling" of the cosmos (cf. Jer. 23:24; Isa. 6:3; Ps. 33:5; 72:19; 119:64). But this does not mean that Israel only participates in God's general "filling" of the world. There is an intensification of the divine presence in the tabernacle compared to the created order (see Fretheim, *The Suffering of God*, pp. 61–65). This concentration of God's presence means that Israel is the special recipient of the divine blessing, though the emphasis falls on the promise. At the same time, God's filling of the cosmos means that God is *both* near and far (Jer. 23:23) and cannot be said to be confined to Israel's precincts (see at 35:1).

Additional Considerations

The tabernacle serves additional functions besides that of being a vehicle for divine presence. Leviticus and Numbers give greater detail regarding these functions and show how the tabernacle serves the community well as it continues on its journey (on the tabernacle in other literature, see Koester). Most prominently, the tabernacle is:

1. A place where *sacrifices and offerings* would be presented, though in this context their atoning purpose is associated almost exclusively with the priesthood (chap. 29). An exception may be 30:10, where the day of atonement seems to be in view (cf. 28:38; 29:38–42). This absence may be due to the fact that Israel's apostasy is yet to come. But the priesthood is put in place for the administration of the offerings (detailed in Leviticus 1—9). The specific function of the priesthood is specified here in terms of the receipt of oracles and bringing Israel "to continual remembrance before the LORD" (28:12, 29–30; 30:16; cf. Isa. 62:6). These texts suggest an activity that is primarily intercessory, representing the people before God, yet

serving as "watchmen" for God, bringing to the divine attention matters of earthly consequence.

2. A place where God would *meet and speak* with Moses (25:22; 29:42) and meet with the people (29:43). The tabernacle thus functions much like the old tent of meeting, as a place of revelation (cf. 33:7–11); Moses retains his mediating role in the new structure (cf. 34:34–35). At the same time, this ought not be reduced to a speech event, as if the only important thing were the words spoken. God's meeting but not speaking with the people suggests a focused presence that has an import beyond the verbal encounter. The combination of the divine "dwelling" and "meeting" ought not be considered incongruent, just as God is present everywhere in creation but reveals self in particular theophanic encounters from time to time.

On their journey through the wilderness, God gives Israel two basic institutions, *the law and the tabernacle.* These gifts are alike in that both are portable, both are designed to bring some order out of the disorder, both give shape to life when the center has trouble holding. They provide *an ethical shape and a liturgical shape.* And it is just such a formfulness to life that is sufficient for the journey through wildernesses that never seem to end. Psalm 119:54 captures this dual-shaped reality for Israel: "Thy statutes have been my songs in the house of my pilgrimage"—law and tabernacle, in the wilderness, on the way.

At the same time, the process, the journey, is regularly punctuated with *the sabbath* (see at 16:1–36; 20:8–11). Therein is rest from the rigors of the journey. The sabbath plays an important role in the making of the tabernacle (31:12–17; 35:2–3). The workers keep the sabbath, resting from their labors. They step back from their own creative activity to celebrate and recognize publicly the work of the divine Creator. The sabbath brings out the underlying rhythm of creation; to keep the sabbath is to be in tune with a fundamental rhythm of life. The sabbath also connects with the descriptions of the making of the tent, showing the pleasures that can be received from giving oneself over to a task. There is a sense in which, by involving one's self in all the joining and weaving of the tabernacle, one is involved in the creating of a new world. Hence the value of the sabbath as a sign (31:17; cf. Gen. 17:11). Keeping the sabbath is a sign in the present of the eventual realization

277

of that new creation which God, through Israel, is bringing into being. The exceptionally strong penalties for breaking the sabbath seem to connect with this creational function, especially in view of the apostasy in chapters 32—34. The shape of the future of God's creative work in and through Israel is at stake.

PART EIGHT

The Fall and Restoration of Israel

Exodus 32:1—34:35

Introductory Issues

Within the setting provided by chapters 25—31, chapter 32 is a sudden, sharp blast of cold air. It is Genesis 3 all over again. The garden scene becomes a tangled mess. Harmony turns to dissonance, rest to disturbance, preparedness to confusion, and the future with God becomes a highly uncertain matter. The reason for this is stated clearly: the people of Israel have taken the future into their own hands and compromised their loyalty to Yahweh through the construction of an idol.

Chapters 32—34 have been informed by various streams of traditions and a number of redactions (see Deut. 9:12–29 for a parallel version), but no scholarly agreement has been reached as to their identity. For our purposes, we work with these chapters as a redactionally unified narrative. Given the strong connections to creation traditions in Exodus, not least in the tabernacle sections, it is likely that these chapters function as a fall story for Israel. Israel's own history is seen to parallel the experience of all humankind.

While this final redaction is not socially or historically disinterested, the discernment of the setting is difficult. This raises the question of the relationship of this material with I Kings 12:25–33 (cf. Ps. 106:19–20; Hos. 8:5; Childs, pp. 558–562). The thematic and verbal links indicate that they are interdependent in some way. At the least, the problem with a molten calf idolatry was perceived not to be peculiar to one historical period. This coincides with the presence of such images elsewhere in that world and their likely impact on Israel. It may be that Jeroboam's institution of such a cult was originally acceptable but soon became syncretistic. That experience probably informed the redaction of a story of idolatry from an earlier period, giving it a polemical cast against both monarchical and Aaronide circles. A parallel may have been drawn between the calf apostasy and the idolatry that led to the fall of Samaria (and possibly later applied to the fall of Jerusalem), with comparable issues concerning forgiveness and the future of Israel as the people of God.

The word of these chapters is, finally, a hopeful one, as they move from sin and judgment to restoration. Their overall flow is largely determined by an ongoing dialogue between Moses and God. The role of the intercessor is seen to be a key to preserving the community from annihilation, but finally the future of Israel is seen to rest solely in God, who is gracious, merciful, and abounding in steadfast love (34:6–7). Interweaving these themes is a lively concern for divine presence and how it is that God will be present to Israel, thus keeping a close tie to the surrounding tabernacle narratives.

Exodus 32:1–6
The Golden Calf

At every key point the people's building project contrasts with the tabernacle that God has just announced. This gives to the account a heavy ironic cast. (1) The people seek to create what God has already provided; (2) they, rather than God, take the initiative; (3) offerings are demanded rather than willingly presented; (4) the elaborate preparations are missing altogether; (5) the painstaking length of time needed for building becomes an overnight rush job; (6) the careful provision for guarding the presence of the Holy One turns into an open-air object of immediate accessibility; (7) the invisible, intangible God becomes a visible, tangible image; and (8) the personal, active God becomes an impersonal object that cannot see or speak or act. The ironic effect is that the people forfeit the very divine presence they had hoped to bind more closely to themselves.

At the heart of the matter, the most important of the commandments has been violated. Israel has been disloyal to its God. The problem is thus fundamentally not one of disobedience to a law code; it is a matter of unfaithfulness to the God who had bound himself to a people. Israel has violated the established relationship (see at 20:3–4).

A recurring phrase in this section is "who brought you out of the land of Egypt." Moses is the subject in the mouth of both people (32:1, 23) and God (32:7; 33:1); God is the subject in Moses' speech (32:11–12); and the manufactured god is according to the people (32:4, 8). This usage will provide important clues to the flow of the narrative: Who will be responsible for Israel when Israel is being irresponsible?

The issue presented initially in chapter 32 is that of a leadership vacuum. Without proper leadership the people can flounder. Here they complain that their leader Moses has been absent for too long; they are impatient to move on. Consequently, they confront Aaron, who was given the responsibility of leadership in Moses' absence (see 24:14). The people demand that he make an image of "a god" to "go before" them to lead them to the promised land (their first words after 24:7!). Without hesitation Aaron accedes to their request. He takes the people's Egyptian gold (the status symbol of their deliverance), shapes it, and makes an image. The calf image is represented as Aaron's idea, no doubt picking up on a ubiquitous symbol of deity in the ancient Near East.

The people do not thereby simply request a substitute for the absent Moses, a divine figure for "the man." Nor are they seeking a substitute for Yahweh. The phrase "go before" is never used with Moses elsewhere in Exodus, nor with an unmediated Yahweh. It is used only of God's messenger (14:19; 23:23; 32:34; cf. 23:20; 33:2) or God in the pillar (13:19), identified with the messenger in 14:19. This suggests that the people are requesting *an image of the messenger of God* (not a substitute). Up to now the messenger has been understood as a living representation of Yahweh but not separable from Yahweh himself (see at 3:1–6). By imaging the messenger, they make the representation concrete and accessible, hence having a greater

281

independence from Yahweh. The people's confessional statement ascribing the exodus deliverance to this divine figure (32:4, 8) thus carries some truth (see 14:19, 24); it indicates that they understand this divine messenger already to have had some history among them. But it clearly implies a failure properly to acknowledge Yahweh's role. The larger context consistently states that Yahweh alone is to be *confessed* as Israel's redeemer from Egyptian bondage (see 29:46; 20:2; 19:4; 18:1, 8–10).

The people's emphasis on the absence of Moses means that he is the one who has mediated such divine leading heretofore (they understand the truth of 3:10; cf. 14:31). The construction of an image of the divine messenger would give that figure a more permanent place at the lead of the community, no longer dependent upon Moses' mediation. It would also provide a visible, tangible element to compensate for the absence of Moses' leadership.

Yahweh is not being set aside. At least this is what Aaron understands by the "feast to Yahweh" in verse 5. Aaron's proclamation to that effect suggests that the people also so view the matter. The people also proceed to engage in acts of worship that, except possibly for the "play," are appropriate, indeed reserved for Yahweh. Hence the messenger of God has been elevated to a status alongside Yahweh in the allegiance of the people (and hence the plural reference to "gods").

The goal of the exodus deliverance, that the people be freed to serve Yahweh (see 3:18), has taken a disastrous turn—the people also serve another and give that other the doxologies for their deliverance. The people's action, of course, is in direct violation of 20:4. But the word "disobedience" is not adequate for what has happened. This action is a fundamental act of disloyalty to the God who had delivered them and entered into an intimate relationship with them.

The confusion of God with the messenger is not an uncommon problem for communities of faith. Time after time people have lifted up those who speak and lead for God and given them virtual divine status. They give their primary allegiance to the messenger, sing their praises of the messenger, and ascribe to the messenger what only God can do. It is a serious, if often subtle, form of idolatry. It can also be a problem for the messen-

282

ger, who might subtly encourage or unknowingly submit to such kinds of thinking.

Exodus 32:7–14
The Repentance of God

The sections that follow (through chap. 34) present a veritable "mosaic" of traditions that has been built up to provide a multifaceted look at the efforts of God and Moses to come to terms with this apostasy. A certain roughness in the transition from one unit to the next literarily portrays the complexity of the situation and the difficulty in finding a proper resolution. This is comparable to other experiences of brokenness in human relationships. Even God is presented as one searching for the appropriate response, but always in consultation with Moses. One is reminded of the divine question voiced at a later apostasy of Israel (Hos. 6:4): "What shall I do with you?"

Yahweh's reaction to this apostasy is immediate, directed to Moses, the mediator, rather than to the people; it is freighted with irony. They are "your" people whom "you" brought up from Egypt. God here mimics the words of the people, first quoting their statement that Moses delivered them, then that the "god" has. In between is a sharp statement of the apostasy: contrary to the divine word, they have worshiped a graven image. In effect, God informs Moses that, if this is what the people want to believe and confess, let them. But, with emphasis provided by a new introduction, if they wish to make confession of a deliverer other than Yahweh, then they will have to bear the consequences. God does not treat such unfaithfulness lightly and so asks Moses to leave him alone so that judgment can be exacted on this recalcitrant people.

A key phrase for interpreting this passage is "let me alone" (v. 10; see Childs, p. 567). For such a word to make sense, one must assume that, while God has decided to execute wrath (see v. 14), the decision has not reached an irretrievable point; the will of God is not set on the matter. Moses could conceivably contribute something to the divine deliberation that might oc-

283

casion a future for Israel other than wrath. In fact, God seems to anticipate that Moses would resist what is being said. At the least, it recognizes that what Moses might say about God's decision places some limits on what it would be possible for God to do. God here recognizes the relationship with Moses over having an absolutely free decision in this matter. The devastation of Israel by the divine wrath is thus conditioned upon Moses giving God leave to do so. While the reader cannot hear the tone of the remark, "let me alone," it may well refer to the isolation desired to suffer grief. But God thereby does leave the door of Israel's future open.

At the same time, the future for Israel is placed in high jeopardy. God has made a preliminary decision to "consume" them as a people. What form this might take is not stated, but 34:7 (see 32:33) may give the reader some clues. It is not a sudden annihilation but a removal from within the sphere of God's special care and concern. This would entail letting the effects of the brokenness have their way with the people. In other words, Israel is staring into the face of a future far more devastating than any experience of bondage in Egypt.

One should consider the following factors in trying to sort this through. For one thing, this reaction of God is exploratory, shared only with Moses in a preliminary way. It is possible, in fact, that God was testing Moses in some way, seen not least in God's reference to Moses' future (v. 10). Would Moses take his own future and run? But the divine repentance (NRSV, change of mind) in response to Moses' intercession seems seriously genuine; it is a change in divine direction.

Another approach seems preferable. Israel has openly and willingly entered into a relationship with Yahweh. The people have agreed that this relationship is to be an exclusive one, entailing the service and worship of Yahweh alone. To use an analogy found elsewhere in the Old Testament, Israel has entered into a marriage relationship with Yahweh with all that that entails in terms of faithfulness. Amos 3:2 is of some help here: You only have I known of all the families of the earth, therefore I will punish you for your iniquities. An analogy with divorce may be helpful: normally, its effects on the persons involved will be more dire than the effects that follow upon the breaking of a relationship that is not so close and intimate. To make such a commitment to Yahweh is a serious matter. The

284

benefits are considerable, but at the same time the effects of brokenness will be all the more severe if and when rejection of Yahweh occurs. Those who make the choice for Yahweh and then depart from it are worse off than if they had left it alone. It is at such moments when one can understand why Israel on occasion wanted to be back in Egypt.

Remarkably, Moses does not accede to God's request; he does not leave God alone. In fact, he speaks on behalf of the people (see Ps. 106:23; Jer. 18:20), though he has not yet seen for himself what has happened. The boldness of his reply indicates something of the nature of the relationship between God and Moses. God has so entered into this relationship that such dialogue is invited, indeed welcomed: *God is not the only one who has something important to say.* Moses' argument is stunning in its directness, but without excusing Israel in any way (cf. Num. 14:11–20). It is reminiscent of the lament psalms, particularly those designed to motivate God to act (see Ps. 13:3–4; 79:9–10). His argument is threefold; he states two matters in question form and concludes with three imperatives.

1. An appeal to *God's reasonableness.* God has only just delivered this people (Moses has the confession straight!), and so what sense does it make for God to reverse that action so quickly? The assumption on Moses' part is that God is the kind of God who will take into account factors of reason and logic in making decisions and considering options.

2. An appeal to *God's reputation.* Moses raises the concern: What will the neighbors say? A recurrent theme throughout the narrative has been that God has acted on Israel's behalf in order that the Egyptians and others might know that Yahweh is Lord (see 14:4, 18; 9:16). What would they now think, if God destroyed them (see Num. 14:13–16; Deut. 9:28; Ezek. 20:14)? Moreover, in the commandments (see at 20:7) God has shown himself to be concerned about reputation and the contexts in which the divine name is used. If God were to destroy this people, would not that place the divine purpose with respect to non-Israelite peoples, indeed God's very name, in some jeopardy?

3. A reminder of *God's own promise*—to which God has personally sworn!—to this people that their descendants would be multiplied (not killed off!) and that they would inherit the land. God has made a commitment to Israel, and would not God

285

be following the same course as the people by going back on such a promise? It is a matter of God being true to self. Moses extends this argument somewhat beyond what God had said would be done. God had in fact promised Moses, "Of you I will make a great nation" (v. 10). Hence God does have those promises in mind. There would be a way for God to remain true to these promises in and through Moses, but that would be like starting with Abraham once again.

What status do these arguments have for God? They are certainly not matters that God had not considered before. But to have them articulated in a forceful way by God's own chosen leader gives them a new status. Moses, by his entry into the discussion, brings three new factors to bear on the situation: his decision or will, his energy (!), and his insight. These factors make the situation different from what it had been moments earlier. God is open to what Moses has to say and takes Moses' contribution with utmost seriousness, honoring it as an important ingredient for the shaping of the future. If Moses wills and thinks and does these things, they take on a significance that they do not carry when treated in divine isolation. It is not a matter of Moses' winning the argument but of a relationship that God takes seriously.

God's response to Moses is immediate and direct. In fact, the narrator does not have God verbally respond to Moses; he only reports what God does. God "changed his mind [niham] about the disaster [RSV, repented of the evil] that he planned to bring on his people." In the Old Testament, God never repents of sin; all of God's actions are considered appropriate and justifiable. Rather, divine repentance is the reversal of a direction taken or a decision made. But God does repent of evil. Evil (ra') has reference to anything in life that makes for less than total well-being, including divine judgment and its effects (cf. Jer. 18:7–10; 26:3, 19). Hence God's repenting of evil has reference to a decision to reverse the preliminary decision for judgment. It is to be noted that this does not entail removal of all forms of judgment (see vv. 33, 35) or forgiveness of the people's sin. Moses' continued intercession with God for their forgiveness (32:30–34 and 34:9) shows that that is yet another step for God to take (see Fretheim, "The Repentance of God: A Key to Evaluating Old Testament God-Talk," *Horizons in Biblical Theology* 10:47–70 [1988]).

286

The God of Israel is revealed as one who is open to change. God will move from decisions made, from courses charted, in view of the ongoing interaction with those affected. God treats the relationship with the people with an integrity that is responsive to what they do and say. Hence human prayer (in this case, intercession) is honored by God as a contribution to a conversation that has the capacity to change future directions for God, people, and world. God may well adjust modes and directions (though not ultimate goals) in view of such human responsiveness. This means that there is genuine openness to the future on God's part, fundamentally in order that God's salvific will for all might be realized as fully as possible. It is this openness to change that reveals what it is about God that is unchangeable: God's steadfastness has to do with God's love; God's faithfulness has to do with God's promises; God's will is for the salvation of all. God will always act, even make changes, in order to be true to these unchangeable ways and to accomplish these unchangeable goals.

Exodus 32:15–29
The Leadership of Moses

In verses 7–14 the narrator has portrayed Israel's apostasy from God's point of view. Moses' response has been totally dependent upon the divine perspective. Verses 15–35 now portray the same situation from Moses' point of view. Initially, special emphasis is given to the tablets that Moses brings with him. They symbolize the completed covenant, "the work of God," written in stone by God himself. They are intact; the covenant is not broken from God's side.

But when Moses first hears and then sees for himself what has happened, his reaction is more severe than God's: Moses' anger actually does "burn hot" (v. 19; cf. v. 10); Aaron does not succeed with Moses as Moses did with God (v. 22). Only now does he break the "work of God" (at the place where the covenant was concluded), symbolizing from *his* point of view that the covenant is broken. One wonders why there was none of this anger when he was informed by God of these events. He

287

equivocates with Joshua, not telling him what he already knows. Nor does he tell the people about his intercession with God and its effect; in fact, in verse 27 he speaks a word for God that has no basis in the previous conversation. This suggests that the narrator intends to overdraw Moses' reaction as one who is somewhat too zealous on behalf of Yahweh. In any case, Moses moves quickly on various fronts in an effort to turn the situation around, confronting people, religious leadership, and God.

1. *Confrontation and elimination* (vv. 19–20). Moses reduces the calf to powder and forces the people to drink water polluted with the remains (the plague of v. 35 may have been an effect). Not only is the calf destroyed, it suffers the ignominy of being dispersed more and more until it is reduced to human waste. The scene is full of wordless action as Moses becomes the executor of judgment. Unlike God, Moses consults with no one and gives no explanation.

2. *Calling leaders to account* (vv. 21–24). Only then does Moses call Aaron on the carpet, making it clear in no uncertain terms that, whatever the people have done and said, he is responsible for what has happened (though Aaron by citing the confession seeks to show—correctly—that Moses is not free of responsibility). Moses has a high view of the accountability of leaders; Aaron has failed to measure up (see Deut. 9:20), an opinion the narrator confirms (v. 25). The decision that God was forced to make in 4:14–15 proves to be momentous. Aaron minimizes his own role, even suggesting that the calf materialized all by itself! The conversation with Aaron is abruptly terminated. Once again Moses' silence is foreboding. The reader expects action.

3. *Exacting punishment* (vv. 25–29). This incident is redactionally represented as Moses' reaction to *Aaron's* failure. The people are represented as anarchic, "running wild" (is more than idolatry in view?); they would rather be enslaved or unbridled than free. But the blame is laid on Aaron; his leadership has left them open to the slander of their enemies—note the concern once again for reputation (see Ps. 22:6–8).

Moses invites the entire community to make a public stand: do they belong to Yahweh or not? The issue is the same as that articulated by Elijah in I Kings 18:21: "If Yahweh is God, follow him; but if Baal, then follow him." No coercion is involved, no

288

threat is expressed; it is an invitation. This is not a call for theological judgment or community loyalty; it is a call for commitment to Yahweh alone. It is noteworthy that the subsequent slaughter could have been avoided at this point if everyone had answered positively. The issue is no longer whether they had participated in idolatry (see the "all" in v. 3) but whether they were now willing to declare themselves for Yahweh. The great majority of people, however, remain unmoved; their silent indifference to the call is deafening. In other words, this is an *intensification of the apostasy* evident in the golden calf episode; it is revealing of deep levels of disloyalty.

The Levites respond positively as a group, forsaking their past and choosing now to be loyal. They immediately receive an unexpected task from God through Moses. They are to be the executors of divine judgment on those who did not respond to Moses' call. Each Levite is apparently to kill a representative number of those who did not respond. About three thousand (a stereotyped number, cf. Judg. 16:27) are killed "according to the word of Moses." Modern sensitivities may get in the way of our interpretation of this method, but it is continuous with other texts (see Deut. 13!; cf. I Kings 18:40; II Kings 10:17). For this juncture in Israel's life, when its entire future is at stake, radical sin is believed to call for radical measures; continued life for the community is believed to be possible only through the death of some. Declining Moses' call to stand for Yahweh is not an open matter for Israel. The relationship with God even takes priority over all other relationships (see Luke 14:26).

Such methods are obviously not available to modern communities of faith, even if their future should ride in the balance. But the seriousness with which Israel takes the matter should occasion critical reflection by those of us who live in an age where virtually anything that goes by the name of religion is tolerated. Perhaps a Jonestown or two could be averted.

In the absence of Aaronic leadership, the Levites exemplify it "under fire." By their actions they demonstrate that they are suitable for leadership positions in Yahweh's service. We cannot be certain how much of the tumultuous history of the priesthood may be reflected here. Aaron is not removed from the priesthood earlier bestowed (chap. 29), though the Levites are lifted up to share leadership. The far-reaching effects of good or

289

bad leadership on the community of faith is not unique to Israel; it has been amply evidenced in the course of the entire history of the people of God.

Exodus 32:30–35
Will God Forgive?

4. *Making atonement* (vv. 30–34). Moses continues an agenda that keeps death and life closely intertwined, pleading with Yahweh to forgive the people. The actions of verses 25–29 are not deemed sufficient for a restoration of relationship. The move that Moses takes now is not the death of many for the people's sin (the word occurs eight times in five verses!) but (for all practical purposes) the death of one. His request to be removed from God's book is a vivid (not literal) reference to those who are God's elect people (see Ezek. 13:9; Mal. 3:16). Whatever one might say regarding Moses' zeal, he himself here assumes the ultimate responsibility of the leader. The earlier divine repentance had at least cut off the possibility of Israel's destruction. But the issue of forgiveness and the nature of the God-Israel relationship remains uncertain. With that goal in mind, Moses first of all seeks to obtain forgiveness for the people's sin through his intercession. But if this is not acceptable, Moses offers up his place among God's elect for the sake of the people's future.

The divine response is not easy to fathom. The key is to understand this section as a less than final divine decision (as 32:10 was earlier). God refuses to accept Moses' offer (see 23:21)—though no judgment is made regarding the *principle* of one atoning for the many—declaring that all sinners are to be removed from the register of the elect people of God. Inasmuch as all have been implicated in this apostasy, this decision includes everybody. This is not a reversal of the divine action of 32:14, which simply entailed that the people would not be destroyed. Here the point is that, though the people would continue to survive and God would hold to his promise of giving them the land (v. 34), they would no longer be the elect community. As is implied in the fuller statement of verse 34 in 33:2–3, such a divine decision would entail the absence of any special divine care and protection for this community. God would not go with them as their God and would visit them for purposes of judgment for their sin (see 20:5). That is to say, their sins would have deleterious effects upon them according to the normal moral order of things. Forgiveness and the alleviation of judgment effected thereby would not be available to the people (see at 34:7).

This time Moses' intercession is not successful. God is not moved to back off from this decision. The narrator concludes this more abstract point in concrete fashion in verse 35, illustrating the effects of the decision that God has just made and the failure of the intercession. God visits the people with a plague; but that is a far cry from verse 10! The people's apostasy has left them exposed to the inevitable effects of their sin and, in particular, Aaron's sin. God will see to the promise of a land, but the people's future is bleak indeed: Israel would no longer be God's elect people.

But God's decision and that bleak future are not yet written in stone. Moses is not yet done interceding and God is not yet done responding. God has not closed down other possibilities. Yet, at this moment in the story, life for Israel looks very precarious indeed. Ceasing to be God's elect ones is not a sham possibility.

The fact that verses 30–34 sketch out real possibilities for God and Israel, and yet (in view of what happens in chap. 34) do not constitute the end of the matter, raises *a sharp hermeneutical issue.* This text is transitional toward a different conclusion; it moves largely within the realm of possibility (as does 32:9–10). Hence one has to use extraordinary care in drawing theological inferences from the text. For example, one cannot use verse 33 to suggest that forgiveness is not available to sinners. God is here represented as one who is sorting out possibilities with Moses, and hence interpretation should not move beyond such possibilities to reality.

At the same time, this text reveals *an amazing picture of God,* a God who enters into genuine dialogue with chosen leaders and takes their contribution to the discussion with utmost seriousness. It is a God who works at the level of possibility, but it is not a God who is indecisive or vacillating, filled with uncertainties. It is a God who chooses not to act alone in such

291

matters for the sake of the integrity of relationships established. God chooses to share the decision-making process with the human partner, in the interests of honoring the relationship with Moses and a final determination that is the best for as many as possible. This is a God who remains genuinely open to the future for an extended period of time. This openness and this patience are revealing of a desire to find the best possible way into the next generation.

We do not know what God would have done if Moses had not entered into the discussion as he did. But the picture that finally emerges from this chapter is that Moses is responsible for shaping a future other than what would have been the case had he been passive and kept silent. This text lifts up the extraordinary importance of human speaking and acting in the shaping of the future. Simply to leave the future in the hands of God is something other than what God desires. Simply to leave the future in the hands of the people is not a divine desire either. That leaves chosen leaders in an uncomfortable position—between God and people, but to such they are called. Moses' way is to be preferred to Aaron's.

Exodus 33:1–6
How Will God Be Present to Israel?

The various traditions commonly recognized in chapter 33 have now been woven together to narrate the progress of the interaction of Moses and God regarding Israel's future in the aftermath of the golden calf debacle.

God's initial word to Moses essentially repeats the command of 32:34, directing him to lead the people of Israel away from Sinai and toward the promised land. Once again the people of Israel are identified as those whom *Moses* brought out of Egypt (see 32:1, 7), a burden that Moses has refused to bear alone (see 32:11), though his integral role has been evident from the beginning (3:10, 12). The expectation is that Moses, having begun the task of leading, will continue in that capacity.

Moses will not have to act alone, but God's role remains somewhat uncertain at this point. One question remaining from

Moses' prayer in 32:10–13 is: Will God fulfill the promises? The answer is positive in some respects. In spite of all that has happened, God will remain true to three recalled promises: God will give the people the land (see 3:8, 17; 6:8); will drive out *(garaš)* its inhabitants (see 23:23, 28–31); and will send a "messenger" to guide Israel on the way (as in 14:19; see 23:20, 23). The move in verse 2 from the messenger to the first person pronoun (as also in 23:20–23; cf. 3:2; 14:19) indicates that the messenger is God himself. It is important to note that there is no basic change in how this is to happen from 23:20–23, 29–30; the golden calf incident has not occasioned a change in God's agenda at this point or in the use of messenger language in its implementation. Though the messenger's tasks are not as fully stated here as in 23:20–23, certainly the basics are the same; the change in God's ways is not to be found at this point.

Then, somewhat surprisingly, Moses is told that God will not go up among them. This has been disjunctive for commentators, largely because the divine presence has been understood univocally. It is important to distinguish among types of divine presence. At the two ends of a continuum are God's general presence in the world and God's intensified presence in theophany. Along that continuum are God's accompanying presence with the people and God's tabernacling presence (for details, see Fretheim, *The Suffering of God* pp. 60–65).

Here the issue has to do only with God's tabernacling presence. This note is sounded again in verse 5 and remains a major theme of the following verses. In terms of the final redaction, this means that the divine promise of 29:45–46 (see 25:8), that God will "dwell among them," will *not* be fulfilled. This promise was tied to the building of the tabernacle and the faithfulness to God that that implied—they would confess that it was *Yahweh* who brought them out of Egypt (29:46). Inasmuch as the people have built a golden calf instead of a tabernacle, and made a different confession (32:4, 23), that directly affects the fulfillment of that promise. What the people have done (and not done) has adversely affected the relationship with God. The people have removed themselves from the sphere of the dwelling promise; it no longer applies to them.

Yet, in spite of all of this, God will be gracious and move toward the fulfillment of other promises. Indeed, God's not dwelling among the people is expressed as a concern for their

293

well-being: God's close presence may destroy them (do the people in their remorse exaggerate this in v. 5?). God does not want to be confronted with an occasion to exercise the divine wrath. This is a marvelous picture of divine reluctance! This is not just because they have been sinful (God later chooses to dwell with a sinful people). Rather, if the people should continue to be apostate, and their stiff-neckedness suggests that is a real possibility, the situation may revert to 32:9–10; and this time they may not be saved from the divine wrath. Amos 3:2 may help explain this: if they are no longer treated as God's elect people (as 32:33 and 33:16 imply will happen if this is not resolved), then whatever they might do would not be called apostasy anymore. If, however, God were to dwell among them as the elect, then the principle enunciated in Amos would apply. Hence it is best for *both God and Israel* for God to keep distance. A future for the people as those among whom God had chosen to dwell (and all that that means in terms of election, see 33:16) is on the verge of being lost.

This is to be related to the command to leave Sinai (which does not occur until Num. 10:11), the place of God's dwelling (see 19:4). The command to build the tabernacle is, in effect, God's decision to move his dwelling from Sinai to a portable sanctuary that moves constantly among the people (25:8). The tabernacle was to become a "portable Sinai." God's directive that the people leave Sinai without a tabernacle means that God's dwelling would remain on Mt. Sinai rather than among the people. This does not mean that God would be absent from the people, anymore than God was absent from them prior to Sinai. God will continue to lead the people and to drive out the inhabitants of the land before them. But God will not dwell among them.

Yet God leaves the future open. According to verse 5, God has not finally decided the issue; there is some hope. It is as if the God who has been spurned waits to find some new way into the future. The people who wait find themselves accompanied by a God who waits. God commands them to remove their festive dress and jewelry, signs of their redeemed status. What they stripped from the Egyptians they are themselves stripped of (see 12:36). This suggests that the people thereby are to place themselves in a kind of limbo; they set aside their past, and any special future with God is recognized as precarious. *They stand*

294

betwixt and between. It is no wonder that, when the people hear this "evil word," they engage in abject mourning, and not only take off their status symbols, they *leave* them off. This obedient response to God's command, together with their *on-going* remorse, may be one important sign to God that affects "what to do to you."

Exodus 33:7–11
Face-to-Face

Commentators have often considered this section disruptive in the present context. Others have sought to find a way of integrating it into this context, while recognizing its origins in a different tradition (e.g., Childs, pp. 589–593; Moberly,). We align ourselves with the latter approach, albeit differing in the basic interpretation.

In its present context, this section serves a number of purposes. Literarily, it serves to retard the action of the narrative to some degree, keeping the question of what God shall do at a level of continuing uncertainty. It also functions as a retrospective: this is how things have been in the recent past. It is likely that the narrator thought Israel had such a sanctuary during the pre-Sinai period (16:33–34; 18:12, 19; cf. 18:7; 23:19), that Moses brought inquiries before God on behalf of Israel (18:19), and even that God appeared to Moses in a cloud in the sight of the people, though at some distance (16:7, 10). While historically the references in chapters 16—18 may be anachronistic, in their present context they provide some continuity with 33:7–11. It is possible that this practice is understood to extend into the present moment (Childs, p. 592, who claims that the tent is outside the camp to be separated from the apostate people). This is unlikely, however. If God's tabernacling presence were now no longer possible, how could God's theophanic presence continue unaffected? Rather, this is a picture of how things used to be.

As a retrospective, verses 7–11 function in this context to show forth two primary matters:

1. The portrayal of the people is highly positive. They regu-

295

larly seek the Lord, attentively respond to Moses as their leader, and "everyone" engages in appropriate acts of worship (in some ways this is continuous with the obedient response of v. 6). It is difficult to imagine a more striking contrast with the behaviors of the people in chapter 32. This picture is integral to the development of the conversation between Moses and God. Israel has had some history of maintaining worship practices that are 180 degrees removed from the golden calf; their potential for faithfulness is evident.

2. Moses' status as leader and mediator is highlighted. It has not yet been noted what Moses' response will be to God's words of verses 3–6. Given his activity on behalf of the people in chapter 32, will he enter again into the breach between God and people (see Ps. 106:23)? These verses emphasize Moses' role as a mediator between God and people and testify that the relationship between God and Moses is very close. God and Moses are "friends"; they speak "face to face." Face means something different here from what it does in v. 23. It is not a reference to God's very self. Rather, it refers to the unmediated relationship between God and Moses. God's will and word are conveyed directly to him, a level of immediacy not available to the people as a whole. The God-Moses relationship is presented as one that holds some promise for working through this critical time in Israel's history. Will God go with this people or not? Moses and God will now "have it out."

The portrayal of verses 7–11 is thus a way of introducing some hope into a precarious situation. The past is not irrelevant for the future; there is a quality of relationship there that bodes well for future possibilities.

Exodus 33:12–17
God's Decision to Dwell with Israel

This picture of Moses' uniquely close relationship with God immediately leads into the report of Moses' intercession on behalf of the people (v. 12). Yahweh responds to three different pleas from Moses, each carrying the interaction one step farther. Moses is responsible for extending the conversation in each instance, and God reacts to him in remarkably open ways. God graciously honors the perspective of the chosen leader concerning the shape of Israel's future (for a more negative view of this conversation, see Brueggemann).

Moses begins and ends his first statement with an imperative: See, Consider! He brings up some of God's own words (v. 12; not unlike 32:13), and with some forcefulness ("you" is thrice used emphatically). God has told Moses to bring up this people but has not informed him how this is possible (this recalls earlier complaints, 4:10; 6:12); certainly Moses cannot do it by himself. This is probably a not too subtle hint to God to decide (see v. 5) whether God will in fact be going up among them. God has told him that he has found favor in God's estimation (the phrase occurs five times in vv. 12–17), and God knows him by name ("know" is also used five times). These phrases are references to God's choice of Moses to be the leader of Israel (see Gen. 6:8 for the usage of the first; Amos 3:2; Isa. 43:1; 49:1 for the second).

Given this special relationship with Moses, God should show him the divine ways, that is, what God's intentions are in this situation. If Moses had been more blunt, he might have said: "What is going on here? What are you going to do?" If Moses does not know more, he may do the wrong thing and incur God's disfavor. It is a quite natural request, given the God-Moses relationship. Then, after this focus on himself, Moses repeats the imperative with which he began: consider (see) that this nation is *God's* own people (a phrase repeated twice in v. 16). This reference to Israel is not an afterthought but a strategic move; if God understands the importance of his relationship with Moses, what Moses thinks about the people is also important. Moses thinks that Israel continues to be God's special people in spite of what they have done.

To this, God responds (v. 14), informing Moses of his intentions. The divine presence (literally, face) will go (RSV and NRSV's "with you" is not in the Hebrew text) and *Moses* will be given rest from all that troubles him about these matters (see 32:10). The reference to God's "face" is prominent in this narrative (vv. 14–15, 20, 23; cf. at v. 11). It can function as a personal pronoun, or refer to the divine presence at varying levels of intensity, or refer to God's very self. A fundamental issue for Moses is what God means by it in verse 14.

INTERPRETATION

Moses' response in verses 15–16 suggests that it is not yet clear to him what commitment God has made regarding *the people*. This divine reply seems focused only on himself as an individual. Nor is it clear what is entailed in the divine presence—is it in fact a *dwelling* presence? If God were not to go, then there would be no sense for the people to continue on their journey. In verse 15, Moses leaves the object of God's presence open. His subsequent words, especially his twice-spoken "I and your people," indicate that he wants to make sure that the people are included in God's promise of verse 14. For how else shall it be known that they, both himself and the people, have found favor in God's estimation. For only with God's constant, dwelling presence among them are they distinctive among the nations (see 11:7). Only then will they know that they are the elect people of God, "your people," those upon whom God has looked with special favor. If God does not respond positively to this request, all of this will be a lost venture, with no future of consequence. They would not be without God's presence altogether (the promises of v. 2 are real), but their special place in God's design for the entire world would no longer be in place.

God's response (v. 17) relieves some of the tension built up in the narrative. God honors Moses' request, assuring him that all that he has asked for will be done: God will be a constant presence with the people. The reason: God knows Moses by name and Moses has found favor with God (forming an inclusio with v. 12). God's response is in the singular, implying that it is because of Moses' own standing with God that God decides for the people and determines to be a constant presence among the people as a whole. Because Moses *is known* by God, Moses is now given to *know* God's decision. Once again God is shown to be responsive to what his servant Moses has had to say, who does not adopt a take it or leave it attitude toward such matters. God will take into account what such human beings think and say and incorporate that into a renewed shaping of the future. The future is thus shown not to be all blocked out; God is open to moving from decisions made in view of human words and deeds in consonance with the gracious divine purposes.

298

Nevertheless, the issue between God and people is not finally resolved. It is not clear from verse 17 whether the situation of 33:3 will obtain. The people are still stiff-necked, which makes the future with God less certain than is desirable. And so Moses pursues the conversation still farther, but it will take God's redirection of his question to bring the matter to final resolution.

Exodus 33:18–23
God Will Be Gracious

In the direct manner we have come to expect, Moses makes another request of God: "Show me your glory." (Moses is now silent until 34:9.) Glory *for Moses* refers to the face/presence of God no longer enveloped by the cloud (cf. 16:10; 40:34) or the fire (see 24:17). This is a request to see God's very self. He wishes to be assured that God will dwell among the people in all his fullness without leading to their death. In effect, *this is a request for a sign that God himself will truly dwell among them without judgment.*

God grants Moses' request only in part, for the reason that human beings cannot see God and live (v. 20); but God also redirects the question. Instead of speaking of glory, God speaks of goodness. Goodness has a more abstract mien (as does 34:6); it carries the matter beyond any simple tangible manifestation to a statement about *what kind of God this is.* What will serve as *a more genuine sign* to Moses is not some direct view of God but a specific indication of the "good" character of this one who has given the divine name Yahweh to Israel (see at 3:14 on God's giving the name). After all, a direct view of God will not say much at all about God's character. God could be a monster. In other terms, any *seeing* that is granted to Moses must be accompanied by a *knowing* if it is going to be truly revelatory of who God is and what God is about. It is more important to know what kind of God this is than to see that God. Hence Moses must not simply use his eyes, he must use his ears to hear the *proclamation.* It is in fact the proclamation of the very nature of Yahweh that will prove to Moses that God will be gracious in response to what Israel has done.

299

Hence *all* of God's goodness will pass before Moses, and the name Yahweh will be proclaimed to him (as in 3:14–15). The paralleling of goodness and glory in verse 22 means, then, that glory has been redefined for Moses (see 14:4, 18 for the connection between glory and knowing). Glory includes also a "proclamation" of the very nature of God, encompassed in the proclamation of the divine name (34:6–8). That "I" which "passes before" Moses will be *a speaking God.* The glory of God is something that Moses will both see (though only in part) and hear. The God whom Moses sees is the kind of God about whom Moses hears directly.

This does not mean that the spatial considerations in 33: 21–23 are to be spiritualized. There is a visible appearance of God in the center of the text that cannot be argued away. Moses will use his eyes and will see. The anthropomorphic language for God is consistent with the human form of other theophanies, but it is unique. God's own hand is used to prevent Moses from seeing the divine face! When God has passed by, God will take the hand away and Moses will be able to see God's back but not God's face (referring not generally to God's presence but to God's front side, God's very self). The significance of the back may well relate to what one would see of a God leading the people on their journeys.

Insofar as this theophany is parallel to that of chapters 19—24, the theme of "seeing God" is parallel to 24:9–11. It may be that the golden calf debacle means that the sight of God, though now given, will be somewhat more muted or impressionistic because of what has happened. There can be no return to Eden or Sinai. God's fullness cannot be seen. Such partial sight may also be meant in those instances where God is said to be seen (see Judg. 6:22–23; 13:22–23), though Num. 12:8 is more reminiscent of 24:9–11 than this text. But what is now true for Moses will also be true for Israel; God will dwell among the people, but it will be less than what it would have been had the apostasy not occurred.

It is important to note that verse 20 does not say that God *cannot* be seen. Rather, it assumes that God can be seen, but one cannot live if this happens. The issue is always a matter of life for the human beings involved, not God's visibility. Nowhere is it suggested that *God* is being protected or shielded or that God's sovereignty would be compromised by sight. God expresses no displeasure with Moses' request. In fact, while

300

shifting the grounds of the request, God positively moves with Moses throughout. Moses has no claim on such a divine vision, however. That God allows Moses a vision at all is a demonstration of God's mercy and graciousness. God's freedom is thus a freedom *for* Moses (see below on 33:19).

Other dimensions of this theme may be implicit here. It refers to the epistemic distance between God and human beings, structured into the created order for the purpose of preserving human freedom (and hence life). For God to be fully present would be coercive; faith would be turned into sight, and humankind could not but believe. God's presence cannot be obvious; there must be an element of ambiguity, such that disbelief remains possible. A sense of God's mystery must be preserved. This text shows that even for Moses there is an essential mystery in the confrontation with God.

Exodus 34:1–8
A God Gracious and Merciful

For two full chapters the aftermath of Israel's apostasy has been played out. It is still not clear how God will make good on the promise given to Moses in 33:17. The resolution that now comes in this appearance of God is given to Moses alone. A gracious and merciful God will go beyond justice, forgive the people, and welcome them back into relationship, but this time without any conditions whatsoever.

Once again the two tablets inform us of the status of this relationship. God commands Moses to replicate the earlier tablets so that God can write on them the same words as before. This symbolizes God's openness to covenant with Israel once again, and God takes the initiative with Moses to move toward that end. When Moses procures the tablets and presents himself before God, God passes before him and proclaims the name of Yahweh. As a virtual exegesis of this name, God proclaims a summary statement regarding the nature of this God with whom Moses and Israel now have to do on the far side of apostasy.

301

INTERPRETATION

The confessional statement in verses 6–7 occurs many times in the Old Testament in various forms (see Num. 14:18; Neh. 9:17; Ps. 103:8, 17; 145:8; Jer. 32:18–19; Nahum 1:3) and in numerous echoes (see Deut. 5:9–10; I Kings 3:6; Lam. 3:32; Dan. 9:4). It appears in a variety of traditions and types of literature. While its origins are obscure, there is no reason to suppose that it is not at least pre-Deuteronomic. It is important to note that this statement has a certain abstract, even propositional character. It cuts across the Old Testament as a statement of basic Israelite convictions regarding its God. It thus constitutes a kind of "canon" of the kind of God Israel's God is, in the light of which God's ongoing involvement in its history is to be interpreted.

What is the function of this confessional statement in this text? We have seen something of its revelatory function for Moses. It is also important to relate it back to an earlier partial version of the statement in 20:5 as well as to 23:21. The new elements here are the references to God as "merciful and gracious, slow to anger, and abounding in steadfast love and faithfulness," and "forgiving iniquity and transgression and sin, but who will by no means clear the guilty." The reference to judging is removed from the beginning of the formulation to the end and is not accounted among the divine attributes listed in verse 6. Wrath is not a continuous aspect of the nature of God but a particular response to a historical situation. The divine jealousy is missing from the formulation, and though it will be strongly emphasized in 34:14, it is there no longer tied explicitly to judgment on Israel. Also omitted is the conditional phrase "who love me and keep my commandments" with respect to the showing of steadfast love.

This comparison shows that the fundamentally new emphasis in 34:6–7 is on the divine mercy and forgiveness and patience. The doubling of the emphasis upon God's steadfast love and the omission of the conditional elements stress the unconditionality of the divine love to Israel. The additional reference to not clearing the guilty, in the context of forgiveness, means "but not neglecting just judgment" (Durham, p. 450). The retention of the visitation of iniquity—even extending the generations—is a continuing recognition of the moral order (see at 20:5).

302

Exodus 34:9
Prayer for Pardon

Moses immediately sees the import of this divine word and responds in awe-filled worship—once again it is a gospel word that prompts worship (4:31; 12:27). He then picks up on the new element that has been articulated by God: once again he asks God to forgive the sin of the people (v. 9). Only this time it is "our" sin and iniquity; Moses now includes himself in a way he did not in 32:32. Moses' request for God's tabernacling presence, given the divine response in 33:17, indicates that the primary force of the prayer is for forgiveness: go with us and pardon our sins. It is a prayer that keeps God's undergirding presence *and* forgiveness together. Without forgiveness, then 33:3 would come into play; God's intimate presence would only result in Israel being consumed.

Moses' prayer explores even more deeply these adjustments in God's own self-proclamation. They have fundamentally to do with a change in the divine relation to Israel's sinfulness.

Such adjustments are to be understood in a way similar to the divine statements before and after the flood story (Gen. 6:5–7; 8:21; see Moberly, pp. 91–92). This story also climaxes in God's entering into a covenant with those who are preserved alive, yet still sinful. God decides to go with the world, come what may in the way of human sin and wickedness. Even more, God makes this promise, not simply in spite of human failure, but precisely *because* human beings are sinful (Gen. 8:21). Human beings are as sinful after the flood as they were before. The way into the future cannot be said to depend upon human goodness and loyalty. If this were the case, then God's judgment would once again be the order of the day. Even more, sinfulness so defines humanity that, if human beings are to continue to live, they must be *undergirded by* the divine promise. And so it is *because* of human sinfulness that God promises to stay with the world.

303

This is also the force of the prayer of Moses in verse 9. Moses asks God to go with Israel, not simply in spite of the people's stiff-neckedness (so NRSV) but *because (ki)* it is such a people. The four references to Israel as stiff-necked provide a clue to this interpretation ("stiff" has the same root as one of the words for Pharaoh's "hard" heart). Its first use in 32:9 gives the *reason* for God's judgment (comparable to Gen. 6:5–7), and its use in 33:3–5 indicates that God's tabernacling presence would only subject such a people again and again to judgment. Moses' prayer assumes that Israel will always be a stiff-necked people; it is the nature of its very being in the world that it cannot extricate itself from such a condition. But it is precisely *because* Israel is such a people that it *needs* God's close presence and constant pardon. It must be so undergirded if it is to continue to be God's inheritance (=elect ones) in the world. Hence, rather than requesting simply a concession to Israel's stiff-neckedness, a sort of divine "Oh, all right, I'll do this anyway," Moses gives a deeply positive cast to his prayer: God's grace and mercy are requested for a people who stand always in profound need of just such divine action. Only because of such a God, who chooses to dwell among the people and stands ready to forgive, can a stiff-necked people move into a future worth talking about.

It is noteworthy that Moses does not appeal to any repentant act on Israel's part as a basis on which God should move to forgive (though 33:5–6 at least indicates remorse on Israel's part and hence speaks to future possibilities). The only matter to which Moses appeals is his own history with God, who has declared that Moses has a favorable status (v. 9; 33:12). Thus, while the divine forgiveness is grounded in the divine mercy (see below), the divine favor granted Moses is not believed to be irrelevant (so also Noah in Gen. 6:8; 7:1; 8:1). There is a sense in which the offer of Moses in 32:30–31 is accepted by God, though without requiring Moses' removal from God's elect ones. Moses is the mediator of the atonement for Israel's sin (cf. the action of Noah in Gen. 8:20–21).

To draw out the parallels with Genesis 6—8 still farther, the relationship between God and Israel is seen to stand on the same footing as God's relationship to the entire world. God's actions toward Israel *are not unique:* this is the way of God *with the world.* As God backs off from total destruction, and extends promises to a sinful world, so God "repents" and extends the

304

chosen relationship with Israel. In both cases, the divine action is undeserved, grounded in God's graciousness mediated through an intercessor. It may thus be claimed that it is *as creator* that God makes these moves on Israel's behalf; this is God's way with the world generally. God's creation-wide ways are here realized at the microcosmic level. Yet Israel's *particular* participation in this divine way with the world has a special place; it holds promise for the *particular* participation of other peoples (see below on Jonah). God takes this way with Israel for the sake of others. Indeed, 34:10 has this world already in view: the nations will see the work of the Lord in Israel (see 9:16; 19:5-6; 33:16).

Moreover, God introduces a new element into the divine-human relationship with Israel. For the first time in the canonical Old Testament, and unlike Genesis 6—8, divine forgiveness becomes a fundamental way of relating to sin (v. 7 contains the three most prominent words for sin in the Old Testament!). It is to be noted that this theme is hardly in view in chapters 25—31. This text thus becomes a witness not only to God's openness to change in view of the divine history with the world but to *the foundational function* that divine forgiveness is to have for the community of faith, indeed for the world. What had earlier been stated as a divine impossibility (23:21) is now proclaimed (!) as a new way of God's relating to sinful creatures.

The idea for such a direction in the divine ways seems to be introduced first of all by Moses (32:32)! There is a sense in which this is so. This would not be the first time that God picks up on a suggestion from Moses as a way of moving into the future (see at 32:7–14). At the same time, the following factors need to be taken into account. These make it clear that Moses' response is grounded outside himself.

1. Especially important is God's statement in 33:19 regarding the divine freedom to be gracious and merciful, which now comes to fruition. This verse indicates that this divine decision is freely chosen by God. God's concern is *not* to stake a claim for a divine freedom *from* Moses or Israel, a freedom to be gracious toward some but not others if God so wills. It is a declaration of God's freedom *to move beyond previously stated stipulations* and reach out in mercy. Childs (p. 69) calls attention to the fact that the same idiom is used in 3:14, which he translates, "I am there, wherever it may be . . . I am really

there." A comparable translation of 33:19 would thus be: I will have mercy on you, . . . yes indeed, I will have mercy on you. This is a statement of God's graciousness *for* Moses, God's freedom *for* others, not *from* others. But it is granted only at God's initiative. It is a divine declaration that God will be gracious to Moses in responding to his requests. God's own "proclamation" in 34:6–7 makes the basis for the divine decision clear: God makes this gracious move toward Israel because it is the divine nature so to do. The repeated divine name, Yahweh, stresses this identification.

This is a statement which carries a force similar to that of the book of Jonah: if God desires to have mercy even on such a renegade people as the Ninevites, God is free to make that move without being subject to Jonah's charge of being merely indulgent or unfair (see Matt. 20:1–16). At least one point of the book of Jonah (which quotes Exod. 34:6–7 at 4:2) is that the divine freedom available to Israel is also available to the worst of the "non-chosen" world.

2. But why, then, the sharp statements earlier in the text about a seeming *absence* of divine patience and mercy (23:21; 20:5–6; cf. 20:20)? Mercy can be seen as *genuine mercy* only if it is not built into the structure of the relationship from the beginning. If it had been made clear from the outset that, of course, God is merciful and could be counted on to be gracious and forgiving toward any apostasy, that would be *indulgence, not mercy*. Such would take away from the seriousness, indeed the uncompromising character of God's claim on Israel's undivided loyalty. In fact, it could be said that apostasy would not be able to be identified as truly apostasy if it were initially couched in terms that could be interpreted in any way as equivocal.

Hence an initially uncompromising statement (to which the people agree!) is necessary for three reasons: *(a)* It reveals apostasy for what it truly is. It is an act of unfaithfulness and disloyalty, no ifs, ands, or buts. The depths of Israel's sinfulness are made evident to one and all. This is stressed in the use of "stiffnecked" throughout the narrative, even at the point of the renewal of the covenant in 34:9. There is no goodness in them, no partial faithfulness, on the basis of which they can lay a claim before God. That can come only from outside themselves. *(b)* It reveals the genuine character of the divine mercy. Only

306

when one is genuinely faced with death can one begin to see what mercy is truly all about. *(c)* More precisely, it enables grace to be seen truly as grace. The command's uncompromising clarity and the people's agreement to be unequivocally committed to Yahweh mean that they cannot lay any claim on God for lenience. There is no basis to appeal to some ambiguity in the command or some situational ethic, no room to maneuver around some vagueness in the margins of the demand. They are deserving only of death. Only then can grace be seen for what it in fact is: an incredible gift, extended only at the divine initiative.

3. Why, then, is the extensive dialogue between Moses and God necessary before the gracious divine response is extended? This makes it clear that God is neither obligated to make this move (as we have seen) nor somehow an "easy mark," as if forgiveness were "God's business," available in some heavenly vending machine. The dialogue stands as a reminder that God will not bear an apostate people forever (see Num. 14:12–25; Isa. 1:14; Jer. 44:22; Josh. 24:19). There is no predictability or inevitability about the divine grace. This serves as a reminder that the community of faith ought not live close to the margins of God's patience (cf. Rom. 6:1).

The revelation of the "divine back" to Moses (33:18–23) is a vivid picture of this character of the divine graciousness. Even Moses is not able to get an unambiguously clear picture of the divine goodness, so as to be able to lay claims on God. For all of God's willingness to respond to Moses' intercession on behalf of the community of faith, forgiveness is finally rooted in the divine grace; it is not at the beck and call of human beings, even trusted mediators.

Exodus 34:10–28
A New Covenant

Finally, God is not represented as making this move reluctantly. Verse 10 speaks of an almost exuberant divine response to this new situation. God will do marvelous things on behalf of Israel. The word "create" (NRSV, "perform"; *bara'*), used

307

throughout Genesis 1, is believed to be the most appropriate language for this divine activity in Israel. What God is doing for Israel is an act parallel to the creation of the world! This act is of such an unprecedented nature that only creation language, combined with language of marvel and awe, can adequately describe it. While the identification of the awesome things God does for Israel is debated—but the oft-repeated promises of 34:11, 24 would hardly fit such a description—it would appear to have reference to the work of God in forgiving a sinful people (see Micah 7:15–20; Moberly, p. 94). In this reading, Moses' prayer has a specific response; it does not have to be assumed. This work of God occurs "before your [Moses'] people" (gathered below the mountain), and it will be recognized as an act of such renown that it will come to the attention of other peoples (see above).

This suggests that verse 10 does *not*, strictly speaking, refer to a renewal of the covenant of chapters 19—24. While there is continuity in the tables of the law (34:1, 4, 28), at least one decisively new element in this text is not present in chapters 19—24. Whatever its tradition history may have been, this is a *new* covenant grounded in a new act of God on behalf of Israel. God places the relationship with Israel on a new footing. It is now grounded in an event that is as profoundly "full of wonder" as what God has done in and to Egypt (see 3:20; 15:11): undeserved divine forgiveness of an apostate people. In contrast to chapter 24, this covenant is not characterized by any formal response from Israel. The new covenant is in place simply because God has determined that it be so. Hence the nature of God's covenant with Israel has changed. It is now no longer one to which the people agree. God simply promises in verse 10 to make this covenant and to do this marvelous thing on behalf of the people. No conditions are attached. Entirely at the divine initiative, at a moment in Israel's life where it is most vulnerable and can call on no goodness of its own or any other human resource, God acts on Israel's behalf: its sins are forgiven. *This is an entirely new reality for Israel, indeed for the world.*

Verses 11–26, originally perhaps from another covenant-making tradition, in their present context could be considered a restatement of the law of chapters 20—23 in summary form as an accompaniment to the making of a new covenant. More precisely, however, these materials are centered on issues relat-

308

ing to the proper worship of Yahweh alone. That is to say, they are respondent to the particular form of Israel's apostasy: disloyalty to Yahweh as manifested in idolatry and false forms of worship. Given the nature of Israel's failure, these are the matters to which the people must attend in a special way if they would be faithful to their God. It is not that the laws outlined in chapters 20—23 are no longer valid; these are the ones that now need emphasis. This shows once again how the law relates to particular historical circumstances.

Moreover, it is to be noted that verses 11–26 are an admixture of command, exhortations to faithfulness, and promises, often interweaving elements from 23:10–33. While the section begins with a statement concerning God's *command,* divine promises virtually enclose the section (vv. 11, 24). The messenger of 23:20, 23; 32:34; and 33:2 is no longer in view; it is God himself who will be about the promises. As in 20:22–26 and 23:20–33, issues of divine and human loyalty are interwoven. God does not expect loyalty *from* Israel apart from declaring the divine loyalty *to* Israel. It is only from within the context of divine faithfulness to promises that human faithfulness is possible. Israel is called to be faithful, but it knows that this call comes from a God who is *for them,* not against them or standing over them as a threat. In the face of Israel's apostasy, the promises of 23:23, 27–31 are repeated. The God who gives the law is the God who makes unconditional promises.

The divine exhortations to Israel are centered on issues of loyalty to Yahweh, comparable to 23:24, 32–33. While God will drive out the inhabitants of the land, Israel is not to fall prey to the idolatrous enticements of those who remain. Missing entirely from this section, however, are the conditional elements of 23:21–22. Israel for its part is to be observant of various aspects of worship designed to protect its faithfulness to Yahweh, especially given a coming situation where the temptation to apostasy will be faced once again.

The seriousness with which Israel's undivided loyalty is stated is made clear by the strong, double reference to *divine jealousy* (v. 14). Indeed, God names himself with the metaphor Jealous, indicating that Israel's faithfulness is a matter close to the divine heart. This is not simply a formal matter with God, it touches God's very emotional life. It has to do not only with what God expects *from* Israel but, with an inescapable refer-

309

ence to the divine inwardness, what God feels *for* the people—jealousy by definition has both an inner and an outer reference. But *the inner reference is the prior one.* God cares deeply about Israel and, *because of that,* cares about what Israel does with its allegiances. This is a serious matter indeed. But Israel stands as the forgiven people of Yahweh, and God will go with this people into the future, come what may. What might happen should the people choose apostasy once again is not stated, though the fact of the divine jealousy means that God will not, indeed cannot, remain unmoved by such a turn of events (see Num. 14:20–24). Because of the nature of jealousy, however, it will mean that God's being moved will entail both pain and anger.

Verses 27–28 have long puzzled commentators, both who is to write (see 34:1) and what is to be written (are "these words" the same as the "ten words"?). It seems likely that verse 27 refers to the preceding materials, *both law and promises,* as is the case in 24:3–4. Thus the divine expectations of the people do not stand isolated from God's own commitment to them. Their obedience will constantly be undergirded by the divine promise. The certainty of this is not concluded with a divine-human handshake; God has Moses put it in writing! Verse 28*b* is likely an inclusio with verse 1; God writes the ten commandments down once again, clarifying that these words still remain very much in the picture for Israel.

Exodus 34:29–35
Word and Body

Verses 29–35 report Moses' return from the mountain to the encamped people of Israel. What receives special attention is not Moses' instruction of the people, as important as that is, but the shining appearance of his face (the verb can also be translated "horned," leading to many renderings of a horned Moses, e.g., Michelangelo; Chagall). It had its origins in the context of God's speaking with him (v. 29), of which Moses was initially unaware (and hence not of his own doing). Moses wore a veil to conceal this shining, except on two occasions: when

310

God was speaking with him in the sanctuary (see 33:7–11) and when he spoke God's words to the people. In other words, the face of Moses is *visibly* shining (i.e., unveiled) whenever there is a communicating of the word of God. No reason is given for Moses' wearing a veil when a communication of the word of God is not involved; it may entail a recognition that Moses was not always functioning in this capacity (no doubt to the relief of both Moses and people!). Verses 34–35 show that this is a continuing reality for Israel, beyond this time and place. This suggests that we have to do with a concrete theological symbol, not a historical reality.

While the significance of this shining is much debated, it likely is concerned with two matters: (1) It gives a prominence to the mediator of the word of God in the community of faith. There is a reflection of the effulgence of the glory of God himself in the face of Moses. As such, it is made clearer that Moses is speaking for God. Once again (see 19:9) God sees to an external means by which the mediator of the word of God can be shown to be authentic to the larger community. Appearance does make a difference to words, commanding greater attention and respect. Even more, it shows that Moses is not simply a speaker for the word of God; in some sense he *embodies* that word. The people thus do not only hear that word being spoken, they *see* it standing before them. There is conveyed in *Moses' own body* something of the nature of the divine communication to the community.

There are affinities here with the appearance of the messenger of God in theophanies (see especially Judg. 13:6; Exod. 3:2). In effect, Moses now functions as a divine messenger. In this connection, the reference to Moses' face ties this narrative back to chapter 33 and the issue of the face of God. We are told in 33:11 that God speaks to Moses face-to-face. Yet it is twice stated that God's face cannot be seen in all its fullness, even by Moses (33:20, 23). One might then say that *Moses' shining face is the vision of the face of God which is available to the community of faith* (see the comparable language for Jesus in II Cor. 3:18; 4:6 in a context that works with this Exodus passage; see also the story of Jesus' transfiguration in Matt. 17:1–8). Finally, it might be noted that the use of "horn" language may be intended as a deliberate correlation of Moses and the golden

311

calf. As such, this may convey to the people (especially in view of 32:1) that their need for a mediator of the word is sufficiently present in Moses; there is no need for a nonliving image.

2. The shining conveys something of the nature and significance of the word of God being communicated. The embodiment of the word conveys that which is concrete, tangible, with distinct implications for the life of those who hear that word. The human response can never simply be to believe or speak; it must also mean to do, to reembody the word in the world. Moreover, the word is imaged in a shining, a radiance, a brilliance, an incandescence, a fieriness. As such, it evokes freshness, vividness, intensity, and splendor. The word has to do with light and brightness, not with darkness and dullness. Because it is Moses' skin that is affected, the image may also be one of ruddiness. As such, it evokes ardor, zeal, vigor, and vitality. The word has to do with warmth and passion, not coldness and apathy. All in all, the shining evokes an understanding of the word of God that is living and active, munificently present among the people for their good. The reference to God's face shining on the people in the Aaronic benediction (Num. 6:25; see Ps. 80) places this understanding into the ongoing worship life of the people. There they are assured of the *constancy* of the shining face of God.

Moses' shining face anticipates the filling of the tabernacle with the divine glory in 40:34–38, foreshadowing that glory in both its radiance and its veiledness.

PART NINE

God Fills the Tabernacle

EXODUS 35:1—40:38

Israel in an Advent Mode

The discussion of the tabernacle at 25:1 applies also to this section, which presents a new opportunity for obedience in Israel.

Chapters 35—40 portray in detail how the commands given by God to Moses in chapters 25—31 were executed (according to the logic of construction rather than the order of sanctity). Just as that account concluded with a note on the sabbath, so this section begins with sabbath-keeping. The enclosure of chapters 32—34 with sabbath references means that God's grace and mercy shown to an apostate Israel make it possible to pick up the narrative where it was earlier interrupted. The construction of the tabernacle can begin at once. God's promise to dwell among the people remains intact (cf. 25:8; 29:45).

We have noted that the tabernacle sections are best understood when an exilic provenance is in view. The extensiveness of the repetition of material from chapters 25—31 lifts up two issues. It assures Israel that, just as God once before went forward with plans for a sanctuary in the wake of apostasy, so God would again. It would be a sign of hope that a new sanctuary is in their future and that God would indeed dwell among God's people once again. But it also places considerable stress on human obedience. Chapters 35—40 never tire of stating how the divine instructions were carried out in precise detail; there are eighteen references to Moses doing as God commanded.

313

INTERPRETATION

It is important that this obedience be properly understood. Given the apostasy, such obedience is *an external demonstration of loyalty to Yahweh*. Obedience arises out of a heart and spirit properly turned toward God, as the emphasis on that theme makes clear (35:5, 21–22, 29; 36:2). Obedience is thus rooted in faithfulness; the external activity is internally motivated. The actual building can proceed only because of the generous offerings brought by everyone (note the inclusive reference in 35:22; cf. 38:8) to the Lord, the "LORD's offering" (35:5, 21–22, 24, 29). They respond with far more than is necessary (36:5–7). A worshipful act thus precedes the obedience and the construction activity. Even more, the human activity is seen to be finally rooted in divine inspiration (35: 30—36:2; cf. 31:1–11). God makes such obedience possible in and through the gifts bestowed upon individuals. Given these factors, there should be some confidence regarding the proper worship of Yahweh in the future. There would be little room for compromise with idolatrous propensities with such a combination of divine inspiration and the human response of generosity and faithfulness, leading to a relatively controlled worship environment. As ancient Israel under Moses was faithful, so also should the Israelites in exile be. As it once was, so it should be again.

It is important to note that these chapters are not a description of the completed tabernacle but of its being made. The emphasis is on the joining and threading and making, and then finally on its being assembled. The point is not contemplation of a beautiful object, as much as that may be the case, but on the obedient activity needed to make it so. The image presented is thus not a static one but a dynamic picture of preparation for the coming of God to dwell in their midst. *The community is in an "Advent" mode.* It is not that the people's preparedness causes God to dwell among them, however. God's dwelling in their midst is a matter of the divine initiative and promise (see 29:45). Yet the people's faithful response rather than disloyalty is an important factor in what becomes possible for God. This is clearly related to the effect of Israel's apostasy on the divine presence (cf. 33:1–3), and parallels with the exilic situation may also be noted (cf. Ezek. 8:6; Micah 3:4; Matt. 25:1–12).

314

The Tabernacle as Body of God

This emphasis on the divine initiative is also highlighted by the role of Moses in 40:35, for whom there is no room in this newly filled sanctuary (cf. I Kings 8:10–11). Moses' activity is not responsible in any way for God's dwelling. The tabernacle is for God for the sake of Israel, not for human beings, however important. What Moses does is dependent upon God's call from the tabernacle (25:22; Lev. 1:1).

When all is ready, God comes to dwell among the people in the completed tabernacle. The sanctuary is not simply a symbol of the divine presence, it is *an actual vehicle for divine immanence,* in and through which the transcendent God dwells. The concern for consecration and an appropriate setting for the Holy One makes it clear that *the tabernacle does not collapse presence into immanence.* The God who is present is present as the transcendent one. It is *as* the Holy One that God is present. God remains transcendent in immanence and related in transcendence (see at 25:1 and Fretheim, *The Suffering of God,* pp. 70–71). Israel's God now dwells, with intensity and at close range, in Israel's very midst. God actually takes up space in Israel's world. At the same time, the God who "fills" the tabernacle also "fills" the cosmos (Jer. 23:24; Isa. 6:3; Ps. 33:5; 72:19). On the one hand, this makes it clear that Israel's place of worship is not the only place in the world where God's presence can be found. God cannot be so confined; God is both near and far. Yet there is no other *specific place* in creation that is said to be filled up with God; the focused choice of place by God provides for an intensity of presence that is not true of the creation generally. The tabernacle may thus be said to be a kind of *material "body" for God.* It is no wonder that the New Testament can pick up this language of fullness and use it for God's bodily dwelling in Jesus (Col. 1:19; 2:9; Eph. 1:23; John 1:14–16).

Moreover, Israel's God is not present just in isolated mo-

315

ments of Israel's life, or only to key leaders, but is present to the community as a whole on an ongoing basis. God continues to lead the people in all of their journeyings (see Num. 9:15–23; 10:11–13). The dwelling of God is not a static, immobile, unchanging presence. There is movement with this God, a movement that signals the comings and goings of Israel (on the continuing use of the verbal as well, see Num. 9:18–20). The people are now no longer subjected to a changeless system, to an increasingly dispiriting bondage. They are followers of a God who is on the move, in whose service true freedom and joy are to be found.

BIBLIOGRAPHY

1. For Further Study

BARR, J. "Story and History in Biblical Theology." *Journal of Religion* 56:1–17 (1980).

BLOOM, H., ed. *Exodus* (New York: Chelsea House, 1987).

CASSUTO, U. *A Commentary on the Book of Exodus* (Jerusalem: Magnes Press, 1967).

CHILDS, B. S. *The Book of Exodus: A Critical, Theological Commentary*. OLD TESTAMENT LIBRARY (Philadelphia: Westminster Press, 1974).

CLEMENTS, R. E. *Exodus*. CAMBRIDGE BIBLE COMMENTARY (Cambridge: Cambridge University Press, 1972).

CLINES, D. J. *The Theme of the Pentateuch* (Sheffield: JSOT Press, 1978).

COATS, G. *Rebellion in the Wilderness: The Murmuring Motif in the Wilderness Traditions of the Old Testament* (Nashville: Abingdon Press, 1968).

————. "The King's Loyal Opposition: Obedience and Authority in Exodus 32–34." In *Canon and Authority: Essays in Old Testament Religion and Theology* ed. by G. W. Coats and B. O. Long (Philadelphia: Fortress Press, 1977), pp. 91–109.

COHN, R. L. *The Shape of Sacred Space: Four Biblical Studies* Studies in Religion, 23 (Chico, Calif.: Scholars Press, 1981).

COLLINS, J. J. "The 'Historical Character' of the Old Testament in Recent Biblical Theology." *Catholic Biblical Quarterly* 41:185–204 (1979).

DAUBE, D. *The Exodus Pattern in the Bible* (London: Faber & Faber, 1963).

FOX, E. *Now These Are the Names: A New English Translation of the Book of Exodus* (New York: Schocken Books, 1986).

FREEDMAN, D. N. "Divine Commitment and Human Obligation." *Interpretation* 18:419–431 (1964).

GERSTENBERGER, E. "Covenant and Commandment." *Journal of Biblical Literature* 84:38–51 (1965).

HYATT, J. P. *Exodus*. NEW CENTURY BIBLE (London: Oliphants, 1971).

BIBLIOGRAPHY

McCURLEY, F. R. *Genesis, Exodus, Leviticus, Numbers* (Philadelphia: Fortress Press, 1979).

MENDENHALL, G. *Law and Covenant in Israel and the Ancient Near East* (Pittsburgh: Biblical Colloquium, 1955).

PLAUT, W. G., and B. J. BAMBERGER. *The Torah: A Modern Commentary* (New York: Union of American Hebrew Congregations, 1981).

RAD, G. von. *Moses* (London: Lutterworth Press, 1960).

RAISANEN, H. *The Idea of Divine Hardening* (Helsinki: PFES, 1972).

RAMSEY, G. *The Quest for the Historical Israel* (Atlanta: John Knox Press, 1981).

RYLAARSDAM, J. C. "The Book of Exodus." In *The Interpreter's Bible*, ed. by G. A. Buttrick et al. (New York: Abingdon Press, 1952), 1:833–1099.

STAMM, J. J., and M. E. ANDREW. *The Ten Commandments in Recent Research* (London: SCM Press, 1967).

VAN IERSEL, B., and A. WEILER. *Exodus: A Lasting Paradigm* (Edinburgh: T. & T. Clark, 1987).

WALZER, M. *Exodus and Revolution* (New York: Basic Books, 1985).

WHYBRAY, R. N. *The Making of the Pentateuch: A Methodological Study* (Sheffield: JSOT Press, 1987).

WILDAVSKY, A. *The Nursing Father: Moses as a Political Leader* (University, Ala.: University of Alabama Press, 1984).

2. Literature Cited

ACKERMAN, J. "The Literary Context of the Moses Birth Story." In *Literary Interpretations of Biblical Narratives*, ed. by K. R. Gros Louis, J. Ackerman, and T. S. Warshaw (Nashville: Abingdon Press, 1974), pp. 74–119.

BLENKINSOPP, J. "The Structure of P." *Catholic Biblical Quarterly* 38:275–292 (1976).

BRUEGGEMANN, W. "The Crisis and Promise of Presence in Israel." *Horizons in Biblical Theology* 1:47–86 (1979).

BURNS, R. J. *Exodus, Leviticus, Numbers.* OLD TESTAMENT MESSAGE SERIES (Wilmington, Del.: Michael Glazier, 1983).

————. *Has the Lord Indeed Spoken Only Through Moses? A*

Study of the Biblical Portrait of Miriam. SOCIETY OF BIBLI-
CAL LITERATURE DISSERTATION SERIES (Atlanta: Scholars
Press, 1987).

CHILDS, B. S. (See Bibliography 1.)

COATS, G. W. *Moses: Heroic Man, Man of God* (Sheffield: JSOT
Press, 1988).

COOTE, R., and D. ORD. *The Bible's First History* (Philadelphia: Fortress Press, 1988).

CROATTO, J. S. *Exodus: A Hermeneutics of Freedom* (Maryknoll, N.Y.: Orbis Books, 1981).

CROSS, F. M. *Canaanite Myth and Hebrew Epic: Essays in the
History of the Religion of Israel* (Cambridge, Mass.: Harvard University Press, 1973).

DAMROSCH, D. *The Narrative Covenant* (San Francisco:
Harper & Row, 1987).

DRIVER, S. R. *Exodus.* CAMBRIDGE BIBLE (Cambridge: Cambridge University Press, 1911).

DURHAM, J. *Exodus* (Waco, Tex.: Word Publishing, 1987).

EXUM, J. C. "You Shall Let Every Daughter Live: A Study of
Ex. 1:8—2:10." *Semeia* 28:63–82 (1983).

FISHBANE, M. *Text and Texture: Close Readings of Selected
Biblical Texts* (New York: Schocken Books, 1979).

FREIRE, P. *Pedagogy of the Oppressed* (New York: Herder &
Herder, 1970).

FRETHEIM, T. E. *The Suffering of God: An Old Testament
Perspective.* OVERTURES TO BIBLICAL THEOLOGY (Philadelphia: Fortress Press, 1984).

———. "The Plagues as Ecological Signs of Historical Disaster."
Journal of Biblical Literature 110 (1991).

———. "The Priestly Document: Anti-Temple?" *Vetus Testamentum* 18:318–329 (1968).

———. "Suffering God and Sovereign God in Exodus." *Horizons in Biblical Theology* 11:31–56 (1989).

GREENBERG, M. *Understanding Exodus* (New York: Behr-
man House, 1969).

GUNN, D. "The 'Hardening of Pharaoh's Heart': Plot, Character and Theology in Exodus 1—14." In *Art and Meaning:
Rhetoric in Biblical Literature,* ed. by D. J. Clines, D. M.
Gunn, and A. Hauser (Sheffield: JSOT Press, 1982), pp. 72–
96.

HANSON, P. D. "The Theological Significance of Contradiction

Within the Book of the Covenant." In *Canon and Authority*, ed. by G. W. Coats and B. O. Long (Philadelphia: Fortress Press, 1977), pp. 110–131.

HARAN, M. *Temples and Temple-Service in Ancient Israel* (Oxford: Clarendon Press, 1978).

HARRELSON, W. *The Ten Commandments and Human Rights.* OVERTURES TO BIBLICAL THEOLOGY (Philadelphia· Fortress Press, 1980).

ISBELL, C. "Exodus 1–2 in the Context of Exodus 1—14: Story Lines and Key Words." In *Art and Meaning: Rhetoric in Biblical Literature*, ed. by D. J. Clines, D. M. Gunn, and A. Hauser (Sheffield: JSOT Press, 1982), pp. 37–61.

JACKSON, B. S. "The Ceremonial and the Judicial: Biblical Law as Sign and Symbol." *Journal for the Study of the Old Testament* 30:25–50 (1984).

JANZEN, J. G. "What's in a Name? 'Yahweh' in Exodus 3 and the Wider Biblical Context." *Interpretation* 33:227–239 (1979).

JOSIPOVICI, G. *The Book of God: A Response to the Bible* (New Haven: Yale University Press, 1988).

KAPLAN, L. " 'And the Lord Sought to Kill Him' (Exod 4:24): Yet Once Again." *Hebrew Annual Review* 5:65–74 (1981).

KEARNEY, P. J. "Creation and Liturgy: The P Redaction of Ex. 25–40." *Zeitschrift für die alttestamentliche Wissenschaft* 89:375–387 (1977).

KOESTER, C. *The Dwelling of God: The Tabernacle in the Old Testament, Intertestamental Jewish Literature, and the New Testament* (Washington: Catholic Biblical Association of America, 1989).

LEVENSON, J. *Sinai and Zion: An Entry into the Jewish Bible* (San Francisco: Harper & Row, 1987).

———. *Creation and the Persistence of Evil: The Jewish Drama of Divine Omnipotence* (San Francisco: Harper & Row, 1988).

McCARTHY, D. J. *Old Testament Covenant: A Survey of Current Opinions* (Richmond: John Knox Press, 1972).

———. "Exodus 3:14: History, Philology and Theology." *Catholic Biblical Quarterly* 40:311–322 (1978).

MANN, T. W. *The Book of the Torah: The Narrative Integrity of the Pentateuch* (Atlanta: John Knox Press, 1988).

MEYER, L. *The Message of Exodus* (Minneapolis: Augsburg Publishing House, 1983).

MILLER, P. D., Jr. *The Divine Warrior in Early Israel* (Cambridge, Mass.: Harvard University Press, 1973).

MOBERLY, R. W. *At the Mountain of God: Story and Theology in Exodus 32—34.* JSOT SUPPLEMENT SERIES, 22 (Sheffield: JSOT Press, 1983).

NICHOLSON, E. W. *Exodus and Sinai in History and Tradition* (Richmond: John Knox Press, 1973).

———. *God and His People: Covenant and Theology in the Old Testament* (Oxford: Clarendon Press, 1986).

NOTH, M. *Exodus, a Commentary.* OLD TESTAMENT LIBRARY (Philadelphia: Westminster Press, 1962).

PATRICK, D. "The Covenant Code Source." *Vetus Testamentum* 27:145–157 (1977).

———. *Old Testament Law* (Atlanta: John Knox Press, 1984).

PIXLEY, G. *On Exodus: A Liberation Perspective* (Maryknoll, N.Y.: Orbis Books, 1987).

PLASTARAS, J. *The God of Exodus: The Theology of the Exodus Narratives* (Milwaukee: Bruce Publishing Co., 1966).

PROPP, W. *Water in the Wilderness: A Biblical Motif and Its Mythological Background* (Cambridge, Mass.: Harvard University Press, 1988).

SARNA, N. *Exploring Exodus: The Heritage of Biblical Israel* (New York: Schocken Books, 1986).

SCHMIDT, W. H. Exodus. BKAT, II 1–3 (Neukirchen-Vluyn: Neukirchener Verlag, 1974–1983).

WILSON, R. "The Hardening of Pharaoh's Heart." *Catholic Biblical Quarterly* 41:18–36 (1979).

YODER, J. H. "Exodus and Exile: The Two Faces of Liberation." *Cross Currents* 23: 297–309 (1973).

ZEVIT, Z. "The Priestly Redaction and Interpretation of the Plague Narrative in Exodus." *Jewish Quarterly Review* 66: 193–211 (1975–1976).

321